D1053127

The History and Theory of
Environmental Scenography

Theater and Dramatic Studies, No. 3

Bernard Beckerman, Series Editor

Brander Matthews Professor of Dramatic Literature
Columbia University in the City of New York

Other Titles in This Series

The History and Theory of
Environmental Scenography

by
Arnold Aronson

UMI RESEARCH PRESS
Ann Arbor, Michigan

Produced and distributed by
UMI Research Press
an imprint of
University Microfilms International
Ann Arbor, Michigan 48106

Library of Congress Cataloging in Publication Data

Aronson, Arnold.
The history and theory of environmental
scenography.

(Theater and dramatic studies ; no. 3)
Revision of thesis (Ph.D.)—New York University, 1977.
Bibliography: p.
Includes index.
1. Theaters—Stage-setting and scenery. I. Title.
II. Series. III. Title: Environmental scenography.

PN2091.S8A73   1981   792'.025'09   81-11677
ISBN 0-8357-1224-9   AACR2

For my parents
Louis and Anna Aronson

Contents

List of Illustrations

Preface

The impetus for this study grew out of an awareness that the fairly recent movement known as environmental theatre had a long, but largely ignored tradition. At first, my intention was to document those historical performances which had an influence on, or were analogous to, contemporary environmental performance. It quickly became apparent that these were not merely a few significant performances but dozens, perhaps hundreds. And that was without taking into account the wide range of non-Western, traditional, and pre-neoclassical theatre which was and is frequently environmental. Furthermore, with the exception of Michael Kirby's essay on environmental theatre in his *Art of Time*, there was not even a clear definition of the form. Consequently, this study attempts to define environmental theatre and, through a broad survey, place it in historical perspective.

The major difficulty in doing such a broad survey is that its parameters are hard to determine. There seems to be no point at which it can be said that all information has been thoroughly exhausted. For every performance that is mentioned here, some scholar will know of another such production that predates it. There is, unfortunately, no one name to search out, no single, inclusive library entry that will yield all the relevant information. For discovering records of past environmental productions I was dependent on the recommendations of fellow historians and frequently on sheer accident and coincidence—happening across a magazine article when it was least expected, for instance. Because of this, it is sure that there are many important productions that chance has not led me to discover.

There seems to be more of an historical awareness of non-frontal staging in France than elsewhere. The best writer in this field is Denis Bablet who has, in his books and articles, been developing a history of modern scenography.

For their guidance and help in locating materials and putting me on to important performances I would like to thank Michael Kirby and Mel Gordon. I would also like to thank Bernard Koten of the Bobst Library for his help with the NYU Slavonic Collection, Richard Schechner for giving me access to his personal files, and Roma Scharoun and Thomas Malionek for help in translations. I would also like to thank Brooks McNamara and Kate Davy for their patience and help in the writing of this work.

Thanks to the following people, publications, and institutions for permission to reprint the following illustrations:

Ron Blanchette, photographer, 88

David Braithwaite, *Fairground Architecture*, 2

Michel Corvin, *Le Théâtre Recherche entre les Deux Guerres*, 80, 81

The Drama Review, 1, 84, 85, 90, 95, 106, 113

Fred Ederstadt, photographer, 108, 109

André Emmerich Gallery, 41

The Finnish Embassy, 24

The Norman Bel Geddes Collection at the Hoblitzelle Theatre Arts Library, the University of Texas at Austin, by permission of the executrix of the Norman Bel Geddes Estate, Edith Lutyens Bel Geddes, 9, 10

Mel Gordon, 63

Matt Heron (Black Star) photographer, 107

George Honcher, photographer, 112

Intermède, 79

Jean Jacquot, *Les Voies de la Création Théâtrale*, 94, 104

Allan Kaprow, *Assemblage, Environments and Happenings*, 82, 83

Mrs. Lillian Kiesler, 34–40, 42, 43

Basil Langton, photographer, 89

Library of Congress, 74, 75

Babette Mangolte, photographer, 91

Myśl Teatralna Polskiej Awangardy 1919–1939, 72, 73, 76–78

Rare Books and Manuscript Division, The New York Public Library, Astor Lenox and Tilden Foundation, 16

Jacques Polieri, *Scenographie Semiographie*, 25, 46, 47, 97–102

Maurice Pottecher, *Le Théâtre du Peuple de Bussang*, 3

Jerry Rojo, 110

Theodore Shank, photographer, 86

Theatre Arts Monthly, 4, 65

Theatre Crafts, 111

Theatre Design and Technology, 71

Travail Théâtrale, 103, 114

1

The Scenography of Environmental Performance

In the Spring 1968 issue of *The Drama Review* Richard Schechner, then editor, published an essay entitled "6 Axioms for Environmental Theatre."[1] Using such diverse examples as Happenings, street theatre, political demonstrations, ritual performances, the theories of John Cage, the productions of Jerzy Grotowski, the architectural schemes of Frederick Kiesler, World's Fair pavilions, and his own production of Eugène Ionesco's *Victims of Duty*, presented in New Orleans the previous year, Schechner outlined and codified an approach to theatrical production that stood in direct opposition to what had generally been accepted as conventional staging since the eighteenth century. The examples he was able to offer clearly indicated that the approach to staging which Schechner described was neither new nor unique, but the term he coined—"environmental theatre"—was both.

The phrase caught on quickly, enhanced no doubt by the somewhat scandalous success of *Dionysus In 69*, an environmental adaptation of *The Bacchae*, directed by Schechner later that year. Since that time, environmental theatre has been popularized largely through Schechner's writings and the productions of his Performance Group. Once an approach to art is identified it seems to acquire a new visibility, and the assortment of environmental productions which took place during the sixties suddenly assumed the status of a movement. Critics began to apply the term with great facility and, like the term *Happenings* before it, *environmental theatre* entered the vernacular with broad and indistinct references while at the same time it was over-specified or limited by its practitioners.

Basically, the word *environmental* is applied to staging that is non-frontal. Proscenium, end, thrust, alley, and arena stages are all frontal in that a spectator observing a performance rarely has to look more than forty-five degrees to the right or left in order to view the whole production. Certain of these stages, such as the arena, will provide somewhat different perspectives for viewers, and some will make the spectators more aware of each other, but in all cases the audience is facing "forward" and is generally focused on the same space and action. Any performance of which this is not true—in which the complete *mise-en-scène* or scenography cannot be totally apprehended by a spectator maintaining a single frontal relationship to the performance—must be considered non-frontal or environmental.

This point can be demonstrated further in terms of framing. A frame around a painting, while being, of course, a physical demarcation, acts, in a sense, as a symbolic demarcation as well. It indicates that the space inside is different from the surrounding space. A stage is also framed, whether by an elaborate proscenium arch or a circle created by a crowd of spectators. It is understood that the stage area represents a different reality from the audience area. In the case of a non-illusionistic performance, say, a nightclub comic or even a lecturer in front of a class, the stage still represents a specialized place, providing central focus. As long as there is a single frame and the spectator remains outside it, the performance is frontal. If, however, the spectator is somehow incorporated within the frame, surrounded by the frame, or surrounded by several distinct frames (as in scatter staging which employs several stages throughout a given space), the performance becomes environmental.[2]

If these definitions allow the elimination of certain productions from consideration as being definitely non-environmental, they raise questions about a great many more which seem to be only "partially environmental." Stanislavski, who for many represents the quintessence of the fourth-wall, illusionistic style of staging, once said that he wanted the audience at *Three Sisters* to feel as if they were guests at the Prozorov household. If a spectator at the Moscow Art Theatre should truly feel this way, how does this experience differ from that of the spectators at Grotowski's *Doctor Faustus* who sit at the table with Faustus as his guests, or from The Performance Group's production of *The Tooth of Crime* in which the spectators move with the character Hoss from his kitchen to his bedroom in different parts of the theatre? Clearly, these examples represent differing aspects of environmentalism and there is no single answer. The Stanislavski example is definitely frontal and entails purely psychological involvement, while Grotowski represents an incorporation of the spectator within a frame, and the third is a kinesthetic incorporation—encouraging the spectator to experience the stage space physically, much as the performer does.

Since this study attempts to define environmental theatre in terms of spatial relationships, it is necessary to classify environmental productions clearly by the degree to which they move from frontal to totally non-frontal staging—a continuum of environmental theatre.

There are two ways in which a spectator will be unable to view a performance frontally: he may be placed more or less in the center of the production so that the actions or just the decor extend beyond his frontal line of vision; or the performance may be fragmented so that it occurs in two or more discrete locations—what can be termed multi-space staging. A multi-space performance can occur in locations separated by some distance (as in Meredith Monk's *Vessel* which took place at three sites in Manhattan), or at a single location partitioned or compartmented to create distinct and separate areas (as in Allan Kaprow's *18 Happenings in 6 Parts* in which the performing space was partitioned so as to create three rooms).

To begin with, let us consider the first possibility—a continuum of surrounding staging in which the spectator is incorporated to some degree into the scenographic frame. At what we may call the frontal end of the continuum are those productions which do not surround the spectator in any way—the arena or proscenium stages—and at the other end are those productions which totally envelop the spectator. Beginning near the frontal end we might consider certain outdoor performances. Although most open-air theatres—the Shakespeare-in-the-park theatres, the historical pageant theatres to be found throughout the South and Southwest, and of course the Greek theatres, for instance—are nothing more than frontal stages moved outside, many spectators have probably had the experience of feeling that the surrounding natural features—the sky, trees, distant mountains, or even buildings—were somehow incorporated into the setting.[3] Some productions reinforce this feeling by referring to these features or, if possible, physically including them in the performance. *Tecumseh*, an historical pageant at Chillicothe, Ohio, for instance, is set before a cliff. The performance commences at sundown with an actor riding a horse down the cliff and onto the stage. If the spectator perceives the natural background as part of the setting (and it is irrelevant whether this perception was intended by the production or not), then, by extension, he may feel surrounded by the setting. The sky above the stage, for example, is equally above the spectators; the greenery behind the stage may wrap around the spectator area as well.

The pre-existing surroundings may be described as a found environment. Found space, which is frequently used as a setting for environmental performance, is any given area, interior or exterior, that is used in its existing state for performance. It is not physically altered in any significant way. Since a found environment characteristically contains no preordained stage or audience areas—these are determined by the use of space within the performance—the spectator can perceive the environment as a total space shared by himself and the performers. Max Reinhardt's famous production of *Everyman* was staged in front of the cathedral at Salzburg, Austria. The cathedral, a found environment, provided a backdrop, but, as will be seen in Chapter 3, the cathedral plaza in which the spectators sat and the surrounding buildings *seemed* to become unified into one performance space. Trisha Brown's *Roof Piece*, a post-modern dance that was staged on and watched from various rooftops in New York's Soho district, is another example (see Chapter 8). Rather than seeing certain roofs as stages, the spectators most likely perceived themselves as surrounded by an environment of rooftops, some of which supported performances.

It might be possible to talk of a purely frontal performance in a found environment, a booth stage in a market square, say, but this takes into account only the *quality* of the space. Environmental staging, at least as defined here, can be discussed only in terms of the *use of space*.[4]

In the uses of space discussed so far, the spectator has not had to alter his relationship to the performance itself; it remains essentially frontal and the perception of environment is largely in the mind of the viewer. This may be called perceived environment.

Frontal   **Non-frontal**
Perceived
environment

There are certain plays or performances, however, which directly imply that the spectators share the same space (and time) as the performers. In Clifford Odets' *Waiting for Lefty* , for instance, audience members are treated as if they were cab drivers at a union meeting and actors address the spectators directly as co-workers. The Royal Shakespeare Company's production of *Marat/Sade* tried to create the feeling that the spectators were the audience of the play-within-the-play—spectators at the asylum at Charenton. Regardless of the success of such illusionistic devices as those just mentioned, the performance implies that the auditorium is part of the stage environment. While the performer-spectator relationship is still frontal, the perception of environment is now suggested by the performance itself and can be referred to as implied environment.

Frontal   **Non-frontal**
Perceived   Implied
environment   environment

Early in this century, when scenographic experimentation was largely directed towards alternatives to the proscenium stage, many architects attempted to unite the stage and auditorium spaces either scenically or architecturally, a trend which continues to the present. In an architecturally unified space the stage and auditorium are enclosed by the same architectural elements: wall, ceiling, floor.[5] Historical precedents for this may be seen in reconstructions of Elizabethan private theatres and in the Restoration stages in which spectator boxes continued along the forestage walls and the same lighting sources lit both the stage and auditorium. In the twentieth century a somewhat similar effect was consciously sought in such theatres as the Redoutensaal in Vienna and the Dalcroze theatre at Hellerau, Switzerland (see Chapter 3). Although performances in these theatres were frontal, and the plays did not necessarily implicate the spectators spatially, the audiences were actually in the same physical space as the performance. When compared to the proscenium this seemed, at the time, to eliminate the sense of a frame. Today, with the so-called black box or open-space theatres being fairly common, new spatial conventions have developed and frontal performances in these spaces are generally not seen as even semi-environmental.

Scenic unification of a given space is a result of the transformation of that space. Transformed space is the corollary to found space; it is the result of the physical alteration of a given area for performance. On one level this can consist of the extension of onstage scenery into the auditorium, or it can be as elaborate as the construction of a total environment that encompasses the audience. Richard Foreman's *Le Livre des Splendeurs*, for instance, was staged in Paris in 1976. There were strings, well known to anyone who has seen his plays, extending from the stage to the balcony, thus connecting the stage and auditorium. For Reinhardt's American production of Karl Vollmoeller's *The Miracle*, designer Norman Bel Geddes transformed the interior of the Century Theatre into a gothic cathedral (see Chapter 3). Besides the arches and stained glass windows, Geddes covered the aisles with slate and disguised the seats as pews. The degree of transformation differed in the two cases but they represented the same impulse. Scenically the stage and auditorium became a connected, if not unified, space and the spectator, while watching the otherwise frontal performance could not therefore take in the total scenography. Although physical decor is the most obvious means of creating a unified space, sound and smell have sometimes been used as well.

Frontal			**Non-frontal**
Perceived environment	Implied environment	Unified space	

Many factors enter into the audience's acceptance of unified space. There is, of course, the question of degree—*The Miracle* is far more elaborate than *Les Livres des Splendeurs* in its unification. And there is a question of juxtaposition and reinforcement. The spectators at *The Miracle* were still seated in standard theatre seats. At a Performance Group production, on the other hand, spectators sit on wooden stairs, scaffolds, and platforms also used for, or identical to, performance areas, and thus may feel more incorporated into the environment. Regardless of how complete or successful the unification of space, however, it is still possible for a spectator to divorce himself from the surroundings and to perceive as performance only the actions of the performers themselves. But if the performers begin to surround the audience, then the spectators can no longer view the performance as frontal.

Although any performance, of course, may be staged so that the performers encircle the spectators, there are certain types of stages specifically designed to permit this. The caliper stage, for example, is a pincer or tonglike stage that partially wraps about the front of the audience. With a caliper stage the sensation of being surrounded will exist only for those spectators forward of the ends of the stage. Spectators toward the rear of the house will probably perceive the caliper merely as an extension of the otherwise frontal stage. The same experience holds true for spectators at the Noh theatre with the *hashigakari*, or bridge, which runs from the dressing room to the stage, or the Kabuki theatre with its *hanamichi* or runway, into the audience. The experience of being surrounded will thus vary according to the location of the spectator in relation to the stage. We might refer to this partial envelopment as experienced environment.

Frontal				**Non-frontal**
Perceived environment	Implied environment	Unified space	Experienced environment	

If the ends of the caliper stage were extended until they met at the rear of the audience they would form an annular stage—a circular stage that completely surrounds the spectators. With this stage, or an equivalent use of space, all the spectators become equally surrounded. This envelopment, however, exists only on a horizontal plane. The more nearly three-dimensional the environment, the more completely is the spectator surrounded. As with the experienced environment, the sense of envelopment is partially dependent on the location of the spectator within the space, even in the totally surrounding space. In Luca Ronconi's production of *Orlando Furioso*, the action, for the most part, occurs around and among the centrally placed spectators. Since the audience is free to move about, however, it is possible for a spectator to move to a corner of the space and have a generally frontal view of the overall event. Only if he perceives the wall behind him as part of the environment will he still feel surrounded. Ideally, then, the most totally surrounding space would be a sphere with the audience suspended at the center, and throughout this century there have been many proposals for theatres based on this model, although none have ever been built in their proposed forms. From a scenographic point of view, then, the totally surrounding theatre is the most environmental.

Frontal				**Non-frontal**
Perceived environment	Implied environment	Unified space	Experienced environment	Surrounding space

While this continuum is essentially based on the relationship of the spectator to the scenography, it is also possible to discuss environmental theatre in terms of the relationship of the performer to the spectator. On the scenographic continuum the stage frame still remains intact. Regardless of the extent to which the spectator is surrounded or feels a part of the total space, he remains in a clearly defined area outside the performance frame or stage space. It is possible, however, for the performer to break that frame and to begin literally to share the performance space with the spectators.

The first step in this direction is simply the acknowledgement of the audience by the performer. This may be written into the script or it may come in the form of ad libs and the "dropping of character." This is not quite the same as the implied environment in which the performers attempt to include the audience in the illusionistic time and place of the play. It is, rather, a penetration through the frame into the spectator space. The next step, of course, becomes a physical penetration of space which is most commonly seen in the form of performers in the aisles. As with the architecturally unified space, the effectiveness of performers in the auditorium as a means of destroying the stage frame was greater when the practice was novel, earlier in this century. Now, with the exception of such performances as *The Connection* or certain Happenings which are, or seem to be, occurring in the same time and space as the event itself, performers in the auditorium tend to be seen primarily as an intrusion into audience space. (In much arena and thrust staging it is necessary for the actors to enter via the aisles. In these cases it is regarded as a convention and the aisles are employed either as an extension of the stage or as "backstage" areas which are not "visible.")

The sense of shared space can be further enhanced if performing areas are created in and among the spectators. If these take the form of permanent stages at several points in an auditorium or spectator area, the result is known as scatter staging. As the distinction between spectator and performance space becomes less definable—as there is a greater sharing of space—it becomes increasingly difficult to establish frontal relationships, and the performance, therefore, can be considered more environmental. A progression in this direction may be seen in a comparison of The Performance Group's production of Sam Shepard's *The Tooth of Crime* and Luca Ronconi's production of *Orlando Furioso* (see Chapter 9). In *Tooth* the audience could move anywhere within the space. There were, however, areas—certain platforms and bridges—that at times reverted to use as localized spaces. One platform became a bedroom, another, the kitchen. If spectators occupied any of these areas when they were needed, the performers simply asked them to move. In *Orlando*, on the other hand, the audience stood about in a large, open rectangular area which was also the place of most of the action. Other than a platform stage at either end, there were no preordained performance sites. Performers on floats were pushed into the space and the audience made way and regrouped around the floats when they were in position. In a truly shared space there is no predetermined performance area, no predetermined audience area. The performers, by virtue of their actions, establish temporary playing spaces (usually frontal) in the midst of the spectators.

A traditional example of this "negotiation" can be seen in the performance of the English mumming play which usually occurs in the found space of a home or tavern. In a standard version the Presenter enters and says: "Room, room, brave gallants all,/ Pray give us room to rhyme."[6] This is the cue for the formation of the playing space. In some versions each performer enters the room independently, walking about in a circle to delineate the space. Other versions have a character entering with a broom and sweeping out a circular area, pushing back spectators as he does so.[7] Modern groups, like the Bread and Puppet Theatre, function in much the same way, although they may use less ritualized techniques.

The shared space cannot rightly be placed on the continuum we have established since it is really a function of the *performers*' relationship to space while the continuum deals with the *spectators*' relationship to space. In all the examples provided by the continuum so far, environmental scenography has been determined largely by the extent to which the spectator was, or perceived himself to be, surrounded by elements of the setting. Shared space is determined by the degree to which the performer uses the entire space of the theatre or performance area. It is possible for the performer to penetrate the audience space—to create a shared space—at any one of the points we have established along the continuum. Shared space can exist in an implied environment or a surrounding space. We can say, however, that shared space is generally more environmental than space which is not shared because it tends to place the spectator in the center of the action.

There are two other elements that can enter into the discussion of both shared and surrounding space: movement and simultaneity. As indicated by the examples of *The Tooth of Crime* and *Orlando Furioso*, the audience may move about with the performance. This movement may affect a spectator's perception of space, and the degree to which he perceives it as environmental, but as long as he remains within a defined or contained space (as in *Tooth* and *Orlando*) movement on the part of the spectator does not make the piece either more or less environmental. Simultaneous performance, on the other hand, will generally make it impossible for a spectator to view the entire production frontally and therefore it increases the environmental nature of a performance.

Before moving on to multi-space performances it is necessary to consider one more aspect of shared space environments. With the exception of simultaneous performances, is there really such a thing as environmental performance in a shared space? All the examples given seem to suggest that shared spaces give rise to a series of frontal performances. The answer may be found in the idea of the perceived environment. Most performances tend to transform the space which surrounds them in the minds of the spectators. When the mummers enter the parlor, for instance, that room ceases, in effect, to be a parlor and becomes instead a performance space which is then shaped by the actors. The fact that only one part of the space may be used for the actual performance is irrelevant—the whole space is transformed for the duration.[8] Parades offer another example. Although ostensibly frontal performances, they transform pedestrian space into festival space and alter the normal patterns of movement on a street. Many spectators may even perceive everyday street facades as a theatrical backdrop. This same transformation of space occurs in most found environment productions.[9]

As mentioned earlier, a second form of environmental theatre involves multi-space staging—the physical separation of the segments of a performance. While the concept of discrete locations may be taken to mean clearly defined areas within a single space—say, two pools of light on a darkened stage—for our purposes "discrete locations" are two or more areas physically separated in such a way that they cannot be simultaneously perceived by a spectator. This is not an absolute definition, however, since there are degrees of discreteness. In Allan Kaprow's *18 Happenings in 6 Parts*, for example, a single room was partitioned into three discrete spaces by translucent dividers. Although the spectator perceived or accepted this as three "rooms," it was possible for a spectator in one space to glimpse parts of the other rooms through doorways. The translucent walls also allowed light and shadows from other spaces to be seen. In Ronconi's *XX*, spectators in each of twenty connected cubicles could hear activity in adjacent compartments although they could not see them. Thus, even discreteness is a function of use and perceptions.

It is not really possible to develop a continuum for multi-space staging as we have done for surrounding space environments. Although multi-space performances employ space in several different ways, the degree to which they are environmental is not determined by the number of discrete places used, or the distance between each discrete space. A multi-space production could, for instance, employ a series of frontal spaces, as Meredith Monk more or less did in *Vessel* (see Chapter 8). What becomes significant in such cases is the relationship of the performers and spectators to the spaces—to what extent they move between areas.

An audience for a multi-space event may, as a group or in parts, move from space to space. Or the spectators may be fragmented and stationary—a section of the audience remaining in each discrete location for the duration of the performance. The performers, likewise, may remain in one location or move from space to space. This allows, then, four combinations of performer-spectator relationships: stationary audience-stationary performance; stationary audience - moving performance; moving audience - moving performance; moving audience - stationary performance.

Stationary audience - stationary performance. The result of this combination is two or more related but independent performances presented sequentially or simultaneously. Neither the performers nor the spectators could have any experiential knowledge of the total event. While such a situation is theoretically possible, there are no conventional theatrical performances that will serve as examples, although there are a few Happenings and Activities that fall into this category.[10] The scenario of Marta Minujin's *Simultaneity In Simultaneity* (1967) called for three performances occurring simultaneously in Buenos Aires, Berlin, and New York.[11] But even this event was not composed of entirely discrete units since video broadcasts of each performance were to be transmitted via satellite to the other locations. Allan Kaprow's Activity, *Self-Service* (1967), consisted of various events taking place or being performed in Boston, New York, and Los Angeles on twelve different days over a period of four months. Of course, since an Activity is not designed for an intentional audience this cannot really be considered a performance.

Stationary audience - moving performance. Examples of this relationship are best seen in medieval staging, mummings, and most processions. Certain medieval mystery plays were performed on wagons which were moved from point to point within a town. An assembled audience waited at each point. In the traditional mumming, costumed performers move from location to location within the town—often, private homes, although taverns and market squares are used as well—presenting a show at each point. Although each audience sees only the presentation at its own household, the total performance really consists of all the visitations and the movement between these points.[12] This is known as perambulatory performance. If the emphasis of the performance is not on the visitation but on the movement itself, as in parades, the result is processional performance.

Processional performance is the movement of a group of performers between two points, past a more or less continuous line or column of spectators. Processional pageants such as the French Revolution *fêtes* created by Jacques-Louis David, and the royal entries of the Middle Ages and the Renaissance are other examples. Although the stationary audience - moving performance arrangement is most typical of folk and medieval religious performances, there are analogous contemporary examples. In 1967, for instance, members of The Performance Group and others staged an antiwar agit-prop play entitled *Guerilla Warfare* at several locations around New York City (see Chapter 8). Their schedule of performances makes an interesting comparison with the performance schedule of an English mumming troupe called the Antrobus Soul-Cakers:[13]

Antrobus:

George & Dragon, Gt. Budworth	7:30
Cock Inn, St. Budworth	8:00
Wheatsheaf Inn, Antrobus	8:30
Brick & Bottle, Whitley	9:00
Chetwode Arms, Whitley	9:30
Dance in Whitley Schools	10:15

The Performance Group:

10:00 A.M.	At Actors Playhouse, 100 7th Ave. S.
12:00 Noon	United Nations—Dag Hammerskjold Plaza
2:00 P.M.	529 West 42nd, Army Recruiting Center, Times Sq.
4:00 P.M.	ABC, 1330 Ave. of the Americas
6:00 P.M.	Pageant Players support Richard's group at Port Authority

Moving audience - moving performance. In this category both the performers and the spectators move from site to site. An example of this is Tom O'Horgan's production of Megan Terry's *Changes*.[14] In Part One of the three-part piece, spectators were individually taken on tours of several blocks around the theatre. As the performer/guides passed each other they would exchange a few lines of dialogue. Returning to the theatre each spectator was then blindfolded and carried into an environment where he was placed in the middle of a scene. The spectators would then be carried from environment to environment by the performers. In the third part the spectators were carried into still another room where the piece ended in music and dancing. Certain processional and perambulatory performances, both historical and contemporary, involve a moving audience. (Many medieval Church dramas and Jean-Jacques Lebel's *Funeral Ceremony of the Anti-Procès*—see Chapter 7—provide typical examples, as do certain Indian festivals such as the Ramlila.) This form is the most common among contemporary multi-space performances.

Moving audience - stationary performance. Here it is the audience that moves from location to location as the performance remains at each site. For a production of Maria Irene Fornes' *Fefu and Her Friends* in the spring of 1977, spectators gathered in one room and sat on bleachers but were subsequently divided into four groups which would move from room to room to see parts of the performance.[15] The performers remained in the individual rooms and repeated their performances for each new audience. Wolf Vostell's 1964 piece, *You: A Decollage Happening For Bob and Rhett Brown* (see Chapter 7), involved the audience moving from point to point although, in actuality, they were really moving *through* an environment.

So-called amusement environments—fairs and amusement parks—are clearly defined spaces that are broken into smaller individual units devoted to entertainment or performance through which spectators are free to wander. While an amusement environment itself is not theatre, its use of space has been a model for many performance environments, such as Paul Sills' *Monster Model Funhouse* and Ariane Mnouchkine's *1789* (see Chapters 8 and 9). The amusement environment provides an interesting model because its structure allows the spectators a degree of freedom in their movements and choice of performance.

In all but the stationary audience - stationary performance category it is ultimately possible for the spectators to observe the entire performance, provided the performance is presented sequentially (not unlike watching the several acts of a play). If, however, performance is occurring simultaneously in several of the discrete spaces, the spectators not only cannot perceive the entire performance frontally, they cannot ever perceive the entire performance at all. Allan Kaprow's *18 Happenings in 6 Parts* involved simultaneous performance in its three spaces, and when it was performed in 1959 was probably the first modern example of simultaneous performance in multi-space environments. Since that time many multi-space performances in all categories have employed simultaneity.

Certain multi-space performances are presented in obviously unified environments. The twenty cubicles of Luca Ronconi's *XX* (see Chapter 9) were part of a single construction in the theatre auditorium. HaftTan Mountain outside Shiraz became the environment for Robert Wilson's *KA MOUNTAIN AND GUARDenia TERRACE* (see Chapter 9). But those productions which are spread over some distance raise questions about the unification of space. The three locations of Monk's *Vessel*, for instance, were thematically related but were they spatially related? Were they in any way part of a single environment?

In the next chapter it will be seen that many traditional multi-space performances such as mummings and processions employ the town as a found performance environment, thereby unifying disparate spaces through the actions of the participants. In a certain sense, many contemporary performances do the same thing. The Bread and Puppet Theatre, for instance, quite consciously chooses the town over the traditional theatre for specific esthetic reasons, but having done so exploits the qualities of the town in much the same way mummers use the village.

Returning to *Vessel*, we see that Monk was very much aware of the qualities of New York City. The spectators were transported by bus from Part One to Part Two, and Monk had originally intended to place performers along the route. She opted instead to let the natural theatrical ambience of New York streets suffice. The third site was also chosen for its specific New York atmosphere. While the scale of *Vessel* to New York City is, of course, different than that of, say, English mummers to their village, the incorporation and transformation of space are basically the same. For those spectators, at least, who took the bus between locations, or were aware of the surroundings of the parking lot, the city may have become a perceived environment. Ultimately, then, the perception of a multi-space environment as a unified space (unless it is ostensibly physically connected) is dependent upon the spectators.

Frontal performance creates an essentially one-to-one relationship between the performer and spectator; there is a clearly defined boundary between the two. Environmental performance places the spectator at the center of the event, often with no boundary between performer and spectator. The performance frame may be distant and indistinct, and it becomes increasingly difficult to exclude any space or action as non-performance.

In the following chapters environmental theatre is studied from a more or less chronological perspective, beginning with a survey of traditional forms. It will be seen that the historical development of environmental theatre in the twentieth century follows the continuum surprisingly closely— that is, the early attempts were largely in the realm of perceived and implied environments, while more recent forms have involved surrounding and multi-space environments. This is not an exhaustive study; there are dozens, perhaps even hundreds, of performances that could have been included. The purpose here is to chart a development, indicating, along the way, its significant steps. In recent years especially, the number of non-frontal performances has been too great for comprehensive study. It will also be seen that except for some lesser-known productions, documentation has been minimal. Again, the purpose here was not so much to document performances (many are well-documented elsewhere), as to place them in a new perspective. In his introduction to *Theatres, Spaces, Environments*, Brooks McNamara states: "The environmental tradition . . . represents a far more ancient and far more common solution to the problems of organizing space than the critics and historians have supposed."[16] It is hoped that this current study will show that this same environmental tradition has become a prevalent form of scenography in the twentieth century.

2

The Environmental Tradition

This play [Le Jeu de la Feuilée *by Adam de le Hale*] . . . *displays a simple idea, but one that to us is now unfamiliar; it resists any impulse to invent a special "scene," and is content to take place in reality, at the occasion of the performance, and it uses for the background of its action the real inn before which it would be actually played . . . . Beyond this is the overtone suggested of the well-known streets around leading to this inn. . . . Its setting then, is the real world, not a fiction.*

—*Richard Southern*
The Seven Ages of the Theatre

The form of staging that we call environmental theatre is, for the most part, a modern, theoretically-based movement; it is a solution to problems of scenography based on a conscious use and manipulation of space. As we shall see, the roots of this movement may be traced to reactions against the proscenium around the turn of the century. Frontal staging, however, is so dominant in the Western tradition that even after nearly a century of environmental alternatives, many people still have some difficulty in accepting non-frontal scenography. The majority of theatre historians still tend to dismiss environmental performances as little more than eccentric contemporary experiments. It is, therefore, important to realize that non-frontal uses of space have been common throughout the history of theatre and actually dominate much non-Western theatre and certain forms of folk performance. (It should also be realized, however, that traditional non-frontal uses of space are neither conscious nor theoretical. They are practical solutions to spatial problems based on local conditions and conventions and tend to be done without regard to historical precedent. Thus, while there are striking parallels and analogous uses of space, it would be wrong to consider twentieth-century environmental theatre and historical non-frontal performance as part of a continuous tradition.)

While there are few contemporary designers or directors working environmentally who acknowledge an influence from historical forms, a survey of the non-frontal tradition may help place environmental theatre in historical perspective.[1] A detailed history of traditional forms, though, is beyond the scope of this study—it would, of necessity, encompass much of theatre history. Besides, there are already several studies of the use of space in these forms.[2] It is possible, however, to indicate several types of performances and discuss their uses of space.

The play described by Richard Southern at the beginning of this chapter dates from the thirteenth century. Despite Southern's claim that this form of staging is "unfamiliar" to us, the subsequent chapters will demonstrate that this should not be the case—the twentieth century can provide many such examples. What is so surprising, in fact, is the remarkable similarity between the staging of *Le Jeu de la Feuilée (The Play of the Leafed One)* and, say, Reinhardt's *Jederman*. Both use found environments and create a sense of shared space. Both use the town as environment. Since much medieval religious theatre (as well as many folk and popular forms) was occasional, it often employed found environments not normally intended for performance. And, since these presentations were frequently in communities lacking suitable public indoor space, the performances were often outdoors, (or in the case of certain mummings, in private homes). With no preordained or specialized area for presentation, performance space had to be determined by the actions of the participants themselves. The town became a generalized environment in which localized spaces were created through a subtle interaction of performers and spectators.

This may be seen more clearly, perhaps, in another, somewhat different, approach to the town-as-environment, the production of a *Ramlila* spectacle (a drama based on the epic *Ramayana*) at Ramanagar, India.

> Here *Ramlila* performances last for thirty-two days, and the entire text of the epic Ramayana is presented. All of the middle-size town is used as an arena for the processional staging of the epic story. There are permanently built structures of the main locales: the palaces of Ayodhya; the kingdom where Rama ruled; Ashrama of the sage Vishwamitra; Janakpura, where Rama was married to Sita; Panchavati, the jungle hut where Rama lived during the exile and where Sita was abducted by the demon king Ravana; and Lanka, the golden palace of Ravana. These form an integral part of the town's architecture and its landscape. When Rama, along with Sita and his brother Lakshmana, goes to the forest, he has to cross a river; the river flowing by the town is used.
>
> In this processional style of *Ramlila*, the drama moves from one locale to another, and the audience moves along with it. Rama leaves for the forest, and a large audience of some ten thousand people follows him to their first halt with tears in their eyes. To achieve simultaneity of action, the performance often is organized on different physical levels. Thus, the final scene of the epic story, the battle between Rama and Ravana, is enacted on the level ground and also on a raised platform; at the same time, the gods can

be seen sitting on forty to fifty-foot-high platforms, watching the symbolic fight between the forces of good and evil. The scene of the union between Rama and his brother Bharata on Rama's return to Ayodhya after his victory over Ravana is enacted in the main street of the town as a grand royal procession.[3]

The Adam de le Hale play, *Le Jeu de la Feuilée*, using an implied environment, is a single-space, essentially frontal performance. The *Ramlila* uses a multi-space environment, processional performance and a mobile audience. Both effect a transformation of space. Part of the significance of non-frontal folk theatre lies in the ability of such performances to coalesce the several discrete locales of multi-space performance into a single unified space. This unification is fairly obvious at Ramanagar where the setting is incorporated into the permanent architecture of the town, but it is equally valid in more tenuous settings such as the Christmas mummings of England in which costumed performers go from house to house presenting brief folk dramas.

In general, historical or traditional non-frontal performance can be grouped into three broad categories: perambulatory performance, processional performance, and performance environments. The most common form of perambulatory performance, as indicated earlier, is the mumming, which at its most elemental level is a movement of costumed participants from point to point for the purpose of theatrical performances. Generally occurring on or around holidays, a mumming involves members of the community moving from house to house (or from tavern to tavern) to present appropriate skits. Related to this are morris and sword dances, and plough and wooing plays.[4] A traditional mumming usually involves a *quête*, a collection of money or food from the spectators by the performers as well. Since the points of performance are frequently private homes, the performance is often referred to by folklorists as a "visitation."[5] It was suggested in the first chapter that a mumming transforms the visitation point into a perceived environment or shared space; this process is certainly aided by the *quête* which involves a direct interaction with the spectators.

Although the mumming may seem to be little more than a series of independent presentations repeated by a group of performers, the use of the town as environment and the continuation of performance outside the houses or visitation points indicates that the mumming, as a whole, is a single performance event. The mumming may be divided into five parts: 1) the assembly of participants; 2) the movement to the point of presentation or performance; 3) the performance; 4) the exodus (possibly involving the *quête*); 5) the final assembly and dispersal of participants. The middle three segments may be repeated as often as necessary. It is the second part, the movement from point to point, that is most significant in the transformation of space. Herbert Halpert, in his study of mumming in Newfoundland, proposed a "typology of mumming" that included two kinds of movement: "Informal Outdoor Behavior" and "Formal Outdoor Movement."[6] The latter category includes the more formal processions or dances between visitations and such activity indicates that the participants maintain a continuous spirit and attitude of performance beyond the formal presentations themselves. The "Formal Outdoor Movement" clearly fits into the category of the "stationary audience - moving performance."

The "Informal Outdoor Behavior," however, which may border on the paratheatrical, is a better example of the town-as-environment. Richard Southern, for instance, provides a description of a group of German mummers known as the Bavarian Wild Men.[7] On St. Nicholas Eve these masked revelers ski out of the woods and into villages going from house to house making mischief. Spectators watch them, if at all, from behind windows and doors. "There are no words; there is no play," says Southern. "There is no particular place of performance; no stage; no scenery; no playhouse; and no rehearsal. Here there is not even—and this is perhaps the most noticeable lack of all—any assembled audience as such."[8] Here the performance space is limited, though slightly, by the potential audience; the Wild Men can be locked out of the houses. But if, as seems to be the case, their "performance" is carried out regardless of the audience, then their awareness of space is not limited by traditional actor-audience relationships. The village and the woods become an unrestricted performance environment.

Another example is provided by the Polish Vagabonds, a similar group of New Year's mummers, who also use the town-as-environment.[9] The Vagabonds

> assemble at the village brewery. The players come in their costumes . . . When the whole group has assembled, they begin their run into the hills. The gypsy leads the way, followed by the two horses . . . Others in the entourage follow at random. Death swings her cudgel to the right and left while the Devil slides down a hill. As the Vagabonds lash through the hills and valleys, they separate and then meet periodically at the homes of their acquaintances, which in these mountain villages are often far apart.[10]

Such a beginning, together with the ensuing actions, encompasses the entire countryside. The performance space thus becomes the total area within the performers' range of wandering—the entire village area has become a large, unlocalized performance area. Within this space there are no prearranged performance sites. "In another section of the village," the description continues, "the Devil and the Plowman engage in a duel in the snow. As a sleigh full of villagers passes by, their play becomes performance."[11] The unstructured play of the participants becomes shaped as performance and the space involved becomes localized through essentially arbitrary framing devices of the spectators. The boundaries of the performance are delimitated by a subtle interaction between the performer and spectator. This process is really no different from that described earlier for *Orlando Furioso*.

The mumming troupe of St. Stephen's Church in Toledo, Ohio, on the other hand, represents a much more formalized commencement. This group, of Hungarian descent, begins their perambulation with a procession down the aisle of the church on Christmas Eve.

> The shepherds and angels proceed up the center aisle in full costume, hats on, the angels carrying the *Betlehem* [a model church with figurines of the crêche scene, used for keeping the rewards of the *quête*]. The *öregek* ["old ones"], however, do not wear their fur masks and generally hang some steps to the rear during the brief procession.[12]

Aside from a quality of decorum in marked contrast to that of the Vagabonds, there is a definite sense of relationship to the space the performers are using. As in a traditional procession they are bounded on two sides by spectators in more or less inviolable space. This relationship between the performers and the surrounding space remains relatively constant throughout the entire period of their perambulations. It is probably fair to say that in such cases as these, the performers' relationship to the surrounding space is determined at least in part by an individual sensibility regarding the activity—the extent to which the participants consider the event to be a theatrical performance. Another Polish mumming group which performs a King Herod play, for instance, does not consider its activity to be theatre but instead refers to itself as a team or gang.[13] The Toledo mummers, although certainly not lacking the sense of fun inherent in their activity, seem to be more conscious of it as a performance and thus tend to set themselves up in more conventional theatrical relationships to their audiences. This "negotiation" process, and the continual and changing transformation of space, are the primary environmental elements of perambulatory performance.

A sense of shared space is further evidenced in another example, the Indian *Raslila*, a traditional play based on the legend of Krishna. Generally performed in temple courtyards and gardens, all elements of the found environment are employed—gardens, balconies, terraces.[14] The action moves freely throughout the entire space, often passing through the audience. The audience itself moves about to follow the action.

Most mummings conclude with the performers joining the spectator-host in a festival meal, or the spectators joining the performers in song and dance. This conclusion may be seen as a reintegration of the performers into the community, thereby bringing to an end any transformation of space. As opposed to a physical theatre space in which the performance and audience areas remain distinct even when there is no performance in progress, non-frontal folk forms lose their performance aspects the moment the performer/spectator interaction ceases to frame a performance space.

Processional performances may be distinguished from perambulatory performance in that no visitation, in the true sense of the word, occurs; the dynamics of the procession are dominant throughout. Performances are an adjunct of the procession rather than the reverse as is the case with perambulatory performance. Furthermore, these performances maintain the same spirit and quality as the procession itself—they are generally public, emblematic, and allegorical as opposed to the more personal, ritualized mummings. Pageants, spectacles, and certain festival activities are often processional and many may have evolved from once simple processions.

Processional performance is environmental for several reasons. First of all, the total performance involves movement over great distances, generally beyond the frontal visual scope of a single spectator. Like perambulatory performance, processions use the town or its surroundings as performance space, usually transforming the processional route into festival space, and, to some degree, implicating the audience and perhaps even incorporating it into the performance.

Even in the most formalized processions the separation between performer and spectator is often difficult to make, not so much because of unclear physical boundaries, but because there is a frequent crossing-over of roles—either in actuality or in spectator perceptions. The procession, at its basic level, like folk performance, utilizes members of the community performing for other members of the community with the possibility of certain performers and spectators continually changing roles. The performers may even parade in everyday dress, the only theatrical framing devices being provided by a few emblems or banners and by the formal configuration of movement patterns. Thus, the physical boundaries of processional performance are in an almost constant state of flux, depending on the portion of the procession being viewed and the point of view and specific perceptions of the individual spectators.

Despite the processional nature of the parade, the spectator is in an essentially frontal relation to the performance. Depending on his vantage point, he may, of course, be able to obtain some overall perspective of the entire event, or to focus closely on a certain aspect of it over some distance; but his primary view of the performance occurs as it passes. The result is akin to watching a moving panorama, albeit a panorama in which other spectators or the architecture of the town, or the landscape of the countryside provide the background.

The procession tends to move past relatively rapidly, and parade architecture and design, therefore, tends toward the gaudy, colorful, and eye-catching. Because of its transitory nature, the procession must be able to compel focused attention and to convey messages with ease and directness. Passing through a random and frequently very active environment, parade decor must be not only spectacular, but easily comprehensible at a single glance, while being at the same time sufficiently intricate to maintain attention.

The nature of processional performance allows for what Richard Schechner calls "selective inattention."[15] The procession, because it is in some senses multi-focused and simultaneous (units of a parade pass by sequentially, yet several units can be observed at once), does not demand continuous single-focused attention from the spectators. The spectator may, as it were, define his own "performance" by leaving the performance area and returning to it at will, engaging in other activities within the spectator area, and, if his vantage point allows, focusing on different segments of the procession in random order. Although this selective inattention or random focus is theoretically possible in almost any viewing situation, it is most successful in environmental performance because of the multi-focus nature of the event, and often because of the ability of the spectator to move about freely or choose his own viewpoint rather than accepting the forced focal point of conventional frontal theatre.

Even the simplest parade effects a transformation of space. In general, it freezes all movement on the sides of the street or route, focusing attention on the street rather than on the buildings served by the street in the normal course of everyday activity. The multi-focused environment of the street thus changes to a highly directed focus on a sequential procession. The procession serves to transform space; the town becomes a performance environment. As the geographical emphasis shifts, the roles of civic art and architecture and the functions of members of the community also alter accordingly. Certain thoroughfares and monuments of the city which, in everyday use, are not more significant than similar areas, take on special qualities as a result of the festivity. As with the folk performances already discussed, the confluence of costumed performers within a space automatically alters the usual perceptions of that space by spectators.

Aiding in the transformation of space is the spectator himself. The wall of people lining a parade route at least partially obliterates the familiar street facades, thus altering the spectator's perception of an otherwise well-known space. But the spectators are not limited to street level. Surrounding houses and buildings can likewise become vantage points, as was the case with royal entries—the ceremonial procession of visiting royalty and nobility through a city during the Middle Ages and Renaissance. The entries demonstrate many features of processional performance, especially in the shifting roles of performers and spectators. At points along the procession route stages were erected for tableaux or allegorical performances in honor of the royal guest. These stages were sometimes specially erected monuments, but they could also be created from transformed civic architecture such as water cisterns.[16] For the viewing of performances at the processional stops, the best vantage point was the middle of the street opposite the tableau, this place being reserved, of course, for the honored guest and his retinue. Beyond this, the next "best seats," as it were, were in houses facing the performing site. The rest of the crowd had to find space on the street or on rooftops.

Two ostensible consequences of this sort of spectator-performance relationship suggest themselves. First of all, there is a distancing from the performance, since a wall literally exists between the performer and the spectator who is watching from inside a house, discouraging any actual or implied connections with the event. Second there is the transformation of space, which both affects and is informed by altered perceptions: market squares, arches, cisterns and the like are converted into localized performance spaces by the decor and actions of performers, thus transforming the everyday into the theatrical. Private houses, in turn, take on the quality of balconies or private boxes. More than in most types of performance, the spectator at a processional performance is free to shape the performance through his own perceptions by selecting his position, focus, and the degree and duration of his involvement.

Moreover, ceremonial processions frequently had a dual audience or a dual focus of performance. In the royal entry, for example, the primary spectator was the guest of honor—the royal visitor and his retinue. The performances at the presentation points were always directed at him or her. But the larger audience of townspeople saw both the given performance as well as the spectacle of the royal guest. The central spectator became an integral part of the performance and so, by implication, did the general audience. As theatre historian Sheldon Cheney has noted, the royal entries as performances were "none the less dramatic for having decorated streets, palace facades and public squares for their stage; real kings, courtiers, soldiers and slaves for their actors; and an audience that was a living part of the story."[17]

If the royal guest is considered only in his role as spectator, then the royal entry becomes an example of the moving audience - stationary performance category as he travels between prearranged stations throughout the town. In this form of procession, however, an obvious problem of dramatic continuity arises since it is an element of the audience which moves from point to point while the tableau performers are left behind at each stage. There would seem to be a difficulty in maintaining coherence of theme. To the mass of spectators, however, a thematic unity was provided by the continued presence of the honored guest as the focal point of each stage.[18] In this dual role of performer and spectator, the honored guest, moving from point to point, became the center of the pageant. This is an important idea to consider since environmental theatre generally has no physical structure such as a proscenium or arena with which constantly to focus attention and thereby create a forced unity of spectator perceptions.

The *fêtes* of the French Revolution are perhaps the quintessential example of processional/pageant theatre. They often involved hundreds of thousands of spectators and performers and they incorporated simple procession, ceremony, theatrical presentation, rhetoric, and emblematic display (although in deference to the proletarian principles of the Revolution as well as the classical modes of Jacques-Louis David, their principal designer, they tended to avoid an overabundance of rococo allegory).

These events, based on supposedly Roman models, became the blueprint for most political pageantry since that time—most notably they were the basis of the mass spectacles of the Russian Revolution. The pageants had the avowed purpose of legitimizing the revolutionary governments and instilling an appropriate patriotism and fervor in the populace. In this respect they obviously bore a certain relationship to the Renaissance entries. Citing the political philosophy behind the Revolution, David seized upon the true participatory nature of processions: "National festivals are instituted for the people; it is fitting that they participate in them with a common accord and that they play the principal role there."[19] The people thus usurped the role of the royal guest in the entries.

For the festival marking the first anniversary of the storming of the Bastille, tens of thousands participated in building an amphitheatre on the Champ de Mars.[20] A description of the Festival of Liberty in 1792 mentions the slowness of the procession, caused by frequent halts as participants stopped to sing and dance.[21] After the final rituals of the *fêtes* presented on the Champ de Mars, there was a hymn to liberty and the masses embraced each other, dancing around the altar in a demonstration of "patriotic gaiety, perfect equality and civic fraternity."[22]

Perhaps the most grandiose spectacle of this period was Voltaire's funeral procession (or, rather, his exhumation and installation in the recently completed Pantheon) on July 10, 1791. The ceremonial funeral processions—the *Pompe Funèbre*—provided the opportunity for lavish display, and the practice dated at least to the sixteenth century with origins in antiquity. The arrival of Voltaire's sarcophagus turned Paris into a performance environment of sorts, with all the theatres giving special presentations. Other festival activities took place throughout the city as well. The procession itself may have had as many as 100,000 participants and 100,000 spectators, although this estimate came from a highly enthusiastic contemporary source.[23]

Engravings show rank after rank of participants with appropriate banners, medallions, gonfalons, and the like. David had designed the triumphal chair which was drawn by twelve white horses. This spectacular monument dominated the procession. The cortege stopped at the Opéra, Comédie Italienne, the home of the Marquis de Villette (where Voltaire had died), the Comédie Française, and at the Tuileries—an unscheduled stop—to greet the royal prisoners. At each stop there were various orations or dramatic displays.

The cortege included three complete orchestras and quantities of drums and trumpets. It is with descriptions of the French *fêtes* that regular accounts of pageant music become common, although music was always an element of public ceremony. Sound is an intangible component of theatrical performance, but it takes on special qualities in environmental theatre. It has the ability to permeate the environment, thus extending the sense of perception of performance beyond the merely visual aspects. One can hear, for example, a parade coming without necessarily seeing it. March music can regiment disorganized masses, both performers and spectators, into formalized units—it can direct undirected wandering; it can provide focus. The physical vantage point of the spectator will alter aural perceptions. A person at street level will hear each band in a parade in the same sequence that he sees them; someone on a rooftop, however, may hear a melding of sounds that are not coordinated with the visual aspects of the procession.

The performance environment is a structure or unified group of structures that enclose a spectator at a performance and are somehow integral to that particular performance. Thus, a conventional theatre, although enclosing the stage and auditorium, is not really a performance environment. The structure for the *Raslila*, or Krishna play, at the festival of *Bhavana* in India, however, could certainly be considered such an environment (Plate 1).

The playing area, in the shape of a lotus flower, consisted of forty-two "petals."[24] The *Raslila* was simultaneously presented on twenty-one "petals" by twenty-one different monastery groups. Alternating with the acting areas were spectator areas. The performance space also became a communal living area for the participants. The conclusion of the piece was a great procession joined by the spectators.

More common than such specialized structures are the so-called amusement environments—fairs, carnivals and amusement parks which, like perambulatory and processional performance, use the town as environment (or imitate the topography of the town in their layout). Most amusement environments, while containing locations for performance are not performances in themselves. Their significance lies in the manner in which they create, transform or use space as a total environment. The amusement environment represents a transformation of everyday space into festival space, and in so doing it frequently employs spectacular decor, crowd control, and even mass emotional manipulation. Its scenography and its theatrical effect on spectators have provided models for more recent performance environments like Paul Sills' *Monster Model Funhouse* (see Chapter 7), and the general ambience of Ariane Mnouchkine's *1789* (see Chapter 9).

An amusement environment exists when a clearly defined space is broken into smaller individual areas devoted to entertainment or performance, among which the spectators are free to wander. The seemingly haphazard arrangement of compartments is, in actuality, a carefully designed method of spectator control.

Fairs, the basis for most amusement environments, evolved out of a combination of commercial activity and religious celebration.[25] Primitive market fairs were generally held in open areas, usually neutral ground between the territories of two tribes or societies and frequently they possessed no important physical structures.[26] When fairs began to be held in town market squares boundaries were established, creating a specific area which was temporarily transformed by stalls, wagons and the activity of buyers and sellers. As with processions, houses abutting the square might take on special importance. With the introduction of specialized architecture, a market square or an open field thus became an environment of connected but clearly differentiated spaces. By the seventeenth century, amusements began to dominate the larger fairs and hence, the amusement environment evolved.

The placement of a spectator in the midst of an amusement environment must necessarily have psychological or perceptual effects. There is, for example, a tendency toward disorientation, a tendency on which carnival operators have learned to capitalize. Unlike a processional performance in which the spectator may turn his back on the procession and thus on the festival space which it creates, a fairground can be ignored only by quitting the space altogether. Performance, scenic elements and displays assault the spectator at every turn. It is not merely the visual which creates this effect. In the total environment all senses may be affected. Accounts from the Middle Ages and the Renaissance emphasize the great jostling crowds, the smells, and most emphatically the "zealous" or "penetrating noise."[27] More recently, E. E. Cummings eloquently expressed similar sentiments about Coney Island.

A trillion smells; the tinkle and snap of shooting galleries; the magically sonorous exhortations of barkers and ballyhoomen; the thousands upon thousands of faces paralyzed by enchantment to mere eyeful disks, which strugglingly surge through dizzy gates of illusion; the metamorphosis of atmosphere into a stupendous pattern of electric colors, punctuated by a continuous whisking of leaning and cleaving shiplike shapes; the yearn and skid of toy cars crammed with screeching reality, wildly spiraling earthward or gliding out of ferocious depth into sumptuous height or whirling eccentrically in a brilliant flatness; occultly bulging, vividly painted banners inviting us to side-shows, where strut and lurk those placid specimens of impossibility which comprise the extraordinary aristocracy of freakdom; the intricate clowning or enormous deceptions, of palaces which revolve, walls which collapse, surfaces which arch and drop and open to emit spurts of lividly bellowing steam—all these elements disappear in a homogeneously happening universe, surrounded by the rhythmic mutations of the ocean and circumscribed by the mightily oblivion-colored rush of the roller coaster.[28]

This assault on the senses created by the totally enveloping environment is, as we shall see, precisely what certain theatre theorists, notably Antonin Artaud, called for in the twentieth century as an antidote to a theatre become rigid and formal.

Although the spectator at an amusement environment exercises some control over his own movements—again, the selection of his own "performance"—amusement scenography really controls the circulation of crowds. The continuous smooth flow of spectators is essential to the maintenance of environmental unity. David Braithwaite, in his book *Fairground Architecture*, analyzes the design of the fairground and its effect on the spectator's perceptions and actions.

> In architectural terms, the roundabout [carousel] is the pivot. As the climax of movement, light and sound, it is the generator of the total environment, as well as being the setting-out point for the planners. Mechanical evolution has produced a structural form that *side and middle stuff* merely surrounds.[29]

The entrances, he continues,

> are normally contrived to act as funnels. Vistas in the grand manner are rarely possible, but often there are views of fine—if accidental—graphic quality. The suggestion of deeper roundings—the sudden glimpse of a roundabout in motion—are all-important. Vertical features like the "Big Wheel," "Helter Skelter" and "Chair-o-Planes," with their geometric patterns of electric lamps, are valuable advertising symbols—sometimes they are augmented by the beams from searchlights. A good showman will never neglect this visual emphasis, particularly when the ground can be seen from some distance.
>
> The composite plan of Nottingham Goose Fair held in October on the Forest Site is a case in point [Plate 2]. The north and south corner entrances are obvious funnels, the central entry on Gregory Boulevard is a contrived piece of axial planning, whereas the north-west entry has fine accidental vistas. The western approach from Noel Street is like a roller conveyor. There are tight clusters of *round'uns* confining some of the larger riding machines, two central arcades—intimate in scale, and the occasional wide avenue. Shows are concentrated in the south-west corner, their *walk-up* fronts forming an "L." "Helter Skelters," twin "Big Wheels" and the "Steam Yachts" are carefully placed to give vertical emphasis.[30]

From descriptions of almost any amusement environment, it is clear that the crowds are perceived as part of the overall experience. One result of spectator control is that the crowds may become not only part of the decor which helps to transform the space, but actual performers. When the movement patterns and dispositions of the crowd against specialized architectural backgrounds are controlled to some degree, the experience of viewing the crowd on the part of individual spectators becomes a performance of sorts. In the case of everyday experiences one must impose a framing device in order to perceive life as theatre; here the framing device is provided by scenography. As E. E. Cummings suggested, "the essence of Coney Island . . . consists in homogeneity. THE AUDIENCE IS THE PERFORMANCE, and vice versa."[31] And at the 1939 New York World's Fair, one critic remarked: "The greatest discovery . . . was the discovery of the crowd as actor and as decoration of great power. The designers found out that the crowd's greatest pleasure is in the crowd."[32]

Any unified space, of course, can be viewed as an environment. In order for a spectator to perceive it as a specialized or performance environment, however, it is essential that there be a transformation, a change in the perceptual relation of the spectator to familiar space. In conventional performance (i.e., performance on a stage), the stage itself is the transformational agent—it is a frame. The introduction of the stage creates a "theatre" and all the images and attitudes that accrue to audience and stage. When there is no stage—or no focal point for performance—then the spectator must be led to perceive a certain area as a performance environment. This is what the scenography of the fairground does.

Much of the transformation of space is a function of decorative scenic elements and fanciful architecture. These exist to attract spectators to particular booths or other units in the environment and thus exert an influence on the spectator's processes of creating his own personalized performance. As in the procession, individual units vie for attention. Light is also one of the most effective instruments for the transformation of space and the control and creation of environment or localized space. The resort area of Blackpool, England is a classic example of space transformed through light. In the Enchanted Grotto, for example, light and color obliterate the solidity of buildings and create their own new landscape. "Their success (due in part to their exciting vulgarity) shows what can be done to create an effect of fun and pleasure which still has an almost universal appeal."[33] Light not only transforms but is a primary element in delimiting space. From within an environment the glare of lights will obliterate all surroundings, while from the outside they define a specific place within the enveloping darkness. This is why outdoor amusement environments work best at night. "When Blackpool's illuminations are switched on," wrote one observer, the atmosphere of the Pleasure Beach and Funfair is successfully extended for several miles along the whole seafront, transforming buildings which by day are most ordinary into one great landscape of fun and fantasy . . . It is a transformation that converts a northern seafront into something approaching our childhood notion of fairyland; it must rank among the major achievements of environmental design.[34]

The parallels between much amusement park design and architecture and the fantastic designs of many totally surrounding theatres will become evident in Chapter 4.

Although amusement environments provided inspiration and models for certain contemporary environments there is little, if any, influence from most traditional environmental forms or their modern counterparts. The similar uses of time and space in the *Ramlila* and Robert Wilson's *Ka Mountain*, for instance, are purely accidental and arbitrary. But at the same time the similarity indicates that modern non-frontal performance does not exist in a void. Both incorporate and transform found space or else create totally encompassing environments. They provide spectators with multi-focus, often kinesthetic, theatrical experiences that differ significantly from frontal forms. In the following chapters, the development of non-frontal performance in modern Western theatre will be explored and it will be seen that contemporary equivalents of the perambulatory and processional performances, as well as the performance environment, have become part of our modern theatre heritage.

3

Reactions Against the Proscenium

Our theatrical habits make it very difficult to imagine what freedom in staging could mean, and to visualize a new handling of the elements of production. We cannot conceive of a theatre, it seems, except in terms of the present-day stage—a limited space filled with cut-out paintings, in the midst of which actors pace up and down, separated from us by a clear-cut line of demarcation.

—*Adolphe Appia*
The Work of Living Art

Beginning in the latter part of the nineteenth century and continuing into the 1930s, there were many reactions against the proscenium stage both in practice and theory. Although no one specifically suggested a form that might be identifiable as environmental theatre, many, like Appia, called for a freedom, imagination, and experimentation that paved the way for later environmental forms. The experiments were as diverse as stagings in gardens and forests, actors moving through the aisles, and elaborate architectural schemes for altering space. While each theorist presented a different rationale for his particular experiment—an attempt to create greater intimacy, a greater theatricality, or a greater realism—they all had one significant thing in common: all the experimental forms were conscious attempts to alter the spectator's relationship to the performance. The movement was eloquently summed up by Kenneth Macgowan and Robert Edmond Jones in 1922:

Over some fifteen years a growing number of minds have been more or less actively seeking a way towards a new type of theatre. They have been abusing the picture-frame stage, stamping on the footlights, pulling out the front of the apron, pushing the actors into the loges, down the orchestra pit, onto the prompter's box, out upon the runways or up the aisles. They have even gone clear out of the playhouse and into circuses, open air theatres, and public parks. All to set up a new and mutual relationship between the actor and the audience.[1]

Obviously, not all these movements and experiments led to environmental theatre. Outdoor performance at the turn of the century, for instance, was generally frontal, while movement of performers into the auditorium is today considered a cliché that seldom, if ever, achieves the desired effect. Yet seventy-five years ago these were considered radical departures from proscenium staging and they marked the start of the practice of surrounding the spectators, or incorporating them within the performance frame. Some experiments led ultimately to the thrust and arena stages, while other impulses toward reform, as we shall see, remained behind the proscenium and resulted in major alterations of the proscenium stage, including a fragmentation of stage space to achieve new effects, and a reorientation of the performer to the stage space and thus, to the audience.

The impetus for outdoor theatre developed out of the desire for a new classical spirit in the theatre. "In these days when the world is talking vaguely of another great renaissance of the art of the theatre," remarked Sheldon Cheney in 1918, "and is waiting expectantly for the new artists who will express their age as characteristically as the Greeks have expressed theirs and Shakespeare his, one may read a new meaning into the recent revival of interest in the *al fresco* drama."[2] The practitioners of outdoor staging, however, were aware of the limitations as well as the benefits of found environments. As one scholar conceded in 1915, it was not "likely that the use of open-air theatre will change greatly the system of illusion and technique now in use on the stage."[3] But he did note that "the chief service that this theatre will render will be to combine the utilization of nature as a medium, or background of dramatic expression."[4] He was, in other words, suggesting the "perceived environment" aspect of open-air staging. As noted earlier, if it is implied that the vista behind the stage is in some way a part of the production, then by implication the vista behind the spectator is incorporated, as well as is the ground upon which he is sitting. There is a unification of space through incorporation.

One of the earliest instances of the modern outdoor performance occurred in the summer of 1880. In his autobiography, Sir Johnston Forbes-Robertson described a performance of scenes from *Romeo and Juliet* with Helena Modjeska in a rectory garden at night.

A platform was made, near a running stream, with great trees as a background, and a big lawn gently rising from the brook became auditorium ... The lighting came from screened oil lamps and the lucky help of a full moon. No stage balcony scene was ever so beautiful. It was full of mystery and charm, and Modjeska seemed to be inspired by the beauty and novelty of the surroundings.[5]

In this instance the effect of the traditional presentation was heightened by the found environment. A certain transformation of space was effected that might not have been possible with conventional stage techniques. This performance was so successful it led to the founding of the Pastoral Players, a group devoted to outdoor staging.[6]

A similar development occurred in France soon after. Calls for a "people's theatre" had been voiced in Paris since the mid-1880s. Finally, in 1895, an open-air theatre was founded at Bussang by Maurice Pottecher who had formerly worked with the Théâtre Libre.[7] Calling it simply The People's Theatre (Le Théâtre du Peuple), Pottecher mounted productions on a covered platform stage (Plate 3). Although little has been written about these productions, Alfred Vallette, editor of the literary journal *Mercure de France* discussed the concept of outdoor staging in relation to the 1896 production of Pottecher's *Le Diable Marchand de Goutte* at Bussang:

> This idea of open air theatre is not unattractive, and indeed we would wish with pleasure that some audacious young director—M. Lugné-Poe, for example—would take the opportunity to present plays in the parks around Paris, on stages, with the fewest properties possible, two or three times daily during the spring and autumn . . . And it seems that one could play there those pieces unplayable in a theatre, staging Claudel's *Tête d'Or* and certain Shakespearian dramas.[8]

Alfred Jarry also commented on the concept of outdoor staging, though he too provided no descriptions of such performances.

> A few words on natural decors, which exist without duplication if one tries to stage a play in the open air, on the slope of a hill, near a river, which is excellent for carrying the voice, especially when there is no awning, even though the sound may be weakened. Hills are all that is necessary, with a few trees for shade . . . Three or four years ago Monsieur Lugné-Poe and some friends staged *La Gardienne* at Presles, on the edge of the Isle-Adam forest. In these days of universal cycling it would not be absurd to make use of summer Sundays in the countryside to stage a few very short performances (say from two to five o'clock in the afternoon) of literature which is not too abstract; King Lear would be a good example; we do not understand the idea of a people's theatre. The performances should be in places not too far distant, and arrangements should be made for people who come by train, without previous planning. The places in the sun should be free (Monsieur Barrucand was writing quite recently about free theatre), and as for the props, the bare necessities could be transported in one or several automobiles.[9]

It is apparent that Jarry's interest in open-air staging lay more in its social implications than in the scenographic possibilities. While most of these productions remained traditional in their use of space they indicated a restlessness with conventional staging practices. Pottecher's theatre did have one major innovation, however. The rear wall of the stage could be opened, permitting a view of the hillside beyond. Pottecher described his production of *The Passion of Joan of Arc* in which the English camp was set up on the hillside and Joan slowly made her way through the tents and the jeering soldiers onto the stage.[10] The productions at Bussang and elsewhere were a major influence on Romain Rolland and his People's Theatre.[11]

The idea of people's theatre and open-air staging led to the development of historical pageants in England and America by such men as Louis Parker, George Pierce Baker, and Percy MacKaye. From 1905, when Parker produced the Sherbourne Pageant and Baker produced one in Cornish, New Hampshire, until after World War I, there were hundreds of these "community dramas"—massive, outdoor historical-allegorical spectacles, usually put on by members of the community and involving hundreds or even thousands of performers.[12]

The pageants of Parker and MacKaye may have contained some processional elements—Sherbourne, for example, ended with a processional march—but they were, on the whole, static, narrative, frontal events. While such pageants were large (the performance area frequently covered several acres) they were designed to be seen and heard clearly by all spectators and to convey a story. What had once been achieved by a movement from stage to stage throughout a town, as in royal entries and Renaissance pageants, could now be accomplished with lighting and stage machinery. If such pageants were environmental at all it was because of their incorporation of the natural scenery into the production on an emotional if not necessarily physical level. Parker chose his sites with great care. A pageant, he said, was to be "acted in some beautiful and historical spot, which is left without any artificial embellishment whatever."[13] Thomas Dickinson, writing of pageantry in 1915 stated:

> A clean-cut background whether of buildings or trees and hills, is of great value in emphasizing the unity of the pageant. The background of old buildings and ruins, as of Warwick Castle and the background of distant rivers and mountains, as at Quebec, were so adequate that they were indeed a part of the pageant.[14]

This is not to imply that a found environment is inherently beneficial. "In a theatre designed chiefly for pure drama," noted Cheney,

> a vista through the trees or across a lake is likely to prove an interruption of the action, and the more appealing and the more comprehensive the outlook is, the more likely the spectator is to let his attention wander away from the stage and what is happening there.[15]

Many people were captivated by the idea of outdoor theatre, including Edward Gordon Craig, who in 1911 devoted a short essay to Eleanor Duse's suggestion that we should emulate the Greeks and "play in the Open Air."[16] Craig reasoned that by doing this, the "humbug" and "trickery" of the conventional theatre would be eliminated. "The open air is at once the most lawful and the most illegal place in creation," he remarked. "All is allowed there except for the unnatural."[17] Similar sentiments were expressed somewhat sardonically by German critic Raoul Auernheimer in his review of Oscar Kokoschka's *Murderer, the Hope of Women* in 1909. An early Expressionistic play, it was staged at night in a courtyard garden theatre surrounded by hedges and with a row of cyprus trees in the background. Auernheimer commented that the "night sky was without doubt the truest piece of the whole exhibit."[18] Despite the appeal of open air theatre for early twentieth-century theatre practitioners, however, not one of them seemed to have any idea of what we might consider environmental staging. The productions generally remained frontal, and it was apparently sufficient that the natural decor lent an intangible, spiritual quality to the productions that was unattainable in an indoor theatre.

At about the same time that he wrote the essay on open air performance, Craig also wrote "A Plea for Two Theatres" in which he proposed an alternative to traditional staging. Referring to this new form as "ephemeral theatre," he stated that it "could be performed in any and every place, and caprice and phantasy might put together stages one more fantastic than the other."[19] As usual, Craig was not very explicit, but the essay contained two ideas which seemed to become popular soon afterwards. The first, the concept of theatre being performed anywhere—including of course the outdoors—was shortly incorporated by the Futurists and later by the Dadaists.[20] The second concept was that of combining several stages. Again, the idea was not explained, but three possibilities come to mind. The first is a sequence of different stage sets, but this was certainly not a new idea in Craig's time. Second, there could be a simultaneous presentation of several scenes on one stage—that is, in effect, several discrete areas grouped together at one point within a space. (One of the recurring themes of Futurist performance was simultaneity.) Finally, there is the possibility of scatter staging which would play a large role in the works of Erwin Piscator in Germany and Nikolai Okhlopkov in Russia.

Futurism was the first theatrical movement to make systematic attempts at altering the relation of the performer and spectator. In the "Futurist Synthetic Theatre" manifesto of 1915, Filippo Marinetti, Emilio Settimelli, and Bruno Corra proposed to

symphonize the audience's sensibility by exploring it, stirring up its laziest layers with every means possible; eliminate the preconception of footlights by throwing nets of

> sensation between stage and audience; the stage action will invade the orchestra seats,
> the audience . . . Through unbroken contact, create between us and the crowd a current
> of confidence rather than respectfulness, in order to instill in our audience the dynamic
> vivacity of a new Futurist theatricality.[21]

Although the "nets of sensation" were, in one sense, psychological, the Futurists most definitely wished to move across the proscenium and into the auditorium—to perform amidst the spectators. Finding inspiration in the popular entertainments of the day, Marinetti issued the "Variety Theatre" manifesto in 1913. "The Variety Theatre is alone in seeking the audience's collaboration," he proclaimed.

> It doesn't remain static like a stupid *voyeur*, but joins noisily in the action, in the singing,
> accompanying the orchestra, communicating with the actors in surprising actions and
> bizarre dialogues . . . The Variety Theatre uses the smoke of cigars and cigarettes to join
> the atmosphere of the theatre to that of the stage. And because the audience cooperates
> in this way with the actors' fantasy, the action develops simultaneously on the stage, in
> the boxes, and in the orchestra.[22]

Among the attempts to realize this theatre were the "evenings of dynamic and synoptic declamation," which began in 1914. These were performances consisting of music, paratheatrical events, assorted activities, and "declamations" of Futurist poems by several speakers at once.[23] In most of these presentations the hall or gallery in which they were held was totally transformed into a performance environment. The first was *Piedigrotta* by Francesco Cangiullo, presented in a room in the Sprovieri Gallery in Rome.[24] In one corner of the room was something described as a "still life," the walls were hung with Futurist paintings and the room was suffused with red light. The performance consisted of a multivoiced reading alternated with a piano and a procession of dwarfs.[25] The second such evening, *The Siege of Adrianople*, involved three blackboards set up in different parts of the room "to which in succession," wrote Marinetti,

> I either ran or walked, to sketch rapidly an analogy with chalk. My listeners, as they
> turned to follow me in all my evolutions, participated, their entire bodies inflamed with
> emotion, in the violent effects of the battle described by my words-in-freedom.[26]

While Marinetti may have exaggerated the spectator emotions, it appears that the audience became physically involved in a performance that surrounded or moved through them.

Environmental elements, such as processions, could be found in other Futurist presentations, and the idea of touch was a preoccupation of Marinetti's. He began producing "tactile sintesi" (short plays or skits) in the 1910s. In "tactile sintesi" there was no direct contact between the performers and spectators, the sense of touch was supposed to occur in the minds of the spectators.[27] In *The Great Remedy*, for instance, an actress came down from the stage and "almost grazed . . . with her hands" the people in the first row.[28] In the 1921 manifesto, "Tactilism," Marinetti proposed a theatre based on touch in which the audience would touch moving bands and wheels to an accompaniment of light and sound.[29] Such productions necessitated the penetration of audience space or a shared performance/spectator area.

The object of bringing performers into the audience was not merely to surround the spectators but to involve them actively. In *Lights!* the house became dark and remained that way. The cast, if it could be called that, consisted of performers planted in the auditorium who began shouting, "Lights! Lights!" until the whole audience joined in the cry. As soon as the lights came on, the curtain fell.[30] Another fundamentally environmental concept was Fedele Azari's Futurist Aerial Theatre. Described in a manifesto of 1919, this was to be a sort of ballet of airplanes with the sky as a stage.[31] Azari noted that such a theatre would be free of charge, in this case to perhaps millions of people. The maneuvers of the planes were supposed to represent and reflect the states of minds of the pilots. More importantly, performing in the sky placed the presentation in a perceived environment. The performance frame became the horizon which, of course, encompassed the spectator. "The artistic form that we create with flight," wrote Azari,

is analogous to dance, but is infinitely superior to it because of its grandiose background, because of its superlative dynamism, and the greatly varied possibilities that it permits, thereby completing the evolutions according to the three dimensions of space.[32]

The Dadaists, who began their activities in Zurich's Cabaret Voltaire in 1916, adopted many Futurist concepts, among them Tactilism, which Marinetti had presented at the Théâtre de l'Oeuvre in Paris in January of 1921, and the idea of simultaneous presentation of events or activities. Simultaneity may be physically frontal, as in a three-ring circus, but it must be considered at least an antecedent of environmental forms. Simultaneous presentation forces split focus and may create several localized spaces on a single stage, thereby forcing a sort of random disinvolvement on the part of the spectator—a phasing in and out of attentions during any sequential presentation. Conventional performance assumes a continuous attention on the part of the spectator but a simultaneous performance allows the spectator to create his own performance, as it were, by selecting particular moments from different sequences. [33]

Found spaces were frequently turned into performance environments by the Dadaists. A 1920 Dada exhibit in Cologne was held in a courtyard reached by going through a public urinal.[34] In May of 1920 an exhibit of works by Max Ernst was held at the Sans Pareil Gallery in Paris. As with the earlier Futurist exhibit, the event became a performance through the actions of the participants and the entire gallery was transformed into a performance space. The event was documented in *Comoedia*, a contemporary theatre journal.

> With the bad taste that characterizes them, the Dadaists have this time had recourse to horror. The scene was laid in a cellar, all the lights were extinguished in the store, heart-rending groans rose through a trap door, and we could catch some scraps of a whispered conversation: " . . . A poem is an asphyxiation. —In a contest of intelligence, the female cloud always wins. —A game of billiards was placed in the intestines of the cardinal. Etc. . . . Etc. . . ." The Dadaists, without ties and wearing white gloves, paced back and forth. André Breton munched matches, Georges Ribemont-Dessaignes kept shouting: "It's raining on a skull." Aragon miaowed, Philipe Soupault played hide-and-seek with Tristan Tzara while Benjamin Péret and Charchoune shook hands constantly. In the doorway, Jacques Rigaut counted in a loud voice the automobiles and the pearls of the visitors.[35]

In 1921, André Breton, who later founded the Surrealist movement, proposed that the Dadaists take to the streets. A lecture in a garden and a tour of a church conducted by Ribemont-Dessaignes resulted.[36] In Germany there were several "Dadatours," while in Hanover, Kurt Schwitters could be found seated in a tree in front of his home reciting in an invented "bird language," an activity which became a performance when he was observed by visitors.[37] Thus, the Futurists and Dadaists—through their use of found environments, their transformation of ordinary spaces into performance environments, and their presentation of basically non-matrixed performances which depended on spectator perceptions for their unity—were among the forerunners of environmental theatre.

From about 1905 to 1925, the person who had the most influence in altering forms of staging and the relationship of the performer to the spectator was Max Reinhardt. Today he is remembered mostly as a director of spectacles and as producer of the Salzburg Festival. His affinity for circus staging, however, made his productions forerunners of the theatre in the round. Although he used vast arenas, Reinhardt was interested in intimacy, and he often thrust the stage and the actor into the midst of the spectators. He was also one of the first to unify the stage and auditorium architecturally; and, of course, at Salzburg and elsewhere he staged plays outdoors, adapting already existing environments for the productions. Searching, with others of the time, for alternatives to the proscenium, Reinhardt suggested that "good actors today [should] play in a barn or in a theatre, tomorrow at an inn or inside a church, or, in the Devil's name, even on an expressionistic stage: if the place corresponds with the play, something wonderful will be the outcome."[38]

The most famous of Reinhardt's open air productions was *Jederman*,

Hugo von Hofmannsthal's adaptation of the medieval play *Everyman* presented at the Salzburg Festival every year from 1920 to 1937. A long platform stage was erected in front of the cathedral in Salzburg and although the main action was, again, frontal and on what was essentially an end stage, the use of the cathedral and the surrounding city incorporated the spectator into what became almost a medieval pageant. Reinhardt briefly described the production and its effects:

> A stage of boards in front of the Cathedral doors. Heralds who announce the play. Entrance of the actors from the neighboring Squares. The bells of the churches ring. Organ. Choir from the Cathedral. Mystic cries from the church-towers, down from the *Festung* or Fortress and from a greater distance, calling Everyman to death. The Devil springing up from between the spectators' benches to the podium. Faith and the Angel coming out of the Cathedral at the end. The broad Squares fill with a dense crowd of spectators. From the windows of the neighboring monastery, monks and priests: in the first row, the Archbishop and the Cathedral Chapter. Traffic is completely stopped and the whole city listens and watches breathlessly. Wonderful play of light—first, daylight; then sunset; then finally, torches.[39]

Reinhardt had stationed actors in church spires throughout the city and even in a distant castle to call to Everyman. The voice of God came from high inside the Cathedral itself. As evidence of Reinhardt's use of environment, the starting time of the performance would be adjusted so that Everyman's death would coincide with the sunset.[40] Thus, there was, first of all, a transformation of space as the topography and architecture of the town became a theatrical set; second, there was at least one performer among the audience as well as other performers entering on all sides. Finally, the sounds emanating from the Cathedral and the nearby churches surrounded and engulfed the spectator, who was also acted upon by the effects of natural light. One spectator was greatly moved by the "glow of the setting sun, and with the inimitable decorations afforded by the Cathedral pile itself," and further noted that the production was thus so overwhelming that "none of us remembered that it was but a revelation of histrionics—we were in the sway of a grand and imposing religious service."[41] The spectators at the production were literally enveloped by all its aspects.

Reinhardt continued his outdoor productions throughout his life. One of the most notable was the production of the *Merchant of Venice* at the Venice Biennale of 1934. There were two outdoor found-environment productions in Venice that year, the other being Gino Rocca's staging of Goldoni's *Bottega del Caffè* done in the Corte del Teatro at San Luca. *Merchant* was performed at night in the Campo San Trovaso, a Venetian square along the Rio d'Ognissanti Canal (Plate 4).[42] The environment was not entirely a found one, but had added scenic structures by Duilio Torres. Most of the piazza was occupied by seated spectators. Opposite them was a bridge spanning the canal with the steps leading up to the near side of the bridge, forming a sort of proscenium. To one side of the bridge was the casino of the noble Venetians, built for the occasion while on the other side was a small lane at the end of which was a house, left in its natural state and used as Shylock's home. Also constructed on this side was Portia's castle. Reinhardt used natural light and the canal whenever possible; many scenes occurred along the canal banks, as well as on balconies, in windows and on the bridge steps, and arrivals and departures were frequently made via gondolas. For the final scene the lovers appeared in gondolas on the canal, kissing in the moonlight.

In the area of theatre design and architecture, Reinhardt had been experimenting with alternative forms since 1910, often presenting classical plays in a space he considered analogous to the theatre in which they might have originally been produced. *Sumurun* (1910) employed a Japanese *hanamichi*, a runway extending into the auditorium. Both *Oedipus Rex* (1910) and the *Oresteia* (1911) were staged in Berlin's Circus Schumann because, as Reinhardt explained, in such a space "the actors do really move among the audience, there playing out their little drama in the midst of their fellow men."[43] Reinhardt continued to use the circus until World War I because he felt it was the closest contemporary equivalent of the Greek theatre, providing both a certain vastness and a kind of intimacy through the possibility of thrusting the performance into the midst of the spectators. More importantly, it broke the proscenium frame.

As early as 1901, Reinhardt proclaimed:

> For me the frame that separates the stage from the world, has never been essential . . . and everything that breaks that frame open, strengthens and widens the effect, increases contact with the audience, whether in the direction of intimacy or monumentality, will always be welcome to me.[44]

The theatre he envisioned at this time, a dream later conceived as the "Theatre of Five Thousand," was to be "in the shape of an amphitheatre, without curtain or sets, and in the center, . . . the actor, in the middle of the audience, and the audience itself, transformed into *the people*, drawn into, become a part of, the action of the play."[45] Prior to World War I Arthur Kahane, one of Reinhardt's co-workers, expanded on this proposal. "On entering the theatre," he said,

> the spectator feels and is impressed by the possibilities of space . . . No small, strongly circumscribed, impassable frame separates the world of the play from the outer world, and the action flows freely through the whole of the theatre. The peep-show character of the "scene" . . . has vanished.[46]

This, in itself, was essentially a call for the abolition of the proscenium and, as Kahane stated it, it could also be a call for environmental theatre. "The chorus arises and moves in the midst of the audience," he explained,

> the characters meet each other amid the spectators; from all sides the hearer is being impressed, so that gradually he becomes part of the whole, and is rapidly absorbed in the action, a member of the chorus, so to speak. This close contact [intimacy] is the chief feature of the new form of the stage. It makes the spectator a part of the action, secures his entire interest, and intensifies the effect upon him.[47]

As eventually realized by Reinhardt, however, the result—the Grosses Schauspielhaus—was a form of thrust stage.

It is not clear from this description just how the spectators were to be "impressed" from "all sides," the thrust or arena stage still being a frontal arrangement, but the idea of psychological or implied involvement of the spectators is present. The psychological involvement being sought in these cases is different from that of, say, Stanislavski or other Naturalists who, as mentioned earlier, wanted the spectators to feel like "guests" in the household of the characters being portrayed on stage. Psychological involvement with emotions or plot does not necessarily have anything to do with physical proximity. Reinhardt wanted a sense of involvement in the *physical production*. This is precisely the sort of effect described by the spectator at *Everyman*.

In 1919, Reinhardt, together with the architect Hans Poelzig, remodelled the Circus Schumann into a circular thrust theatre with a stalactite-like dome covering the stage and auditorium. It seated some 3500 spectators (Plates 5, 6). Although economics and the given space necessitated certain compromises, this structure realized many of Reinhardt's concepts for the "Theatre of Five Thousand." What had been the ring of the former circus became the orchestra, as in an ancient Greek theatre, and a single bank of seats rose in tiers around three sides of it. Steps led from the rear of the orchestra to a platform stage behind which was a proscenium stage. While the orchestra seemed to place the performance in the midst of the spectators, it was not until the 1920 production of Romain Rolland's *Danton* that actors actually entered the audience space—performers were planted in the auditorium and action spilled over the edges of the orchestra. The character of Danton harangued the audience as if they were citizens of Revolutionary Paris.

Performers in the audience, of course, were not a new concept devised by Reinhardt, nor, as the Futurists had shown, was such practice unique to him. The technique had been used by Percy MacKaye in his pageants and, as we shall see, by certain Russian directors of the period. The most blatant attempt at penetrating audience space, however, was staged by the French director Firmin Gémier. For his 1917 production of *The Merchant of Venice* at the Théâtre Antoine he removed the footlights and built stairs leading into the orchestra. Four stage-level boxes were reserved for performers and allowed access to the stairs. Gémier utilized almost all the doors and aisles of the auditorium.

> I had the actors enter and leave by the auditorium. They came in sometimes by way of the first boxes on the side, transformed into passages, sometimes from the back of the house by way of the aisle which goes around the orchestra, and then they mounted onto the stage. They grazed the spectators. The breeze from their running rustled through the audience. These were no longer imaginary beings, but real. In certain instances, they appeared on a rostrum in the midst of the audience. From there, they called out to the actors onstage, and their sentences flew over the audience. I do not pretend to have discovered these ideas. But I have rediscovered them, in thinking about the shows of Greece and the Middle Ages.[48]

Gémier went on to cite examples from medieval productions such as the *Jeu d'Adam* and was thus one of the few directors to actually base an environmental scenography on historical models. Gémier's rationale is also interesting. Although many conflicting claims would be made for non-frontal staging, most scenographers in the early part of this century felt, as Gémier did, that the destruction of the frame made the production more "real."

While Gémier was penetrating audience space, Reinhardt, despite his few similar attempts, was more concerned with creating a unified stage and auditorium. The Grosses Schauspielhaus had achieved this to some degree with the large dome. But the ultimate unification of stage and auditorium for Reinhardt came with the production of *The Miracle*, a wordless play by Karl Vollmoeller.[49] The play was first staged in London's Olympia Theatre in 1911 and then in 1924 at the Century Theatre in New York. In both cases the aim was to convert the interior of the theatre into a Gothic Cathedral. The illusion in the latter case, designed by Norman Bel Geddes, was nearly complete. After seeing Geddes' plans Reinhardt wrote:

> I must say that this work represents the most tremendous thing ever done anywhere for the theatre . . . If this can be done, I am sure that the decor alone (reproducing, as it will, the awe-inspiring atmosphere of a Gothic cathedral interior, such as none of the New York churches can approach) will cause the greatest astonishment and interest.[50]

Geddes aimed for a total environment that could not be achieved by any found space, and judging from the reverent descriptions of spectators, the desired effect was realized. One admiring architect, however, did note that

> it all looks *real*, being three-dimensional, but it is nevertheless conceived in the spirit of

the painter rather than of the architect. Mr. Geddes' Gothic will not stand rigid analysis, either from the standpoint of style or structure, but he has caught the spirit of the style.[51]

What had been the stage of the Century Theatre became the chancel. The aisles were widened and covered with slate, and the rows of seats were partially disguised as pews. The walls were covered with Gothic arches, stained glass, and clerestory windows; balcony rails were concealed by heraldic banners. All was illuminated by concealed lighting.

Christopher Fry stated in the stage directions to *A Sleep of Prisoners* (1951) that it was to be played in a real church and the play thus makes an interesting comparison with *The Miracle*. In both cases the performance itself remained frontal; it is the scenography that was environmental. In *The Miracle*, illusionistic scenic elements surrounded the audience, but it is questionable whether the spectators ever really believed that they were in a church, let alone within the time and place matrix of the play. An implied environment or a unified space may, in the case of an illusionistic production, have the effect of further distancing the spectators rather than increasing the sense of reality. The spectators may become acutely aware of the disparity between their contemporary dress, for example, and the period sets and costumes of the actors.

In the Fry play, the spectators are in a found environment selected specifically for its relation to the play, yet no precise connection is suggested between the play and the church in which it is performed. The relationship is limited to the associations evoked in the minds of the spectators by the particular church chosen for the performance. A found environment is utilized for its inherent evocative qualities; there is no transformation of space.

The concept of the unified stage and auditorium dates back to at least 1909 and two independent developments. In that year Georg Fuchs, director of the Munich Art Theatre, published *Revolution In The Theatre* and, in Hellerau, Switzerland, Heinrich Tessenow designed a hall for the Dalcroze School of Eurythmics. In his attempts to revitalize the scenic practices of his day Fuchs came close to proclaiming a manifesto for environmental theatre. He claimed that "the function of the stage is to stimulate and to satisfy an overpowering expectation. If we are so aroused that within the confines of convention we can not completely realize this emotion, we must rise above conventions. . . ."[52]

Fuchs went on to attack the separation of performer and spectator, citing historical examples from the Elizabethan and Japanese theatres and adding that "according to their nature and their origin, player and spectator, stage and auditorium are not in opposition. They are a unit."[53] But he concluded that the proscenium was essential:

> Furthermore, since it is in the consciousness of the spectator that the dramatic experience finally becomes a reality, the drama must also create the auditorium. The physical rhythms of the play are transformed at the curtain line into the emotional vibrations which move the audience. Therefore, the proscenium, which is the dividing line between stage and auditorium, is the most important architectural feature in the theatre.[54]

His solution was the "relief stage," a narrow profile stage which brought the performer to the front, eliminating the vast depth of many proscenium stages. Fuchs grasped a fundamental concept of defining space or creating a matrix, yet he seemed, as Appia complained, to have difficulty imagining alternatives to the peep-show stage.[55]

Nonetheless, Fuchs did define a major impulse of the new theoreticians—the unification of stage and auditorium. As it developed early in this century, this unification did not lead directly to the sharing of spectator and performer space, but to an architectural unification in which the stage area was enclosed by the same walls and ceiling and lit by the same source as the auditorium. The result was generally no more than the simple end stage with historical precedents in such models as the Elizabethan private theatres and the Restoration playhouse. Its significance lies in the conscious attempt at a psychological unification of spectators and performers. It was generally believed at the time that this would shatter pictorial illusion and foster a new perception of the 'theatricality' of the stage.

The Hellerau space was famous not only for Dalcroze's school but also as the theatre used by Appia to stage several productions and to develop his ideas. The room was a rectangle with the usually simple stage setting placed at one end (Plate 7). The lighting, designed by A. von Salzmann, consisted of 10,000 bulbs, whose intensity was controllable, placed behind the translucent walls and ceiling of the hall. Thus actors and audience sat in a single room lit by the same source. In 1909 this represented a unique unification of spectator and performer space. Both were contained in a single environment with a performing area that was transformed or localized for each performance.

A similar scheme was developed by Jacques Copeau at the converted Vieux Colombier theatre in Paris just before World War I. Copeau rebuilt the old house into a theatre without a proscenium. In 1919 Louis Jouvet remodelled the theatre again to give it an architectural stage—a permanent, immovable set that was adapted to suit the needs of each performance (Plate 8).

In 1917 Norman Bel Geddes also designed a "prosceniumless" theatre, but it was never built.[56] The stage was to be set diagonally across one corner of a more or less square space; steps radiated out from the stage to the auditorium which was likewise set diagonally across the space (Plates 9, 10).

A curving wall backed the stage like a cyclorama or sky-dome and met a
dome which covered both stage and auditorium.

One other architecturally unified space of note was the Redoutensaal,
built in Vienna in 1921 by Reinhardt in the converted ballroom of a palace.
It was similar in many respects to the theatre in Hellerau except that it
retained its royal ornateness (Plate 11). In the Vienna theatre, also, both
stage and auditorium were lit by the same source. Contemporary critics
remarked on the essential theatricality of the idea. Because the open stage
seemed to prohibit pictorial illusion, they felt that the actors "cannot try to
represent actual people; they can only present themselves to the audience as
artists who will give them a vision of reality."[57]

During the 1920s it was Erwin Piscator who was, perhaps, most
successful in the use of shared-space staging. Although his fame today is
somewhat eclipsed by Bertolt Brecht's, it was Piscator who developed the
notion of Epic Theatre and pioneered much of the so-called mixed-media
performance. Coming of age in Berlin after World War I, he was influenced
by the Berlin Dadaists and adopted a number of their stage techniques and
effects. He also shared with Reinhardt the philosophy behind the Theatre of
the Five Thousand—the desire for a unified mass audience. Through the
introduction and use of film and projections (devices actually used earlier by
Yvan Goll), and elaborate (and often malfunctioning) stage machinery, he
transformed and fragmented the stage, extended its scope and experimented
widely with simultaneity. This led to the introduction of performers into the
audience, surrounding the spectator with scenic elements and scattering
platform stages throughout the auditorium. His unrealized dream was the
total theatre designed by Walter Gropius (discussed in the next chapter)
which would provide total flexibility of staging and a means of surrounding
the spectators.

By 1920 Piscator was staging agit-prop plays, thereby prefiguring a
trend that became popular in Germany later in the decade. Since these were
often produced in beer halls and factories which seldom had a proper stage,
entrances were often made through the midst of the spectators. While
necessity instigated this particular use of space it tied in nicely with his stated
intention to promote "the ideological, dramaturgical, spatial and technical
abrogation of bourgeois theatre."[58]

Although his "spatial and technical abrogations" were not always
environmental, they often employed proto-environmental techniques. *Despite All!* (*Trotz Alledom!*), an historical review staged in 1925, for instance,
through its use of a multi-level stage and film projections, used split focus
and simultaneity. Piscator was also influenced by the German director
Leopold Jessner who was known for dividing the stage into many steps and

levels ("Jessnertreppen"). This innovation was instrumental in the movement toward the fragmentation of the stage and provided the possibility of simultaneous or sequential localized spaces in the same general area.[59]

These influences developed throughout the twenties. Piscator's 1926 production of Schiller's *The Robbers* surrounded the audience with performers who were placed in the auditorium, on steps and overhead on catwalks.[60] This use of simultaneity and multiple playing areas was expanded even more with the 1927 production of Ernst Toller's *Hurrah, We Live!* (*Hoppla, Wir Leben!*) which had eight areas for film and actors and a stage surrounding the audience space. *#218*, produced in 1929, was a play about section 218 of the criminal code, the section dealing with abortion. The play was staged as a public meeting and, like the Futurists, Piscator planted in the audience actors who shouted and made speeches and who were apparently successful in instigating the spectators to do likewise. The performance concluded with a vote among the audience that was almost always unanimous in its rejection of section 218.[61] In its method of involving the audience *#218* was similar to such productions as *The Dawns*, staged by Meyerhold in 1920 (discussed in Chapter 5), which aroused the audience with news of actual Russian civil war battles in progress; and it prefigures such American successes as *Waiting for Lefty*, which would sometimes arouse the audience to a call for a strike. Piscator staged another similar production, *Tai Yang Awakes*, in 1931. For this play, Berlin's Wallnertheater was transformed into a unified space representing a workers' hall in China. There were platform stages throughout the orchestra section and the decor of flags and placards which hung from the walls extended even into the lobby.[62] Piscator continued to use this style periodically throughout his career. His 1959 production of Max Frisch's *The Firebugs* had a central (arena) stage and an outer stage that circled the audience. Another stage was suspended from the ceiling over the spectators and projection screens were placed at various points throughout the theatre.

One other development in the reaction against the proscenium deserves mention here—the so-called space stage. This form was a natural corollary to the multi-level and "prosceniumless" stages and was part of the movement, begun by Appia and Craig, that called for an abandonment of realistic settings and caused a sort of sculpturing of space through light, the use of bodies, and movement. Space stage scenography viewed the stage simply as empty space or as environment in which a central acting area and the actor were emphasized, rather than the peripheral scenery and background as in the conventional box set.[63] Although proponents of the space stage, such as Jurgen Fehling (whose 1921 production of *Man and the Masses* was the most notable success) and Jessner, envisioned essentially an end stage stripped of its usual scenic devices, they were, in effect, advocating the removal of the theatrical scene from the strict confines of the stage house and into open space defined primarily by the performers and by spare and simple scenic devices.

Because the space stage was a generalized concept it was variously defined by its several proponents. The most detailed and "scientific" proposal, however, was set forth by the Austrian architect and designer, Frederick Kiesler. In his manifesto, Kiesler noted that a major shortcoming of the proscenium stage was the inability of a spectator to experience space within it. "Optically, rigid space does not admit of precise cubic apprehension unless it has already been traversed by the observer," wrote Kiesler in 1926,

> so that, when seen again, it is reconstructed with the aid of past experience. Every specific reconstruction arrived at purely from the experiencing of other spaces is inexact and does not suffice for theatrical effectiveness. Space is space only for the person who moves about in it. For the actor, not for the spectator.[64]

His proposal for the three-dimensional stage was presented thus:

> (1) The peep-show stage functions as relief, not as space. The public's shaft of vision pushes the stage space back towards the rear. As is always true of rigid space, it is projected onto the surface of the back-drop.
>
> (2) There is only one space element: motion.
>
> (3) The plastic element of this stage is not scenery, but man. And this is the answer to all attempts at revivifying the stage by so called spatial, plastic stage architecture.
>
> (4) Optically, space can be recognized in four ways: by observation of the ground plan, by rotation of the object, by a reading of the shadows, by the motion of the object.
>
> (5) The actor suggests space by change of position, and plasticity by change of posture.
>
> (6) Seven elements of the stage underlie histrionic unity: surface, space, animate and inanimate material, light, color, sound.
>
> (7) Precision and economy in the organization of the action demand that the curved horizon be represented as flat, once and for all. "I declare myself so far and no further." Respectfully: the stage.
>
> (8) Sculptural problems are always to be solved in three dimensions. The lines are caught and bounded by the six surfaces of the stage: five real surfaces and one imaginary surface, the aperture for the curtain. In the sphere, which is the epitome of the spatial, the stage cube results from the intersection of the six surfaces.
>
> (9) Summing up, one can express the law of construction in the peep-show stage with the formula:

$$C = \overset{\displaystyle\text{Stage}}{\downarrow} \qquad + \qquad \overset{\displaystyle\text{Elements}}{\downarrow} \qquad \overset{\displaystyle\times\;\text{Motion}}{\downarrow}$$

$$C = \frac{G}{ZN \times EW \times NS} + \int_{e}^{u} \left(\frac{F}{M_i^a} + L + R \right) \times \frac{dB}{DT}$$

C = construction
G = sphere
ZN = direction: stage zenith—stage nadir
EW = direction: stage east—stage west
NS = direction: stage north—stage south
$\int_e^u =$ integral between upper and lower limits (in the strength of color, light, sound material)
F = color
M_i^a = material (animate, inanimate)
L = light
R = sound
dB = differential of motion
dT = differential of time

(10) The stage is not a chest with a curtain for a lid. It is an elastic space. But the contemporary stage is still a box, despite curved horizon, trapdoor, and loft, and whether it has or has not a curtain.

(11) When the stage has ceased to be a picture, the play can become an organism. Then the apparently insolvable problem is automatically solved: the systematic cooperation of man and object becomes possible.

(12) Any work of art for the contemporary theatre which goes beyond these limits is to be valued purely as propaganda. As absolute achievement it is a compromise between form and space, play and public.[65]

Although he did not yet advocate a sharing of space he was searching for a means to allow spectators to experience stage space. His space stage and Endless Theatre (see Chapter 4) were results of his experiments, and, as we shall see, make Kiesler the "father" of surrounding space environments.

The many reactions against the proscenium prepared the way for more detailed and comprehensive uses of space. For those persons who lacked the foresight and imagination Appia had asked for, the shattering of the picture-frame stage provided concrete examples of what could be done with space and architecture. The next step was to codify, as it were, the means for sharing and surrounding the spectators' space.

4

Surrounding Space Theatres

The art of the stage is a spatial art, a fact which is bound to become clearer and clearer in the future. The stage, including the auditorium, is above all an architectonic-spatial organism where all things happening to it and within it exist in a spatially conditioned relationship. . . . If . . . we atomize the constricting space of the stage and translate it into terms of the total building itself, the exterior as well as the interior . . . then the idea of a space stage *would be demonstrated in a way which is probably altogether unprecedented.*

—*Oskar Schlemmer, 1927*

Returning for the moment to Cummings' paean to Coney Island cited in Chapter 2, we see a description of a totally encompassing, penetrating, and mesmerizing environment—all the senses are continually assaulted from all sides. All the scenic and architectural components of that amusement park are incorporated into a unified whole, the epitome of the multi-space environment. The unified spaces of Reinhardt and Bel Geddes, or the shared spaces of Piscator and Gémier, worked mostly on a psychological level which could not approach the physical involvement of a Coney Island. In an attempt to recreate this same all-encompassing effect in the theatre, architects and stage designers have been experimenting since the turn of the century with methods of totally surrounding the spectator with the production.

Many of the proposed projects tended toward the fantastic—and consequently, toward the economically unfeasible—and many of the more extravagant projects would have had limited usefulness because they were conceived for a drama that did not yet exist—that would have to be created for the new physical stage. Consequently, most of these proposals remained unbuilt. While the individual theories and rationales behind each project vary, of course, they can all be classified in three basic categories: 1) caliper and annular stages; 2) scatter staging within a free or open space; 3) the so-called architecturally integrated space.

The idea for the caliper stage can be traced to the "tripartite," or three sectioned stage first seen in a project for a theatre designed by Charles-Nicolas Cochin in 1765 (Plate 12).[1] The slightly curved stage was divided into one central proscenium and two side prosceniums. (This itself was of course based on the three "avenues" of the Teatro Olimpico at Vicenza.) Cosimo Morelli actually built such a theatre at Imola, Italy in 1779 (Plate 13).[2] The divisions allowed three separate vistas or three localized spaces on one stage. The tripartite stage (sometimes called a "tryptichon" stage) received little notice, however, until Henry van de Velde incorporated it into the Werkbundtheater at Cologne in 1914 (Plate 14). The theatre was influential partly because the three contiguous stages made it possible to play different scenes in rapid succession—in what scholars of the time considered an Elizabethan style. It also allowed for simultaneous presentation. Furthermore, by eliminating the ornate proscenium of the day, van de Velde partially reduced the sense of stage and auditorium separation. In 1925, a similar stage was presented by Auguste Perret at the Decorative Arts exhibit in Paris (Plate 15), thereby gaining wide exposure for the idea. Because the side stages began to embrace the auditorium in Perret's theatre, it can probably be considered the first caliper stage.

The first proposal for an annular stage seems to have been made by Guillaume Apollinaire in the prologue he added to his play, *The Breasts of Tiresias*, in 1916 (the play had been written in 1903). Complaining about the "antique stage" of the time, he called for

> A circular theatre with two stages
> One in the middle the other like a ring
> Around the spectators permitting
> The full unfolding of our modern art
> Often connecting in unseen ways as in life
> Sounds gestures colors cries tumults
> Music dancing acrobatics poetry painting
> Choruses actions and multiple sets.[3]

The rationale behind this proposal appears fundamentally different from that of previous schemes to alter performer-spectator relationships. While many theatre architects and directors were altering stage space primarily to create a greater immediacy and involvement in the production, Apollinaire seemed to be calling for environmental staging as a means of altering the spectators' basic perceptions.

Later that year, Pierre Albert-Birot, a writer and editor of the short-lived Dada journal *Sic,* proposed the "Theatre Nunique," a theatre quite similar to Apollinaire's idea (Plate 16).[4] Albert-Birot's doctrine of "nunisme" suggested a philosophy in which the humanities would take from past knowledge as well as from new scientific and technological advances to create a sort of scientific humanism.[5] His proposed theatre consequently drew heavily upon technology. Basically, it employed a sort of space stage—"light alone must be the paint of this theatre," he stated.[6] Like Apollinaire, he called for a mixture of acrobatics, buffoonery, pantomime, film and other popular performance elements in production. In his manifesto, "A Propos d'un Théâtre Nunique" (see Appendix A), Albert-Birot stated: "The 'théâtre nunique' must be a grand, simultaneous ensemble, containing all the means and all the emotions capable of communicating an intense and intoxicating life to the spectators."[7] The physical theatre itself was to be an annular stage that rotated, which he explained as "no more than a circus in which the public will occupy the center, while, on a peripheral turning platform, most of the performance will unfold, still connected to the audience by actors scattered throughout the theatre space."[8] While annular stage proposals became fairly common in the twenties, only Polish director Szymon Syrkus acknowledged any influence from Apollinaire or Albert-Birot (see chapter 6).

One person who did have some influence was the Austrian designer Oskar Strnad. In 1915 he began drawing up a plan for a theatre which he presented to Max Reinhardt in 1917.[9] In terms of flexibility and the use of multiple stages, as well as the sense of space it created, the proposed theatre prefigured Walter Gropius' Totaltheater and Kiesler's Endless Theatre; structurally it borrowed from van de Velde and Poelzig (Plate 17). Plans were published in 1920 and were shown at the 1922 International Theatre Exposition.[10] Both Reinhardt and Gordon Craig were excited by Strnad's proposal but despite Reinhardt's efforts on its behalf the theatre was never built.

Strnad believed that "the fundamental element of all dramatic play is to make the infinite aspect of space measurable and understandable, and to make the chaotic and frightening aspects of space comprehensible and felt by means of movement."[11] He felt that Reinhardt and Poelzig were moving in the right direction but were not successful because their theatre ultimately emphasized the separation of the stage and auditorium. Thus, when performers would leave the stage and enter the audience space, Strnad felt, it did not unite the two spaces but was, instead, "painful."[12] Strnad's solution to this problem was to surround the spectators with the stage action—to place them at the center. Furthermore, surrounding them on a horizontal plane was insufficient, Strnad wanted the spectators to feel that they were floating or suspended in space.

A wide, rotating annular stage (*bühnenwagen* or stage vehicle) sur-rounded a steeply raked fixed-seat auditorium (Plate 18). Between the front of the auditorium and the annular stage was a semi-circular forestage (*vorbühne*) which partly wrapped around either side of the auditorium like a caliper stage. The forestage was separated from the annular stage by six columns. Broad steps descending from the forestage led beneath the seating area but in the central portion of these steps was a small platform (*gegenbühne*) that functioned as a thrust stage. Around the annular stage, separated from it by a light trough, was a cyclorama. The pillars seemed to disappear into veil-like curtains (*velum*) at the top, while the steps from the forestage disappeared into the "unknowable" (*unkontrollierbare*) beneath. This was to create a sense of infinite space. "The audience," Strnad stated,

> experiences no concrete space, so to speak, and floats in the unlimited dimensional dynamics of the stage where everything is experience of dimension, a scene for the purpose of the play. . . . Acting may start on all sides: left and right, coming out from behind the notch-boards of the public gallery, from underneath the audience's seats, floating by above in the circular passage, or coming out of some openings and disappearing again through others. Acting and counter-acting, on top and below. Voices from all directions. . . . The actors . . . may fully utilize all the space around them.[13]

Even in this visionary proposal, however, Strnad could not break entirely with traditional architecture: the steeply inclined auditorium and fixed seats precluded action in the rear of the house. The sense of envelopment was thus more psychological than actual and the rotating annular stage served, much as it does in many contemporary annular-stage theatres, as a technological device for changing scenes.

Erwin Piscator, likewise, wanted a flexible theatre for his productions—one which was capable of surrounding the spectators and at the same time would allow the fullest use of technology and other media. He commissioned Walter Gropius, founder of the Bauhaus, to design such a theatre in 1927. The "Totaltheater" was the result, but like Strnad's proposal, it was never built. Unlike Strnad's plan, however, Gropius solved the problem of sight lines by placing the stationary annular stage above the level of the slightly raked auditorium (Plate 19). The annular stage circumscribed an oval auditorium area containing fixed seating. Twelve narrow pillars, between which projection screens could be stretched, separated the stage and auditorium. A deep proscenium-type stage occupied the conventional position, but two of the pillars sectioned it into a tripartite stage "which embraces the forward rows of the audience like a pair of tongs."[14] The great flexibility of this theatre, however, derived from two circular platforms, occupying nearly the entire front half of the auditorium, which allowed the theatre to be used in a proscenium, thrust, or arena fashion (Plate 20). The larger platform could rotate. The smaller platform—within and to one edge of the larger one—could be lowered to the basement, have its seats removed, and resurface as a thrust or arena stage, depending on its position. Gropius explained:

> The smallest turntable can descend to the basement, where the seats can be removed so that it can rise again to serve as an apron in front of the proscenium where it is surrounded by the audience like by a pair of tongs. Consequently, the actor, by descending through the central aisle, can mix among the spectators and return to the stage by moving along the side aisles which circle the auditorium.
>
> But a complete transformation of the theatre occurs by turning the larger turntable 180°. The small sunken platform in the middle of the large turntable is now in the center like an arena surrounded on all sides by the rows of spectators. This can be done even during the performance. The actor reaches this circular area either by stairs from below, by the aisles which . . . lead back to the proscenium, or from the ceiling by means of scaffolding and steps which also allows perpendicular action over the playing arena. . . . I am of the opinion that light projection can make the simplest and most effective modern stage one can build with light and with abstract or objective cinematic techniques (stationary or moving pictures) which render almost entirely superfluous decor and props. In my Totaltheater I have considered the possibilities of projections on all three stages . . . and on the whole surrounding horizon. I want to enclose the entire theatre (walls and ceiling) by film. For this purpose projection screens are stretched between the twelve columns of the auditorium upon which twelve films can be projected from cameras placed behind them, functioning together, so that the audience can thus suddenly find itself in the midst of a raging sea for example, or surrounded by a rapidly advancing multitude. At the same time, another projector suspended from the middle of the room can project on these screens. From here cloud apparatus can project, for example, on the dome of the theatre, clouds, constellations or abstract images. Thus the projection space replaces the projection plane, which we now know only in the cinema. The actual auditorium, neutralized by the absence of light, becomes, by means of projections, a space of illusion, an area of scenic occurrences.
>
> The goal of this theatre consists not in the material accumulation of refined technical tricks; these are available means to insure that the audience will be caught up in the midst of the scenic action, that the spectator will exist only in the space where the action unfolds, and that, being no longer sheltered by the curtain, he cannot escape from the action. . . . It [the theatre] is a great space machine with which the director can form his own personal work according to his creative strength.[15]

Gropius' goal was to destroy the implicit psychological separation of the performer and spectator; to eliminate the flatness of the stage picture and create a dynamic plasticity. In so doing he hoped to encourage the audience to "shake off its inertia." The Totaltheater was to be a "mobilization of all spatial means to rouse the spectator from his intellectual apathy, to assault and overwhelm him, coerce him into participation in the play."[16]

Variations on the Gropius scheme were developed by other Bauhaus members, all united in their desire to alter the spectator-performer relationship and to incorporate the new technology into their work. Echoing Gropius, Laszlo Moholy-Nagy stated:

It is time to produce a kind of stage activity which will no longer permit the masses to be silent spectators, which will not only excite them inwardly but will let them *take hold and participate*—actually allow them to fuse with the action on the stage at the peak of cathartic ecstacy.[17]

The theatre he proposed was a horizontal, vertical and diagonal arrangement of "suspended bridges and drawbridges," and the main performing area was a caliper stage that would "establish . . . a closer connection with the audience."[18] The stage itself became an environment of planes and space—"rotating sections . . . movable space constructions and disklike areas, in order to bring certain action moments on the stage into prominence, as in film 'close-ups.'"[19]

Like Gropius, Moholy-Nagy referred to his concept as Total Theatre. The theatre described was never built, but those elements that could be incorporated into a frontal stage were used in Piscator's production of Walter Mehring's *The Merchant of Berlin*. The sets, however, were a critical failure at the time. Moholy-Nagy tried these ideas once more in a production of *Madame Butterfly*, retaining only the costumes and lighting style of his Total Theatre. When it, too, was a failure, he ceased work along these lines.

Another Bauhaus member, Farkas Molnar, designed a "U-Theatre"— essentially a mechanized thrust stage with certain platforms on hydraulic elevators and others which could move on horizontal planes (Plate 21).[20] This theatre, too, was never built. The "U" shape referred to the configuration of the audience area. What made the theatre environmental was Molnar's significant additions to the scheme. Above the forestage was a suspended platform that could be connected to the balcony of the auditorium by bridges and ramps. In addition, suspended above both the stage and auditorium was "a cylindrical construction movable in all directions" for lighting and projection equipment and for lowering performers and props.[21] A bridge was also attached to the bottom of this cylinder whereby the balcony could be reached, making "aerial acrobatics" possible. There was to be a machine for dispensing appropriate odors, thus increasing the sensual aspect of the production by adding a sensory experience other than the traditional ones of sight and sound, and thus increasing the feeling of total environment. (The use of odors in performance was first tried at the Théâtre d'Art in Paris in 1891.) Perhaps most significantly, Molnar's design placed the spectators on swivel seats, and was thus the first to deal with the problem of sight lines in a theatre with a surrounding stage.

In 1933, Marinetti published a proposal for a "Total Theatre" that seemed to combine almost all the surrounding stage ideas of the previous fifteen years.[22] It included a large circular stage in the center of the auditorium, eleven smaller stages throughout the space, and a peripheral annular stage, allowing simultaneous or sequential action to occur throughout the theatre. Above the central stage was an apparatus for projecting the movement of the sun and moon. The audience could either stand or sit in rotating chairs to watch film, television images, poetry and painting projected on the curved walls of the theatre. Like Molnar, Marinetti proposed the emission of odors which could subsequently be eliminated by a kind of vacuum cleaner apparatus.

Blanding Sloan, an American working on the architecturally integrated space, developed plans for a so-called "Infinidome"—"the only new thing in 20th century theatre construction"—under the auspices of the Federal Theatre Project in the late thirties.[23] Sloan envisioned the project for the San Francisco Exposition of 1938, and later for the New York World's Fair of 1939. The Infinidome was also being considered as a theatre in Springfield, Massachusetts but the demise of the Federal Theatre in 1939 ended Sloan's project.

Drawn up in 1937, the plans indicated a hemispheric dome about 200 feet in diameter (Plate 22).[24] The audience, in a flexible auditorium that could seat from 600 to 1200 spectators, was arranged traditionally in orchestra and balcony sections around a mechanized thrust stage. The dome became a screen for planetarium-like projections of sky scenes, featuring stars and storms, as well as "color symphonies" projected by a color organ keyed to match colors and musical effects which would be heard through a system of speakers that surrounded the spectators, thus placing them in the center of the sound. Like Gropius, Sloan envisioned the technical effects creating "the fury of a sudden storm . . . with a power impossible to the theatre as we know it. Lightning will crackle across the sky and thunder roll realistically through the gloom."[25]

The most significant and comprehensive proposal for an environmental theatre, however, was set forth by Antonin Artaud in his first manifesto, "The Theatre of Cruelty" (1932).

> We abolish the stage and the auditorium and replace them by a single site, without partition or barrier of any kind, which will become the theater of the action. A direct communication will be re-established between the spectator and the spectacle, between the actor and the spectator, from the fact that the spectator, placed in the middle of the action, is engulfed and physically affected by it. This envelopment results, in part, from the very configuration of the room itself.
>
> Thus, abandoning the architecture of present-day theaters, we shall take some hangar or barn, which we shall have reconstructed according to processes which have culminated in the architecture of certain churches of holy places, and of certain temples in Tibet.
>
> In the interior of this construction special proportions of height and depth will prevail. The hall will be enclosed by four walls, without any kind of ornament, and the public will be seated in the middle of the room, on the ground floor, on mobile chairs which will allow them to follow the spectacle which will take place all around them. In effect, the absence of a stage in the usual sense of the word will provide for the

deployment of the action in the four corners of the room. Particular positions will be reserved for actors and action at the four cardinal points of the room. The scenes will be played in front of whitewashed wall-backgrounds designed to absorb the light. In addition, galleries overhead will run around the periphery of the hall as in certain primitive paintings. These galleries will permit the actors, whenever the action makes it neccesary, to be pursued from one point in the room to another, and the action to be deployed on all levels and in all perspectives of height and depth. A cry uttered at one end of the room can be transmitted from mouth to mouth with amplifications and successive modulations all the way to the other. The action will unfold, will extend its trajectory from level to level, point to point: paroxysms will suddenly burst forth, will flare up like fires in different spots. And to speak of the spectacle's character as true illusion or of the direct and immediate influence of the action on the spectator will not be hollow words. For this diffusion of action over an immense space will oblige the lighting of a scene and the varied lighting of a performance to fall upon the public as much as upon the actors—and to the several simultaneous actions or several phases of an identical action in which the characters, swarming over each other like bees, will endure all the onslaughts of the situations and the external assaults of the tempestuous elements, will correspond to the physical means of lighting, of producing thunder or wind, whose repercussions the spectator will undergo.

However, a central position will be reserved which, without serving, properly speaking, as a stage, will permit the bulk of the action to be concentrated and brought to a climax whenever necessary.[26]

It would be of great value to identify the sources which inspired Artaud's scenography. He does not acknowledge any particular influence, although his participation in the Parisian avant-garde would probably have made him aware of the environmental ideas of the first third of the century. In the boldness and specificity of his plan, in any case, Artaud clearly synthesized the ideas and tendencies of the post-war era into a feasible theatrical scenography. Although this passage is often cited as the source of present-day environmental performance, Artaud did not express a single new idea. In fact, he suggested little more than the conversion of a found environment into a unified performance space with mobile seating and peripheral and central stages—all previously proposed ideas. But in so doing he organized most major environmental concepts into a definitive statement about environmental scenography. The conciseness of his concept and, of course, Artaud's profound influence on the whole direction of theatre, account for much of the statement's impact on the development of non-frontal theatre.

While none of the ideas discussed so far in this chapter was ever implemented in the form proposed by its creator, variations of all of them were incorporated into many theatres after World War II. The concept of flexibility, for instance, became the basis of the municipal theatre of Krefeld, Germany, built in 1951 by André Perottet von Laban and Erwin Stoecklin (Plate 23). The basic plan included a fixed annular stage encircling the auditorium above the level of a single bank of slightly raked seats. The stage deepened at the front of the auditorium. Suspended curved wall sections conforming to the curve of the stage could be dropped in at various points around the interior of the annular stage to create a caliper or proscenium stage, or a platform could be extended into the seating area to create a thrust. By placing the seats on the stage and covering the auditorium with flooring at the stage level, an arena was created or, without the seats, a free space.

An alternative to the mobile annular or ring stages envisioned by Albert-Birot and Strnad is a rotating auditorium within a stationary ring. The most successful example is the Pyynikki Theatre of Tampere, Finland (Plate 24). It was built in 1959, not as an avant-garde project, but as a popular outdoor summer theatre. The spectators sit in a rotating, shell-shaped bank of seats. Scenes are set up on the ground or on platforms at intervals around the spectator area, which then rotates to each scene in turn—somewhat like Daguerre's nineteenth-century dioramas.[27] As in all outdoor theatre, the natural decor tends to become incorporated into the scene. One observer remarked that he confused stage sets and actual buildings in the area and "didn't know whether the children on swings in the distance were part of the cast, or Tampere youngsters at play."[28]

Combining the mobile ring stage with the rotating auditorium, Jacques Polieri constructed the Théâtre Mobile for Le Festival de l'Art Avant-Garde at Paris in 1960 (Plate 25).[29] It was a circular theatre thirty meters in diameter consisting of a fixed outer ring, a rotating inner stage, and a rotating central platform fourteen meters in diameter which provided a raked seating area for three- to four-hundred spectators. The spectator platform was situated off-center in relation to the outer ring, so that the inner edge of the ring was five meters from one side of the central platform and ten meters from the other.

Because there were two mobile elements in the Polieri theatre, several combinations of movement were possible. The stage or the seats on the central platform could each rotate alone; the central platform could move in conjunction with the inner stage as a single unit; or the two units could rotate simultaneously but in opposite directions. Because of the off-center position of the central platform, different stage depths were possible through its rotation. When moving in a particular configuration, the spectator experienced a sense of telescopic movement—moving closer to an object and then receding, creating an effect something like the "whip" ride at an amusement park. The spectator's angle of vision could range from 140° to 300° around the stage plane, depending on his position. Polieri believed that this movement of spectators, albeit passive, made them a physical part of the production—their perceptions of space and action were dependent, at least in part, on the imposed positions and movements. Movement, Polieri felt, was the means of bringing dynamism into spectacle. "One of the essential principles of the kaleidoscopic theatre is movement. *All elements of the spectacle are mobile.*"[30] Polieri did not, however, believe in the active participation of spectators. "The theatre of tomorrow," he wrote in 1955, "will be a theatre of introspection and abstraction, utilizing in all ways the whole range of spectacle; an orchestration of sound, light, shapes, color and life."[31] By creating a theatre in which all elements were subservient to decor, the perception of scenic components became the primary goal.

Polieri's Théâtre Mobile concept was incorporated in two theatre projects by other designers—only one of which was actually built. The proposed theatre was designed by Zbigniew Bac, Wiktor Jackiewicz, and others as the studio of the Sebisches National Theatre at Novy Sad, Yugoslavia (1961). It consisted of a gently raked, rotating, circular audience section positioned in the middle of a broad flat stage that filled the room (Plate 26). The other, the Maison de la Culture at Grenoble, France was designed by André Wogenscky and completed in 1968 (Plate 27). It contains two theatres, a large traditional auditorium and a 525-seat studio with a rotating, gradually sloped seating area encircled by a revolving annular stage. A semi-elliptical platform at one side of the ring forms the main stage. As in Gropius' Totaltheater, on which it is based, projection screens surround the annular stage so that the audience can be "enveloped by the spectacle."[32] Other annular stages can be found today in certain American university experimental theatres, notably those at the University of Miami, Trinity University in Texas, and Wayne State University in Detroit.[33]

The second category of surrounding-space theatres is the free or open space, exemplified by the so-called "black-box" theatres—totally adaptable performance areas with stage and seating units that can be arranged in any configuration. The units may range from collapsible platforms to elaborate mechanical and hydraulic stages. Aside from the fact that these types of theatres are unified spaces, there is nothing inherently environmental about them. Proscenium, thrust, and arena set-ups are possible. But such a space, as we shall see in Chapter 9, can be transformed into a total environment, or a scattered stage arrangement can be used.

Some notable free-space designs (never built) were R. von Dobloff's "Free Theatre" (1958), consisting of two flexible spaces and an adjoining, intimate annular stage theatre (Plate 28); Werner Ruhnau's "Mobiles Theatre" (1960) with hydraulic stage platforms (Plate 29)—both submitted in a competition for a playhouse in Dusseldorf; and Jaacov Agam's 1963 design for "a theatre with several stages in counterpoint" (Plate 30).[34] Agam's theatre was to utilize various platforms, open floor spaces, and suspended stages scattered asymmetrically throughout a space of linear geometric patterns.

Both the annular stage and some uses of free space surround the spectators 360° on a horizontal plane. These stages do not, however, significantly involve the spectator from above or below. (Although spectators in a balcony must look down at an angle, of course, and viewers in the orchestra watching a tightrope walker over the stage, for example, must look up, basically these spectators are viewing performances in front of them, not directly above or below.) To create a greater environmental sense in these sorts of theatres, some designers, as we have seen, have added overhead projection screens, suspended stages and scaffolds. In the totally environmental theatre, however, the spectator is placed as if in the center of a sphere with the performance occurring all around him from every conceivable angle. This is the concept inherent in the architecturally integrated space—a theatre whose design incorporates all architectural elements into a unified whole, all of which is accessible to both the performer and spectator. Unlike the unified space which is usually a frontal arrangement with shared architectural elements, the entire interior of the architecturally integrated space becomes simultaneously performance space and spectator area. Even if the spectator is not in the exact center of the structure, he is still inevitably surrounded by the scenographic elements as long as he is within the space.

The term "integrated space" itself was used by Frederick Kiesler in relation to his monumental project, the Endless Theatre. This theatre was originally conceived in 1923 to house the Vienna Theatre and Music Festival the following year. Designed as an ellipsoidal structure within a continuous shell of steel and opaque glass (actually, a double shell that would contain heating and cooling systems) and with a capacity of 10,000, it was meant not only for theatre and display, but was to include hotels, parking lots, and gardens.[35] As Kiesler described it, the interior consisted of

> an interplay of ramp, platform and elevator—an endless showplace throughout the whole space. . . . a continuous intertwining of vast ramps which lead into others on several levels until spectators and actors practically reach the ceiling. The various levels connect through three elevators which are exposed; the elevators are nothing but platforms that take off from one level to another. The players and the audience can intertwine anywhere in space. There, I feel, is a first attempt at an architectural expression of spatial integration. It fully used the construction principles of continuous tension—there was not a single column in the whole structure.[36]

The Guggenheim Museum, designed by Frank Lloyd Wright, with its spiral ramps, captures some of the spirit of Kiesler's design on a much less ambitious scale.

The core of the Endless Theatre was an arena stage (Kiesler's "space stage") with two proscenium or platform stages at either side bisecting the lower seating area and connected to each other by a bridge (Plates 31, 32, 33). There was spectator seating in circular rows, including three rows of stadium-like benches along the perimeter, and standing room on the ramps. These ramps and platforms could be rearranged to allow endless variations in design. The engineering techniques were to be borrowed from bridge building. This project was the first and, to this day, most complete concept for the total use of space by both spectator and performer. Every inch of space was potentially usable in some aspect of production—the inner surface of the structure, for instance, was to serve as a vast projection screen—and the entire space was capable of virtually continuous change. "The drama," as Kiesler said, "can expand and develop in space." In such a structure the spectator is truly surrounded. No longer is there merely a *feeling* of being suspended in space, as Strnad envisioned, but the spectator actually *is* suspended, completely enclosed within an environment.

Kiesler had been designing and sculpting since the end of World War I, and his ideas and projects prefigured almost all forms of architecturally environmental theatres, as well as many theatre planning concepts which were not necessarily environmental. One theme pervades Kiesler's work: continuity. (He refers to it as "endlessness"—the Endless House, the Endless Theatre, the Endless Sculpture.) This concept, as Kiesler used it, became a fundamental aspect of recent environmental theatre.

A conventional theatre is composed of discrete units clearly contained and demarcated—say, a stage space, a backstage, an auditorium, a lobby. Continuity, first of all, suggests no sense of containment but rather a potential for extension or expansion in all directions. Kiesler's "galaxial" mural of 1918 suggests an example.[37] Using what he called the "L and T" exhibit technique—a stabile-like configuration of frames and battens— Kiesler arranged a series of related paintings (essentially a fragmented mural) into a pattern for "continuous viewing." Spectators were not confined to a frontal, linear view but could observe the mural from all angles. Furthermore, the arrangement was not confined within a frame; the mural could grow, and in 1950 Kiesler actually did expand it. A related idea is suggested by his model for a City In Space built for the Decorative Arts Exhibition in Paris in 1925.[38] The model was a construction of intersecting geometric forms, creating an illusion of suspension in space, and with a potential for indefinite expansion.

Another aspect of continuity, according to Kiesler, is inherent in the circle. Whereas an angular shape suggests segmentation and finite space— "A rectangular space is by association and experience a space of confinement," stated Kiesler—a circle seems to be endless (though, of course, it, too, may confine).[39] This was the rationale behind the ellipsoidal continuous shell construction of the proposed Endless Theatre. There was no ceiling or floor, per se; everything was contained by a unified, continuous surface.

Kiesler applied the principles of continuity to his famous space stage (*Raumbühne*). With the peep-show stage the spectator could have no experience of space, said Kiesler. "It appears by necessity as merely a relief. Only to the actor who walks across the stage is it spatial. Here you have the kernel of the situation of space in reality and space as illusion."[40] Through the use of continuity in his scenography, Kiesler hoped to make space accessible on some level to the spectators as well as the actors. Although not all his experiments in this vein led to non-frontal staging, his projects were so unique and complex that a survey of certain major developments seems essential.

He began to deal with the experience of real space in his 1923 production of O'Neill's *The Emperor Jones* in Berlin. The stage for this production was envisioned by Kiesler as a funnel-shaped extension of the auditorium. The scenic elements were designed so that the performer would be perceived in a more three-dimensional aspect and so that the spectators would, he believed, experience the stage space kinesthetically rather than merely illusionistically.

> The stage was elevated. I left the stage open with no curtain. The stage floor was inclined to an angle of 32 degrees. The ceiling was tilted toward the back of the stage by 20 degrees. . . . Rear-stage one saw just a little slit of a cyclorama. There the Emperor appeared, and he walked down the incline of the floor; thus space became visible. As he hears the beat of a tom-tom he tries to escape. He starts to run, and as he moves the transformation of the stage begins. The drum beat gets faster and faster, indicating the passage of time, and time merges into space. I carried this inspiration into the scenery, designing it kinetically and having it move through the length of the play. The sides of the funnel opened up and the ceiling opened. From the sides, flats moved across the stage, turning, moving continuously back and forth. From the ceiling, semitransparent materials in various colors were dropped and made to move rhythmically. . . . [It] was the translation of the beats of the drums into a continuous flow of light, moving scenery, and color.[41]

Designed on the same principles, though never built, was the Optophon, a project for the 1925 Decorative Arts Exhibition which Kiesler wanted to build between the trees along the Seine. It was to be in the shape of a horizontal cross, and where the four wings met was "a mobile-machine for partly abstract or realistic and phonetic plays which would run automatically."[42]

For Kiesler, not only did such designs transform static space into continually evolving space and "coalesce the stage and audience space into a unity," they also expressed a further element of continuity—the dynamic tension between time and space. The continuous movement of scenic elements through space was dependent on the linear progression of the play through actual time. By finding spatial scenic equivalents for temporal elements, Kiesler hoped to achieve a transformation of time into space.

In *The Emperor Jones*, Kiesler was taking the first steps toward the development of an architecturally integrated space by searching for a way to place the spectators in the midst of the production. If the stage was perceived in the manner he envisioned, then the audience would have a psychological experience of actual stage space and actual stage time. Kiesler was one of the first theatre practitioners to be concerned with the experience of actual performance time. In *The Emperor Jones* the evolving scenes were changed in accordance with a real and inflexible time schedule which, although keyed to actions in the script, actually existed independently of onstage activities— scene changes (or, rather, the slowly evolving set) were cued by a clock, as it were, rather than specific words or gestures. Kiesler wanted the spectators to be aware of the relationship between actual time and stage events. Thus, in their perceptions of time and space the audience would have a psychological experience equivalent to the performers' physical experience.

Placing the audience directly on the stage was the next logical step, thus allowing them to experience physically the stage space. This was the theory behind the Endless Theatre. Only by being in a unified and totally shared environment could both actor and spectator experience the same space.

Although Kiesler was in charge of design for the Vienna Music and Theatre Festival, the Endless Theatre was not built, owing to reasons of economy and feasibility. A version of his space stage, however, was built in the Vienna Konserthaus for the Festival. This stage, which was basically the core of the Endless Theatre, was a Constructivist setting of multilevel platforms connected by a spiraling ramp (Plates 34 and 35). An elevator moved through the center connecting all levels. The stage was erected in the orchestra section of the theatre (the seats had been removed), the audience sat in the balcony, and the proscenium opening covered with a white curtain was used as a projection screen. Similar stages were built by Kiesler in Vienna and Berlin for his 1925 production of Wedekind's *Francisca*.

Kiesler came to the United States for the International Theatre Exhibit of 1926 and remained here. His subsequent projects tended to be more feasible than the Endless Theatre and the concept of endlessness came to mean simply the greatest possible flexibility. This flexible-endless theatre idea became incorporated into his next project, the "Universal Theatre"—a double theatre with flexible stage and auditorium space. In its first form the Universal Theatre was to be built in Brooklyn in 1926; then the plan was adapted for a theatre in Woodstock, New York in 1931 (Plates 36-39).[43] Neither one was built. The final version was proposed in 1961; it, too, was never built.[44]

The differences among the three versions have to do mainly with aspects of architecture or auxiliary theatre facilities and are of little concern from an environmental viewpoint. Essentially they included back-to-back theatres, one large and the other intimate, whose stages could be partitioned or combined. If the partition were removed, the seating section of the smaller theatre could be rolled onto the stage, creating an arena in conjunction with the larger house. The orchestra seating in the larger space was on movable platforms which could be rotated so as to create thrust or arena set-ups or even scattered stage arrangements. This section was also surrounded by an annular stage, and, at Woodstock, a second annular stage was designed to encompass the balcony as well. In the "Universal" of 1961, the main stage was encased in a continuous eggplant-shaped shell. Attached to the structure was a thirty-story skyscraper that functioned as a performance complex containing small theatres, television studios and various amenities for performers and spectators (Plates 40-42).

Another unrealized project was a theatre piece conceived in collaboration with the composer Edgar Varese and writer Burgess Meredith that apparently never went beyond the planning stage.[45] Kiesler referred to it as "scenic theatre," and the set was a simplified version of the Endless (Plate 43). The audience was seated arena-style on benches around a flat, oval stage. In the center of the stage was a "table"—a mushroom-like construction that contained projection equipment and could also serve as a "repository for costumes." (Kiesler liked the idea of performers transforming into characters or from one character into another in full view of the audience.) On opposite ends of the arena were two platform stages and there was an annular stage surrounding the whole theatre. Kiesler explained that it was, "a combination of theatre-in-the-round with two proscenium stages and a Japanese ramp."[46] The ceiling was to be underhung with gauze, and for one section of the performance Kiesler envisioned projecting a film of a diving airplane onto the gauze. The image would become larger and larger while at the same time the gauze would descend on the spectators to give the impression of the plane crashing on them. Meredith compared this to the "feelies" in Aldous Huxley's book, *Brave New World*, but, of course, the impulse can also be traced to Marinetti's tactile theatre.

Kiesler's stage work had been very influential in Europe before he came to the United States. In 1923 he became involved with the *de Stijl* group, an art group founded in Holland, and articles by and about Kiesler appeared in their magazine and thus his ideas found their way into both Russia and the work of the Bauhaus.[47] After 1926, however, virtually none of his theatre projects came to fruition. While Kiesler should be known as the "father" of environmental theatre, those who followed his lead failed to acknowledge him. Even in flexible theatre architecture, so common since World War II, there are few who are aware of Kiesler's contributions.[48]

Nonetheless, the spherical-type theatres—the architecturally integrated space—enjoyed great currency during the twenties. In 1924, Andreas Weininger of the Bauhaus proposed his Spherical Theatre (*Kugeltheater*) (Plate 44). It differed from the Endless in that the performance was entirely mechanical. Furthermore, the audience was relegated only to seats on the interior surface of the sphere, making it a sort of spherical arena theatre. The stage was fragmented into a central system of platforms and spiral stairs. Weininger described the space and its theory:

> A sphere as architectonic structure in place of the customary theatre. The spectators, on the inner wall of the sphere, find themselves in a new relationship to space. Because of their all-encompassing view, because of centripetal force, they find themselves in a new psychic, optical, acoustical relationship; they find themselves confronted with new possibilities for concentric, eccentric, multidirectional, mechanical space-stage phenomena.[49]

As with Apollinaire, the impulse here is not merely a greater physical involvement in the production but to alter basic perceptions of space. The idea of "centripetal force" relates Weininger to Kiesler and Gropius in their attempts to shatter pictorial flatness and draw the spectator into a different or new awareness of space.

Similar to Weininger's proposal was Bernard Reder's project for a theatre in a sphere (1961). Reder felt that the sphere was the most satisfactory sculptural form "because it is a perfectly unified and uniform volume with no front or back, no top or bottom, no frontality."[50] His proposed theatre contained a transparent arena stage with transparent sets suspended in the center of the sphere (Plate 45). The spectators were seated in a single row of seats mounted on a spiral track along the interior of the structure. A stationary ramp behind this track provided access to the seats. During the performance, the seats slowly ascended the track, spiraling to the apex of the sphere and then slowly descended on an opposite track, much like the conveyor system in many world's fair pavilions. Thus, during a performance, the spectators viewed the stage from every possible vantage point and angle including from above and below.

As mentioned earlier, most of the so-called total theatres were too specialized or expensive to be constructed privately but they frequently appeared as pavilions at world's fairs and amusement parks. Labyrinth, the pavilion of the Canadian National Film Board at Montreal's Expo 67 was precisely such an example. The audience entered through a dimly lit passage decorated with primitive-looking patterns which led them to an atrium. As the spectators moved along the five tiers of balconies surrounding this space they viewed a film projected on a tall vertical screen and a horizontal screen at the base. The spectators then moved onto a second chamber where they were subjected to special sound effects, music, and lights projected onto mirrored surfaces, all intended to induce "self-contemplation." The third chamber was a more traditional film theatre—the spectators sat facing the screen—but the screen was in a cruciform shape, composed of five screens which did not necessarily show the same or complementary images. Project director Roman Kroitor explained the environment as a means of achieving a greater "film experience as a consequence of one's own physical movement through it, so that the images become part of both an architectural and a linear structure."[51]

Many of the major industrial exhibits at world's fairs since the 1939 fair at New York have relied on totally controlled environments like Labyrinth in which spectators view live or mechanical performances, tableaux or panoramas as they pass through on foot or on mechanized seats and conveyors. At the New York Fair of 1939, the Westinghouse and the Glass exhibits introduced "ambulatory stages" that were hailed as the theatres of the future.[52] These were essentially long, horizontal or winding stages, through or past which the spectators were guided by corral-like structures allowing them to view a continuous, sequential series of actions or tableaux. This kind of total environment was most successfully exploited by Walt Disney both at the recent world's fairs and at Disneyland and Disneyworld.

Even more elaborate are certain contemporary amusement park structures such as the "Fifth Dimension," a fun-house in Ayrshire, Scotland which includes tactile effects in its sensory assault.

This is built up from a number of interchangeable spherical and tubular units in plastic. The exterior is less interesting than the interior, but once inside the visitor is subjected to a series of changes designed to stimulate all the senses except smell. The lighting changes constantly both in colour and intensity, and as the explorer in this dream chamber feels his way from point to point the surfaces he touches and on which he stands vary in texture from smooth to abrasive, warm to cold. Even the floor changes suddenly from concrete to sponge. Assailed by electronically produced sounds, the visitor is thus completely contained in an environment totally designed for its purpose.[53]

Quite similar to this funhouse was a 1967 proposal by German artist Otto Piene for "The Theatre That Moves."[54] Indeed, one version of his theatre, the Theatre of Soft Sensation, was intended to travel with fun fairs.[55] Piene rejected the "vulgarity" of Lincoln Center-style theatre architecture and what he considered the sterility of contemporary performance. His ideas borrowed from Artaud, Meyerhold, Marinetti and others.

Imagine: in these theatres, the stage can be moved and the audience can move. There are no stationary seats. The buildings are essentially empty spaces which can be divided and arranged according to the needs of a production. . . . Any sensual phenomena can be amplified. Loudspeakers and projectors are spread all over the space. Rain and wind and heat and cold can be produced inside the theatre. There will be smells, steam and smoke. Light can blind, darkness soothe; the ground can tremble. The floor can be soft as well as hard. People can lie, sit, stand, walk as they please or as the play requires. Parts of the room or the whole room can move, change shape, ascend or descend so that either the action or the audience or both can change positions quickly or smoothly. (The floor can be hydraulically elevated, and the floor, the walls, and the ceiling can be inflatable.) The air pressure can be lowered or raised. The walls can echo or be sound-absorbent. Everything is flexible, adaptable, erectile, collapsible, portable. . . . Let whole flocks of animals walk in. . . . Let everything from bicycles to tanks drive in. Let flames go up. . . . Can you open the roofs to let balloons, helicopters, planes in and out? Can you open the walls to let the street in?[56]

Jacques Polieri has noted his indebtedness to Disney as well as to Gordon Craig and Oskar Schlemmer. He makes no mention of Kiesler, however, whose Endless Theatre and notions of continuous movement were clearly a prototype of Polieri's Theatre of Total Movement. Like Kiesler, Polieri envisioned a multi-media, "total" theatre that assaulted all the senses, with movement as the essential principle. In 1955 he described the basic impulse behind what he termed the "kaleidoscopic" theatre. "The spectator of the future," he said, is

"in a frame of plexiglass. . . . Surrounded by sound, by light, by colors, by forms, by shadows. . . . The rails of the "performance train" converge, cross, then run parallel for awhile, then separate one from the other in perpetually renewing fireworks and a perpetual festival."[57]

Polieri first proposed the Theatre of Total Movement in 1957 as a realization of those ideas. A second similar version was proposed in 1962 (Plate 46) but neither was built.[58] The building resembled a crystal ball in shape—a circular structure on a concave pedestal. It was to consist of a double shell—the space between the two shells was for storage, properties, sets and so forth, and a control booth was located in the upper portion of the shell. The audience of about 1000 was suspended in the center of the sphere on rotating platforms. In the first version, the spectators were placed on several platforms, shaped somewhat like paddles and hockey sticks, suspended, mobile-fashion, from a rotating core that contained escalators for access. In the second version the spectators were to be seated in revolving chairs on irregularly shaped platforms placed on "telescopic pipes" so that they could be raised to varying heights. The whole interior of the sphere was a performance space of irregularly shaped projection screens and "telescopic stages." Thus, the "spectators [are] in movement at the inside of the sphere and a moving spectacle [is] on the internal faces of the volume."[59]

A simplified version of the Total Movement Theatre was built by the Mitsui group for the 1970 World's Fair at Osaka, Japan (Plate 47). It consisted of a large, mobile, circular platform on which were three telescopic platforms for the public. Access to these areas was by three entrances placed at different levels. A small screen faced each platform so that, at the start of the spectacle, there was a sense of three individual performance areas. The production began with films and projections on each screen but soon expanded so as to surround the spectators on all sides. The audience platforms commenced to move in conjunction with sounds and the rhythms of the projections.[60]

Another project at the Osaka fair was the Pepsi-Cola Pavilion designed and built by some seventy-five artists and engineers working under an umbrella organization called Experiments In Art and Technology.[61] According to the executive coordinator, Billy Klüver, the Pavilion

> represented a new form of theatre space, which completely surrounded the audience and where every part of the space had the same theatrical intensity for the individual. . . . It was a tangible space; the effect was not psychological. . . . Instead, the visitor became part of the total experience.[62]

The structure itself was a white, "false" geodesic dome, 120 feet in diameter—a sort of igloo composed of triangular peaks.[63] This was shrouded in a man-made fog. Visitors entered the dome through a tunnel. They were given "handsets" which received audio signals transmitted from beneath the multi-textured floor (different floor sections were covered with stone, wood, rubber, carpet, artificial turf, and so on). Sounds heard through the handsets were coordinated with the textures—lawnmowers and birds on the grass, city sounds on the asphalt. From the tunnel guests entered the Clam Room—named for its shape—a dark, cave-like room, with flickering lights and shadows in the center. Exiting from the room, visitors walked through a "scintillating shower" of reflected, multi-colored laser light. Stairs led up to the Dome Room whose primary feature was a ninety-foot diameter hemispherical mirror dome designed by artist Robert Whitman. The mirror, because of its shape, produced "real images"—seemingly three-dimensional upside down images as opposed to the conventional "virtual images"—in the space in front of the mirror. A constantly changing environment of light and sound was created by the computer controlled light system, thirty-seven speakers and the unique optical and acoustical properties of the dome.

Aside from light and sound environments there were several performances employing the features of dome which were akin to Happenings and post-modern dances such as Remy Charlip's *Hommage to Loie Fuller* and Rikuro Miyai's *Shadows Left On the Moon* in which a juggler played with the optical tricks of the mirror.

There is perhaps a certain irony in the fact that such radical concepts as the architecturally integrated environment have found their only acceptance in amusement park forms, or that the rotating ring stage is perceived largely as a technological alternative to the revolving stage platform. Designers and directors working with environmental forms in recent times, because of monetary or technical limitations, have often tried to obtain similar effects through a temporary transformation of existing space. Despite the intentions of the various designers mentioned here, it is probable that the spectator in the architecturally integrated space, and especially in the annular stage theatre, will perceive himself *not* as physically involved in the production, but as an island surrounded but distinctly separate from the performance. This, at least, seemed to be the conclusion of many of the Russian designers and directors discussed in the next chapter. While the Constructivist movement, which dominated Russian theatre design in the twenties, was in many ways similar in form and impulse to the work of Kiesler, it tended to shy away from surrounding the spectator, and, as we shall see, Meyerhold ultimately concluded that the arena was the only means of creating intimacy and a sense of shared space.

1. Diagram of the performance area for a *Raslila*
   during the Bhavana festival.

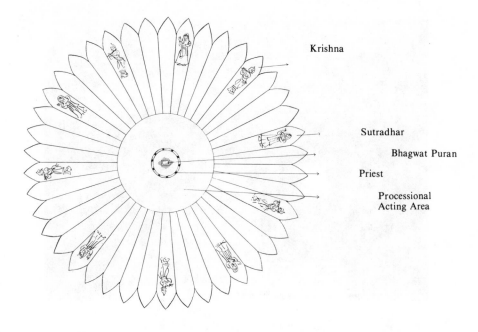

Krishna

Sutradhar

Bhagwat Puran

Priest

Processional
Acting Area

2. Plan of Nottingham Goose Fair.

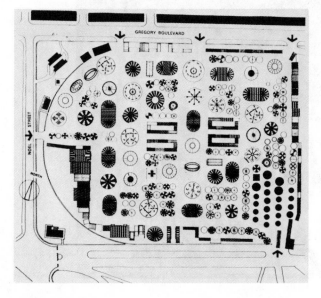

3. Maurice Pottecher's stage at Bussang, France with the back wall opened to provide view of the hillside. (Decor is for production of *Poil de Carotte*.)

4. Reinhardt's open-air production of *The Merchant of Venice* in Venice, 1934.

5. Hans Poelzig's Grosses Schauspielhaus, Berlin; view of the stage.

6. Ground plan of Grosses Schauspielhaus.

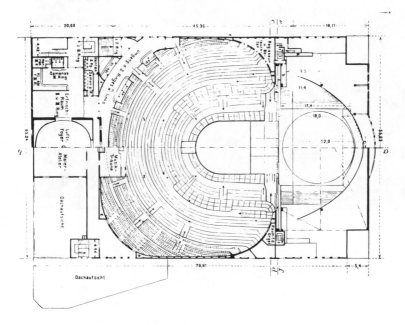

7. The Dalcroze School of Eurythmics's theatre at Hellerau, Switzerland.

8. Jacques Copeau's stage at the Vieux Colombier, Paris.

9. Ground plan of Norman Bel Geddes's "prosceniumless theatre," (1914).

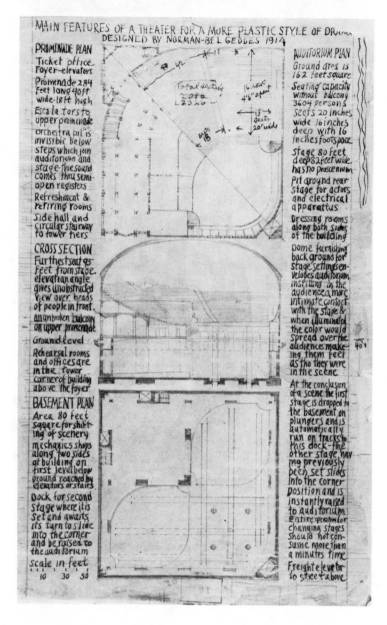

10.   Section of Geddes's "prosceniumless theatre."

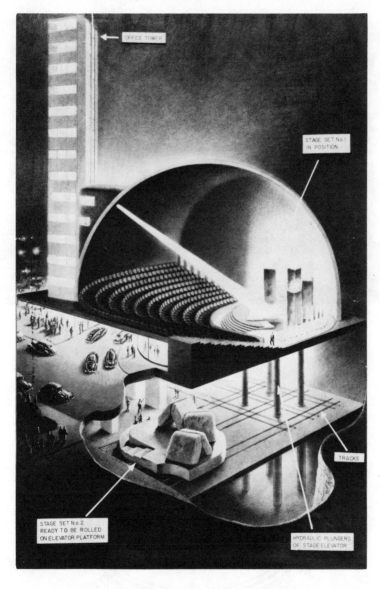

11. Stage of Reinhardt's Redoutensal, 1922.

12. Theatre plan by Charles-Nicolas Cochin,
1765, showing a tripartite stage.

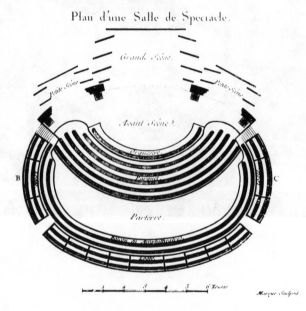

13. Theatre plan by Cosimo Morelli, Imola,
Italy, 1779.

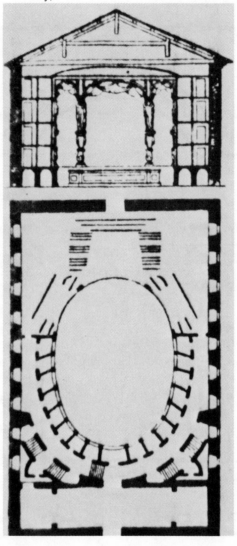

14. Theatre plan by Henry van de Velde for the Werkbundt
    Theater at Cologne, 1914.

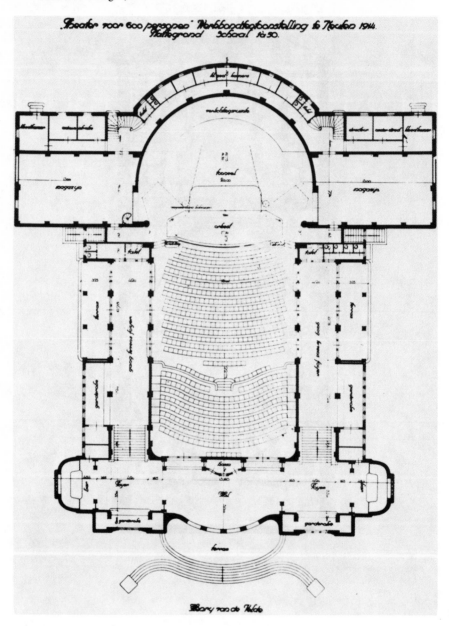

15. Tripartite stage by Auguste Perret for the Exposition of Decorative Arts, Paris, 1925.

16. Ground plan of the Théâtre Nunique by Pierre Albert-Birot.

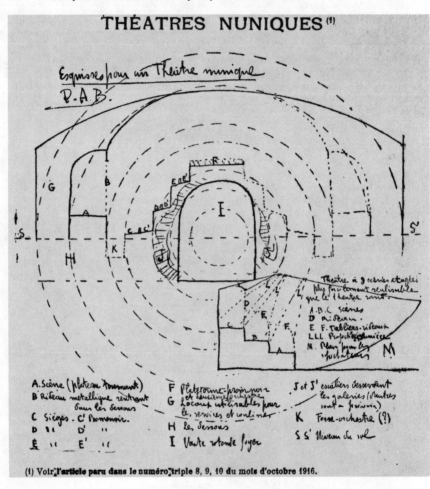

THÉÂTRES NUNIQUES[1]

(1) Voir l'article paru dans le numéro triple 8, 9, 10 du mois d'octobre 1916.

17. Design for a theatre by Oskar Strnad, 1918.

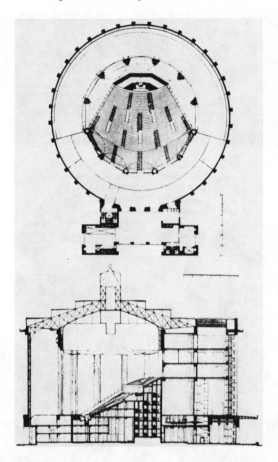

18. Sketch of Strnad's theatre.

19. Model of Walter Gropius's Totaltheater, 1927.

20. Totaltheatre: an isometric view, and plan showing stage in three positions.

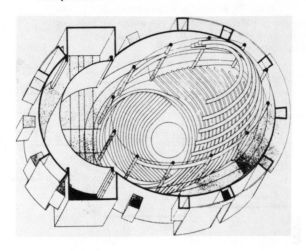

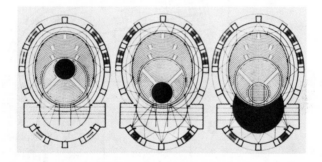

21. Isometric view and plan of Farkas Molnar's U-Theatre,
    1924. Key to plan: A) First Stage; B) Second Stage;
    C) Third Stage; D) Fourth Stage; E) Elevator and Lighting
    Apparatus; F) Mechanical Music Apparatus; G) Suspended
    Bridges and Drawbridges; I, II) U-Shaped Rings;
    III) Balcony; IV, V) Loges.

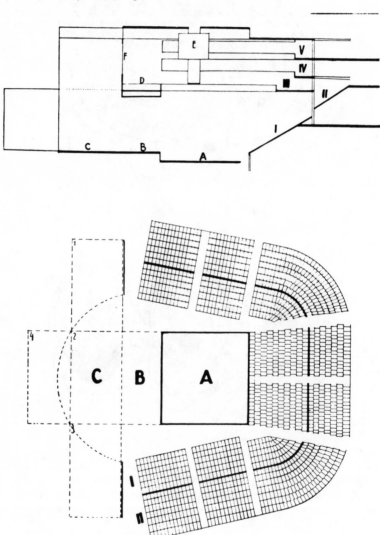

22. Design for Infinidome by Blanding Sloan, 1937.

CROSS SECTION

ABOUT 200 FEET

IDEA and DESIGN by BLANDING SLOAN — 1937

23. Design for a flexible theatre at Krefeld, Germany by Andre
    Perottet von Laban and Erwin Stoecklin, 1951.

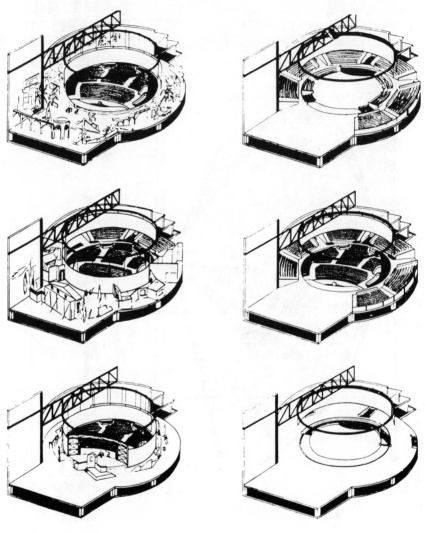

24. Pynnikki Theatre at Tampere, Finland, 1959.

25. Théâtre Mobile by Jacques Polieri.

26. Design for Serbian National Theatre by Zbigniew Bac,
    Wiktor Jackiewicz, Elzbieta Krol, and Krystyna Plawska-
    Jackiewicz. Novy Sad, Yugoslavia, 1961.

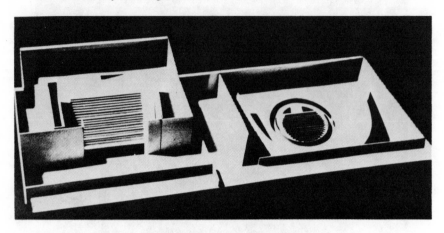

27. Plan and section of the studio theatre of Maison de la
    Culture, Grenoble, France, 1968 by André Woyenscky.

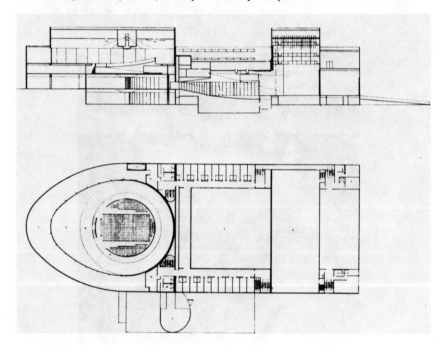

28. Design for a "Free Theatre" by R. von Dobloff, 1958. The "hatched" circular areas and the dark curved lines in the protrusion are for spectators.

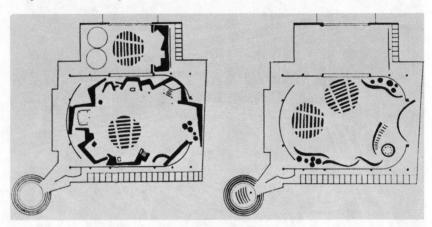

29. "Mobiles Theatre" design by Werner Ruhnau, 1959. The hexagonal areas are for spectators.

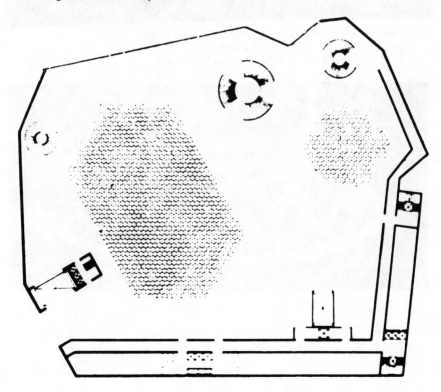

30. Design by Jaacov Agam for a theatre with "several stages in counterpoint," a version of a scattered-stage theatre.

31. Frederick Kiesler's design for the Endless Theatre (section), 1923.
(Collection, The Museum of Modern Art, New York.)

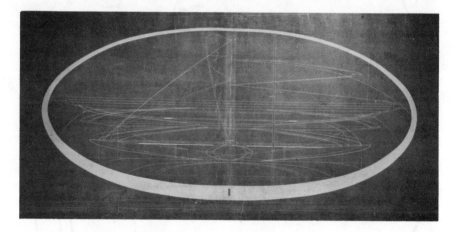

32. Frederick Kiesler's design for the Endless Theatre, 1923.
(Collection, The Museum of Modern Art, New York.)

33. Frederick Kiesler's design for the Endless Theatre, 1923.
(Collection, The Museum of Modern Art, New York)

34. View of construction of Kiesler's "Space Stage" at the
     Vienna Music Festival, 1924.

35. The "Space Stage" at Vienna.

36. Model of a "Space Theatre" for Woodstock, New York, 1931, by Frederick Kiesler.

37. Space Theatre model, view toward auditorium.

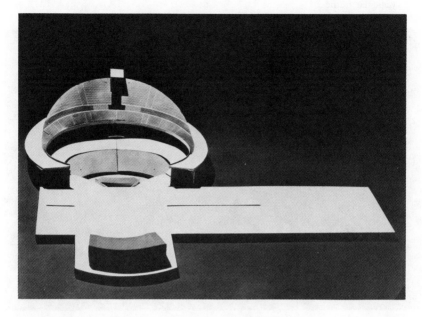

38. Space Theatre model, single stage with auditorium on either side.

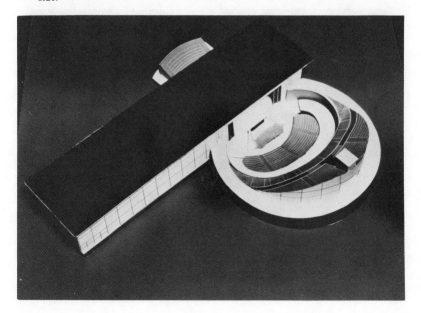

39. Space Theatre model, showing separation of foot and
     vehicular traffic.

40. Model of exterior of Kiesler's Universal Theatre, 1961.

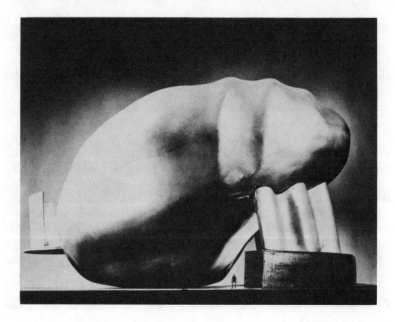

41. Model showing interior of Kiesler's Universal Theatre, 1961.

42. Sketch of Universal Theatre and skyscraper.

43. Kiesler's conceptual sketch of performance space for a theatre project in conjunction with Edgar Varese and Burgess Meredith, 1961.

44. Andreas Weininger's sketch of the Spherical Theatre, 1924.

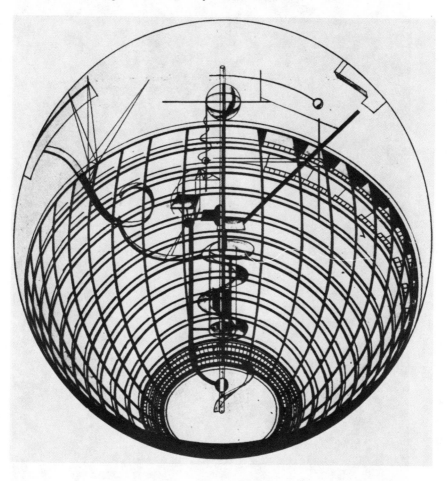

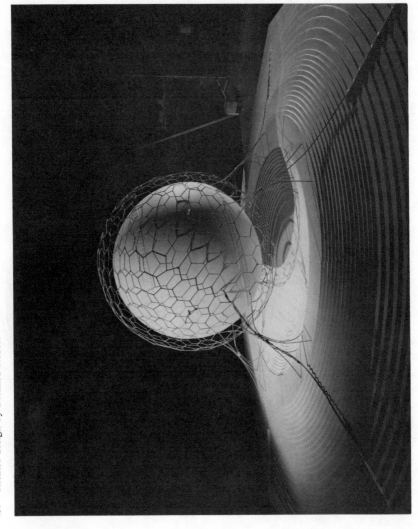

45. Theatre design by Bernard Reder.

46.   Model of Total Movement Theatre by Jacques Polieri, 1962.

47. Adaptation of Polieri's Total Movement Theatre built at
    Expo 70, Osaka, Japan, 1970.

5

Environmental Production In Russia

What the modern *spectator wants is the placard,*
the juxtaposition of the surfaces and shapes of
tangible materials! *To sum up, both we and they*
want to escape from the box of the theatre on to
the wide-open stage. . . .

More than anyone, the Moscow Art Theatre is to
blame for the passivity of the spectator. . . .

—Two statements by
Vsevelod Meyerhold, 1920

The years in Russia from the birth of the Moscow Art Theatre in 1898 to the
eve of World War II represent one of the most phenomenally creative
periods in theatre history.[1] Much of the work done during this time, like that
seen in Western Europe, focused on the problems of unifying spectator and
stage space and achieving a greater plasticity on the stage. Consequently, at
least some of it tended toward environmental staging. This was further
enhanced by developments in the Russian art world, notably Constructivism, which, closely related to the theatre, often provided the impetus and
tools for environmental experimentation. The boldest innovator in theatrical
staging was Vsevelod Meyerhold who not only developed methods of actor
training in opposition to Stanislavsky but ceaselessly experimented with
audience-performer relationships. It was his pupil, Nikolai Okhlopkov, who
in 1932 founded the Realistic Theatre, the first theatre in the world truly
devoted to environmental production (see Chapter 6).

   Except during World War I and the Civil War which followed the
Revolution, Russia was not artistically isolated from the rest of Europe and
new ideas in all of the arts were known and assimilated. Russian directors,
for example, were influenced by the theories and work of Appia, Craig,
Fuchs, Reinhardt, and later, Copeau, Gémier and Dullin, and influences

from Western European art and architecture affected stage design as well. Early examples of non-frontal performance tend to be found not so much in the legitimate theatre as in the activities of the various art groups, many of whose members actively participated in aspects of theatre.

The first Futurist manifesto, for instance, was available in Russia in 1909 and by the time Marinetti himself visited the country in 1914 there was a flourishing group of Russian Futurists.[2] Although they differed in theories, the Russian Futurists, like their Italian counterparts, were consciously outlandish in their everyday activities, parading through the streets in green-striped suits, wearing grotesque make-up and sporting radishes and spoons in their lapels.[3] They, too, held "evenings" in which the readings were purposely inflammatory in order to arouse reactions from the apathetic "bourgeoisie." Galleries and cabarets were used for these performances and the sites were appropriately transformed. The poet Vladimir Mayakovsky frequently read at the Cafe Pittoresque, whose interior was greatly altered by the paintings and sculptures of Vladimir Tatlin, Alexander Rodchenko and Georgy Yakulov on its ceiling and walls, and in its corners.[4] These works surrounded both spectators and "performers" alike while destroying the simple outlines of the room. Constructions were hung from the lights as well, causing unusual patterns of light to criss-cross the room.[5]

Munich was a center of artistic exchange where many Russian artists had gone to study before the war. There, they came into contact with German artists including the nucleus of the future *Blaue Reiter* group.[6] Among the Russians associated with or influenced by this group were Natalia Goncharova, Mikhail Larionov and Alexandra Exter—all of whom worked in theatre to some extent. Several Russian artists, like Vassily Kandinsky, actually became part of the *Blaue Reiter*. The active flow of avant-garde ideas between Russia and Western Europe prior to the War partly accounts for similarities we shall see among such groups as the Russian Constructivists and Suprematists, and the Dutch *de Stijl* and the Bauhaus in Germany.

As in Germany and France, the movement toward a physical unity of stage and auditorium began in Russia as a reaction against the two-dimensional quality of the proscenium stage and the anti-theatricality of Naturalism—specifically against the Moscow Art Theatre. In their search for a greater stage plasticity, many Russian directors and designers turned to Appia, whose influence was evident in the productions of Tairov in the teens and as early as 1907 in Meyerhold's work with Vera Kommisarzhevskaya.[7]

Meyerhold began his career with the Moscow Art Theatre but his anti-naturalist tendencies eventually led to a break with Stanislavsky in 1905. That summer, Meyerhold staged Ibsen's *Ghosts* with the Fellowship of the

New Drama at Poltava. Apparently under the influence of Georg Fuch's *The Stage of the Future*, published the previous year, Meyerhold removed the curtain and footlights for this production, built a deep forestage and used a unit set, thereby taking an important first step toward a unified space.[8]

In the fall of 1905 Meyerhold was hired by Vera Kommisarzhevskaya as a director and actor in her Petersburg Theatre. During his two years there, and in following years at other Imperial Theatres, he continued to exhibit the influence of Fuchs and the Symbolists, frequently using a shallow relief stage and step-like levels. Like Fuchs, Meyerhold believed that the relief stage led to a psychological and spiritual unification of the stage and auditorium. Indeed, observers commented that his means of reaching and involving the spectators was similar to a religious service.[9] Soon, however, psychological unification was insufficient—Meyerhold wanted literally to bridge the gap between the stage and auditorium and to incorporate them physically into one space. In Meyerhold's opinion, this was an essential step in achieving spectator involvement in the production.[10] Consequently, he abandoned the static tableau-like staging of the Symbolists which he believed encouraged spectator passivity and contemplative states.

In the spring of 1910, Meyerhold staged Calderon's *Adoration of the Cross* in the Tower Theatre, a small private theatre in the home of the poet Vyacheslav Ivanov.[11] Here both the stage and auditorium were placed on the same level and entrances and exits were made through the audience. While some of the staging was undoubtedly a result of the physical limitations of the theatre, the use of the aisles for actors was part of the attempt to eliminate the audience-performer dichotomy.[12]

During the fall of 1910, Meyerhold opened the House of Interludes at the former Skazki Theatre in Petersburg. The room was arranged in a cabaret style with the footlights removed and steps built from the stage into the auditorium where the seats were replaced by tables and chairs. Stage action could thus extend into the house. In the production of *Columbine's Scarf* (adapted from Arthur Schnitzler's *The Veil of Pierette*), for example, the character of the Kapellmeister fled through the audience and Gigolo led the wedding guests in a wild polka that wound around the tables.[13] In Znosko-Borovsky's *The Transfigured Prince*, an actor tumbled off the stage during a battle scene and hid under the nearest table, remarking that he seemed to be safe. When the noise of the battle drove him out, he ran through the house shouting, "Every man for himself!"[14] In an adaptation of Molière's *Don Juan*, later that year, at the Alexandrinsky Theatre, not only were the curtain and footlights removed, but the audience remained lit by chandeliers during the performance.[15] The spectators at his production of *The Fairground Booth* (1914) were included in the performance when the performers threw oranges to them.[16]

In all these productions, the spectators were not so much incorporated into the performance as acknowledged by the actors, thus emphasizing the theatrical nature of the event. The spectators were constantly reminded that they were watching a play rather than looking through a peep-hole at real life. Although he abolished many accoutrements of the picture-frame stage in this movement toward unifying spectator and performer space, Meyerhold was reluctant to abandon the proscenium altogether. As late as 1920, he was accused of using the proscenium to separate the stage and auditorium. Replying to this charge, in his inaugural speech to the members of the newly created R.S.F.S.R. (Russian Soviet Federated Socialist Republic) Theatre No. I, Meyerhold paraphrased Fuchs almost verbatim: "For me, the proscenium is far more than just a technical refinement; it is the first step towards the unification of the stage with the auditorium.[17]

The Russian Revolution of 1917 opened an era of great artistic and intellectual experimentation. Marxist concepts were applied to various styles of theatre and the feeling of revolution encouraged experimentation as a means of finding alternatives to existing "bourgeois" forms. Constructivism, perhaps the most original and influential movement to emerge from Russia after the Revolution, found a productive outlet in the Russian theatre of the twenties. After the reopening of the Soviet Union in 1921, Constructivism entered European art circles, primarily through the *de Stijl* group and their magazine. At the same time, the Russian magazine, *Soviet Architecture*, introduced *de Stijl*, Gropius, Frank Lloyd Wright and others to the Soviet Union.

While Constructivism on the Soviet stage was not, in itself, environmental, a fundamental connection existed between environmental and Constructivist ideas. The Constructivists were primarily concerned with the perception, creation, and use of space. In place of the two-dimensional stage picture, they created three-dimensional, utilitarian stage environments for the actor. These environments often strained at the confines of the proscenium, filling the entire stage space and spilling into the auditorium in a dynamic flow that seemed about to engulf the spectators. It seemed that the next logical step would have been to extend the settings into the auditorium creating a unified, if not totally surrounding environment. But this step was never fully taken. Meyerhold had his actors and even cars moving through the aisles, but only the designer El Lissitzky, in his proposal for *I Want A Child* (1926–30), suggested incorporating the spectators into the constructed set.

Constructivism was defined in the Soviet art magazine *LEF*, in 1923, as "The organization of the given material on the principles of tectonics, structure and construction, the form becoming defined in the process by the utilitarian aim of the object."[18] On the stage this impulse resulted in non-illusionistic skeletal constructions, mostly made of wood, that combined ramps, platforms, frames, steps and their necessary structural supports, thus providing acting environments or, in the case of sets with moving parts, "acting machines." The multi-level, fragmented stages permitted simultaneous, multi-focus and montage staging in three-dimensions.[19] For the most part, the Constructivists made no attempt to create a sense of place in their sets, although Varvara Stepanova's set for *Tarelkin's Death*, for example, suggested a prison, and parts of Lyubov Popova's set for *The Magnanimous Cuckold* suggested, in context, a windmill.

Some Constructivist roots are to be found in Suprematism, a non-objective art movement originating in 1913 with Kasimir Malevich's designs for Mayakovsky's *Victory Over the Sun*.[20] The work of the artists in this movement frequently paralleled contemporary European developments, notably Cubism and Futurism. Although Suprematist painting generally consisted of flat geometric shapes, Malevich was also composing perspective, three-dimensional architectural drawings by 1915 which he referred to as "Planits" or "The Contemporary Environment."[21] In the 1920s he translated these drawings into sculptures called "Arkhitektonics" which bore a striking resemblance to Kiesler's proposed "City In Space" and had a similar potential for unlimited expansion. It was such geometrical forms that would provide a basis for Constructivism.

Vladimir Tatlin, a rival of Malevich, coined the term "constructivism" in 1920 in defining the work of his group, then known as the Productivists. To celebrate the success of the Revolution, Tatlin designed the Monument to the Third International (1919–20). Although not designed as a theatre, the intended uses and effects of the space were similar to those of the architecturally integrated environment. Not only was it deemed an appropriate symbol of the new socio-political order, but, in the words of Kenneth Frampton, despite the fact that it was never built, "it crystalized a new consciousness which was to function as a continuous line of thought, sometimes covert, sometimes overt, in the development of European architecture between the two world wars."[22] Made of iron and glass and standing more than half a mile high, it resembled a skeletal Tower of Pisa—an endless spiral into space. Different parts of the structure were to move, rotating at speeds from one revolution per day to one per year. Visitors were to be bombarded with propagandistic films, projections and announcements as they were mechanically moved through the tower. The movement of spectators was paramount. "Least of all must you stand or sit in this building," wrote Tatlin, foreshadowing Reder and Polieri, "you must be mechanically transported up, down, carried along willy-nilly; in front of you will flash the firm, laconic phrases of an announcer-agitator. . . . "[23] On cloudy days films would be projected from the top of the monument onto the haze.

Perhaps the most important architect-designer (in terms of environ-

mentalism) to emerge from this movement was El Lissitzky. Influenced by
Malevich, he began creating his own geometrical forms, *Prouns*, in 1919 but
he was more interested in the creation of three-dimensional space.[24] In 1923,
in Berlin, he installed the first abstract environment, the *Prounenraum*.[25]
The walls, floor, and ceiling of the exhibit room became incorporated into
the display and esthetic experience of the artwork. "All available surfaces,"
noted Herbert Read, "were integrated into a single 'environment.'"[26] Walter
Gropius, among others, noted the influence of this exhibit.[27] Lissitzky was
also concerned with relation of developments in art to the stage. Writing in
1922 about the recent evolution of stage design he noted that stage painters

> began, in accordance with the evolution of paintings, to push forward three-dimensional,
> spatial ideas of decoration. The painters on the stage progressed toward architecture. . . .
> In the latest work by Vesnin, the set for Chesterton's *The Man Who Was Thursday* [at
> Tairov's Kamerny Theatre in 1923], it is interesting to trace how the principles of the
> Tatlin tower have been applied to the theatre. Meyerhold, the director, completely
> abandoned the wings; in the setting for Mayakovsky's *Mysterium buffo* he designs the
> whole expanse of the stage architectonically and extends it into the auditorium.[28]

Lissitzky was more concerned with the illusion of three-dimensional space
than the creation of architectonic space. But rather than using perspective to
create this illusion, he felt it should be achieved solely through the movement
of the spectator or the objects the spectator perceived.[29] Such illusion has no
constraining limits. "We see," he wrote in 1925,

> that Suprematism has swept away from the plane the illusion of two-dimensional
> planemetric space, the illusion of three-dimensional perspective space and has created
> the ultimate illusion of *irrational* space, with infinite extensibility into the background
> and foreground.[30]

Lissitzky never advocated the physical experience of stage space by an
audience; yet, as we shall see, he was the only Soviet designer before
Okhlopkov to propose a spectator encompassing set. In this he seems closely
allied to Kiesler.

Two other Constructivist-related projects bear consideration. One was
the design submitted by Aleksandr and Leonid Vesnin in a 1923 competition
for a Palace of Labor in Moscow (Plate 48). Embodying the flexible theatre
concept, the main 8000 seat auditorium contained movable glass and
aluminum partitions which could reduce the space to an intimate theatre or
allow it to merge with an adjoining 2500 seat lecture hall.[31] There were
moving seat platforms, as well, so that masses of spectators could be brought
near the stage or speaker's platform. The second project was Ivan Leonidov's
plan for the Lenin Institute, part of which was to be a spherical auditorium
for 40,000 people.

After the Revolution, as before, the most radical experiments were being carried out by Meyerhold. Coinciding with the third anniversary of the Revolution, Meyerhold opened his R.S.F.S.R. Theatre No. I on November 7, 1920 in Moscow's Sohn Theatre with an adaptation of Emile Verhaeren's *The Dawns*. Because all of Meyerhold's post-Revolutionary repertoire had political or social themes and messages (added on if they did not already exist in the script), he felt it was now essential for him to bridge the proscenium and involve the audience directly so that the message might be more effective. The atmosphere created for *The Dawns* in the theatre was that of a meeting hall—the walls were hung with placards and the auditorium was periodically showered with leaflets.[32] The proscenium wall was, in effect, destroyed by placing the chorus in the orchestra pit which was reached by steps from the front of the stage. The frame of the stage was thus seemingly bridged—a relatively major step at the time. Also inserted into the script was a herald who reported actual bulletins from the civil war still being fought to the south, thus unifying, however tenuously, the stage with the outside world. Army detachments would frequently attend performances, completely prepared with bands and banners, to react appropriately to these reports or to scenes in the production. One night the herald reported a major Bolshevik victory at the Battle of Perekop in the Crimea and the entire audience rose spontaneously singing the "Internationale."[33] Although the events were not always so fortuitous, there was the attempt to incorporate the audience into the performance.

The second production at Meyerhold's theatre was Mayakovksy's *Mystery-Bouffe*, revised from the original 1918 version. The fronts of the boxes on either side of the rectangular auditorium were removed to create passages from the stage along the sides parallel to the central aisle. A wide ramp sloped from the set (designed by Lavinsky and Khrakovsky) directly into the auditorium (Plate 49). In the final scenes the performers moved into the open boxes, performing actions and speaking to the spectators.[34] At the conclusion the audience was invited to join the performers on the stage. This production was also staged elsewhere as an outdoor spectacle, and it achieved its greatest successes in these performances.[35]

Outdoor performance, of course, reached its peak with the government-sponsored mass spectacles, discussed later in this chapter, but even taking the more conventional dramas outdoors had a great appeal. It seemed appropriate to the proletarian spirit. "The modern theatre wants to move out into the open air," proclaimed Meyerhold in 1920. "We want our setting to be an iron pipe or the open sea or something constructed by the new man."[36] Lissitzky, in 1923, proposed an outdoor staging of *Victory Over the Sun*:

No one seems to pay any attention to the magnificent spectacle of our cities, simply because "everyone" has become part and parcel of the spectacle himself. . . . We intend to erect a scaffolding in a square, accessible and open from all directions. . . . All show objects are brought into motion by means of electro-mechanical forces and devices, with central control in the hands of a single individual who acts as the director of the whole show. . . . At the flick of a switch the sound system is turned on and the whole place may suddenly reverberate with the din of a railroad station, or the roar of Niagara Falls, or the pounding of a steel-rolling mill. . . . Light rays, diffused by prisms and reflectors, follow the movements of the figurines in the play.[37]

Meyerhold's production of Sergei Tretyakov's *The Earth In Turmoil* (adapted from Martinet's *La Nuit*) was first performed at the Sohn in 1923, but like *Mystery-Bouffe* it was done most often and most successfully as an open-air production (Plate 50). An outdoor performance in Moscow included infantry, cavalry and an audience of 25,000.[38] Designed by Lyubov Popova, the production incorporated cars, motorcycles, trucks and a harvester, some of which drove through the auditorium using a wide ramp leading from the stage. One scene in particular, the funeral of a soldier, was reportedly very effective as the coffin was placed on the back of a truck and slowly driven from the stage and through the spectators.[39]

By the early twenties Constructivist settings were typical in the productions of both Meyerhold and Tairov. Because these settings were nonrepresentational ramps, platforms and geometric forms, they could expand continuously, like Kiesler's sculptures. Soon they began to fill the small prosceniums of the old Tsarist theatres. Alexander Vesnin's set for *The Man Who Was Thursday* (1923), for example, filled the entire proscenium opening with a maze of platforms and bridges and appeared about to burst the seams of the stage. Subsequent sets, as we shall see, did spill into the auditorium, and the actors did move through the aisles, but the seemingly logical step of transforming a theatre by means of an all-encompassing Constructivist set was never taken.

Constructivist sets also contained a sense of dynamism, whether the set consisted of moving parts or merely curves and angles suggestive of forceful motion. Many of Meyerhold's designs contained curved or spiral ramps that not only gave the set a particular flow, but conveyed that movement into the house. The ramp in his production of *The Forest* (1924), for instance, was suspended upstage center, swept in an arc stage right and then curved back across the forestage, finally reaching the floor of the central aisle of the auditorium (Plate 51).[40] The set also included extended side stages which brought the action to either side of the front rows. Alexei Faiko's *Bubus, The Teacher* (1925) had both steps and ramps descending into the auditorium (Plate 52). In *The Commander of the Second Army* (1928), Meyerhold used a ramp which began on the auditorium wall in front of the proscenium. It curved back onto the stage in a wide arc following the lines of the back wall of the set and ended upstage center, although the flow was continued by an angled platform from that point to a side stage to the left of the audience.

It was for Sergei Tretyakov's *I Want A Child*, written in 1926, that Lissitzky proposed transforming the interior of Meyerhold's theatre into a unified, audience-encompassing performing space. Had it been built, it would have been, as Edward Braun suggested, the fullest realization of Constructivist ideals ever seen in the theatre.[41] The play, because of its attitudes toward sex, was highly controversial and Meyerhold spent four years trying to get it approved by the censor. In an attempt to facilitate matters he proposed staging it as an illustrated discussion in which the spectators could join.[42] Lissitzky's set, designed with this discussion in mind, was to be constructed in the Sohn Theatre but Meyerhold was so enthusiastic about the model that he felt only a completely new space could do it justice. Plans for a new theatre were begun immediately.

Lissitzky's original design for the transformed Sohn consisted of an arena-type stage with Constructivist ramps and platforms, and aisles extending from the stage through the audience area (Plate 53). The spectators were to sit in two curved sections of bleachers, one placed on what had been the stage behind the proscenium and one opposite at the "back" of the house. In the center was a two-level circular stage, not unlike Kiesler's space stage, but with a hole rather than an elevator through the center. This central stage was partially lit from below. Along either side of the theatre, at a height of about twelve to fifteen feet, were narrow open platforms which could be used for performance. An inclined ramp led from a turret mounted on the upper level of the circular stage to the house left platform. Another ramp on the opposite side of the stage led from the lower level to an area beneath the house right platform. Circling the interior of the theatre above the platforms and audience areas was a banner on which the title of the play was repeatedly inscribed. Steps connected the proscenium seating area with the performance space around the central stage, and clearly designated aisles connected that stage with the "rear" seating area.

While Meyerhold was making plans for his new theatre he continued producing audience-involving plays in the old one, using elements of nonfrontal staging. Vsevelod Vishnevsky's *Final and Decisive* (1931), for example, began with a parody of the Bolshoi's *Red Poppy*, a ballet about navy life, which was interrupted by actors dressed as sailors emerging from the auditorium to present a supposedly more true-to-life naval story.[43] In the final scene the audience was plunged into the effects of a raging battle. Artillery fired blanks directly at the audience, searchlights swept through the theatre, and on a given cue, an actress planted in the audience began to weep. (How she was seen or heard in the midst of this activity is not clear.) The hero, after dying onstage, immediately stood up and addressed the audience:

"Men and women—everyone who is ready to join in defense of the U.S.S.R.—stand up!" And of course, they all did.

The plans for Meyerhold's new theatre, designed by Mikhail Barkhin and Sergei Vakhtangov, was not an architecturally integrated environment but was more along the lines of Reinhardt's and Poelzig's Grosses Schauspielhaus—a deep thrust stage surrounded on three sides by a steeply banked auditorium (Plate 54).[44] Unlike many of the designers and directors we have mentioned earlier who turned to surrounding or shared space concepts in order to achieve intimacy, Meyerhold's years of thrusting the action into the auditorium had led him to believe that true intimacy and stage-auditorium unity were achieved only by surrounding the action with the spectators. He felt, for example, that the annular stage of the Gropius-Piscator *Totaltheater* was little more than a descendant of the Roman Theatre or of Wagner's Festival Theatre at Bayreuth, both of which maintained and emphasized the separation of spectator and performer.[45] Meyerhold's theatre, therefore, placed 1600 spectators in a horseshoe-shaped auditorium around an oval stage with two revolving platforms. There was an automobile access so that cars could deposit patrons directly in front of the seats and so that parades from Red Square could pass through the theatre.

By the early thirties, however, the authorities were demanding socialist realism and putting an end to most experimentation. Many artists, in order to continue working at all, were forced to repudiate their earlier work. Only Meyerhold remained defiant, but his theatre was dissolved in 1938 and he, himself, was murdered in 1939. His new theatre, which was in the process of being built, was converted into The Tchaikovsky Concert Hall.

The firsthand accounts of Meyerhold's productions attest to their dynamism, their ability to elicit spectator reactions, and to the dramatic effect of performers in the auditorium; yet there seems to be a basic conservatism in Meyerhold regarding the use of space. It is as if he were still adhering to certain rules which forbade destroying the sanctity of the auditorium or stage. While advocating the abolition of stage convention he maintained the necessity of the stage. "We must destroy the box-stage once and for all, for only then can we hope to achieve a truly dynamic spectacle," stated Meyerhold in a 1929 speech at Kharkov. "The new stage will have no proscenium arch and will be equipped with a series of platforms which can be moved horizontally and vertically to facilitate transformation scenes and the manipulation of kinetic construction."[46]

"Meyerhold," Okhlopkov said,

> actually cut the continually developing line of revolutionary theatre architecture. He threatened to do away with the stage; he even removed the curtains forever from his stage; but his Constructivism not only retained the stage, but the elaboration of the stage

as an element that Constructivism required. Meyerhold sanctioned the existence of the stage.[47]

He had to. His adherence to specific theatrical theories, the development of a unique acting style, and the insistence upon messages to be conveyed through the production necessitated a distinct and readily identifiable audience and stage. If spectators were incorporated in any way, it was that they were acknowledged observers of a theatrical event who were occasionally asked to take a minor role (catching oranges, singing) in order to complete a dramatic effect.

A few others besides Meyerhold were venturing into environmental forms. Most notable was Sergei Eisenstein, an innovative director whose stage work has been largely overshadowed by his pioneering contributions to the film. In the early twenties, Eisenstein reached the conclusion that all illusionistic art was unpragmatic and anti-revolutionary. Therefore, the stage should present only reality.[48] (Not, however, naturalism which is, of course, illusionistic.) But since a stage is not part of everyday reality, Eisenstein wanted to place the performance in a more realistic relation to the audience.

In his first production, Jack London's *The Mexican* (1920-21), he proposed setting the boxing ring for the fight scene in the midst of the auditorium, as it would be for a real boxing match.[49] Although the fight scene was apparently quite realistic, fire laws prevented it from occurring in the house. The next logical step, then, was to present a play in its natural setting—a found environment—which Eisenstein did in his 1924 production of Sergei Tretyakov's *Gas Masks*, staged in a Moscow gas factory (Plates 55 and 56). The results were not, however, what he had anticipated. The actuality of a real factory heightened the artificiality of the play and created, in his words, a "conflict between material-practical and fictitious-descriptive principles."[50] Eisenstein wrote that,

> The turbines, the factory background, negated the last remnants of make-up and theatrical costumes, and all elements appeared as independently fused. Theatre accessories in the midst of real factory plastics appeared ridiculous. The element of play was incompatible with the acrid smell of gas. The pitiful platform kept getting lost among the real platforms of labor activity. In short, the production was a failure.[51]

It should be remembered that Reinhardt, producing *The Miracle* in New York that same year, and potentially facing the same pitfalls, reconstructed a cathedral in a theatre, thereby capturing the intended spirit and arousing appropriate sensations without overwhelming the overt theatricality with reality. After *Gas Masks* Eisenstein turned to film.

Many workers' groups staged agit-prop plays in the streets, factories, workers' halls, and even in street cars—changing cars at each stop.[52] Those labor organizations which produced plays in theatres frequently borrowed from Meyerhold. The Moscow Trade Union Theatre, for instance, staged Dmitri Furmanov's *Revolt* (1932) with armies marching through the aisles.[53]

There seems to be only one Soviet production that tended toward the architecturally integrated space. This was D. Smolin's *Galelei*, staged in 1937 in the Moscow Planetarium.[54] Although it was apparently a traditional play about the life of Galileo, it employed projections on the domed ceiling which encompassed the spectators and performers in a unified space. As Galileo "trains his invention, the telescope, on the night sky," stated a press release, "the spectators make a fascinating journey in the world of the stars."[55]

It was basically left to the mass spectacles to create a more truly environmental theatre. On the first anniversary of the Revolution an outdoor pageant entitled *A Pantomime of the Great Revolution* was staged in Moscow. This was the first of the many mass spectacles produced throughout Russia during the first few years of the Soviet regime.[56] These spectacles which had a political and ideological appeal, attracted many avant-garde artists as designers and directors. Productions incorporated Cubo-Futuristic sets and emerging Constructivist design concepts, and the spectacles involved tens of thousands of people both as performers and spectators and, most important, often employed the found environments of appropriate historical sites.

The idea of mass spectacles was first voiced in Russia by Vladimir Friche in 1910, but a theoretical ideology for them was set forth by Platon Kerzhentzev in 1918 in *Creative Theatre*, an influential book that went through several printings in the twenties.[57] Kerzhentzev had toured the West and had seen some of Louis Parker's pageants in Britain and such American spectacles as Percy MacKaye's *Masque And Pageant of St. Louis* (1914) and *Caliban* (1916). He was impressed by their "democracy," by which he meant the use of members of the community for production and performing. The idea of incorporating the town and its population into historical drama seemed to Kerzhentzev an ideal way to create mass unity in the uncertain days following the Revolution. "Why confine theatre to the proscenium arch," he asked, "when it can have the freedom of the public square?"[58] The unification of performer and spectator and the abolition of the fourth wall and class-oriented seating, became the ideal Revolutionary metaphor for a classless society.

The pageants and *fêtes* of the French Revolution were studied as examples, and much of the spirit, style and allegorical symbolism of the French pageants was adopted by the Russians. The subject matter for the spectacles was drawn from Russian history, world history, and Communist allegory. Among the larger spectacles were *The Mystery of Freed Labor* (1919) which combined the stories of Spartacus and Stenka Razin, a seventeenth-century Russian revolutionary; *The Trial of Wrangel*, presented by 10,000 Red Army soldiers in a Cossack settlement; and *Toward a World Commune* and *Building of the Commune Tower*, staged in 1920. The spectacles were generally designed and staged by professionals but acted by the citizens and the military who were frequently "volunteered," just as properties were often "requisitioned." Occasionally, if a scenario called for individual performance, a professional actor would play the role, but this was avoided whenever possible. An individual actor, if nothing else, would be lost in a cast of thousands. Both in terms of structure and content, these productions, interestingly referred to as "topographical" theatre, were consciously conceived in terms of medieval mystery and morality plays.[59] They were simplistic and didactic, pitting good (the proletariat) against evil (the bourgeoisie, capitalists, the Tsar, Kerensky). They used multiple stages, often scattered about the town, and the performances moved through masses of spectators on the streets, transforming civic architecture into theatrical sets in the process. Nikolai Evreinov, a playwright, director and theorist, advocated the use of historical and actual sites—found environments— whenever possible as part of the "theatricalization of life."[60] By using these settings Evreinov hoped to stir the memories of the participants and spectators in the spectacles, and the historical events thus recalled could then be consciously reevaluated and appraised.

For the Constructivists, the move to the outdoors represented the abandonment of the confining space of the theatre and the two-dimensionality of its stage for the three-dimensional space of the streets. Also, in keeping with constructivist ideas, utilitarian objects were incorporated into the productions. This sometimes meant no more than the use of military or farm vehicles but was occasionally more elaborate as in I. Korolev's 1924 proposal for a mass theatre:

> My own model shows the rational use of local, street factory and docks equipment, and it is upon such a technical, industrial background that the artist is constructing a mass workers' theatre.
> The construction of a crane is taken as a technical form, fulfilling its industrial task in the course of the working day, and as such its suitability as theatre-decoration for the new theatre is incontrovertible. Its adoption in scene-construction was called for in the first place by the demand for simplified material forms, essential to open-air performances. On the crane three permanent platforms are erected, connected with each other by ladders. These are used as tribunes for speakers, as stages for action, and as places for setting up kino apparatus, radio-sets, projectors, pyro-technical equipment and so forth. Here also can be hung placards bearing slogans, and other accessories. Not much money or material is required to set up such an open-air theatre, which forms a most suitable

background for truly revolutionary, mass performances, at mass sports, carnivals and demonstrations of the workers, and Red Army men.[61]

The Storming of the Winter Palace, produced in Petrograd on the third anniversary of the Revolution, was the largest and most famous of the mass spectacles.[62] The event was staged by Nikolai Evreinov, N. V. Petrov and Alexander Kugel in Uritzky Square in front of the old Winter Palace and combined a symbolic, stylized dramatization of pre-Revolutionary events (the conflict of the Bolsheviks and Kerensky between July and October 1917) with an allegedly realistic recreation of the November 7, 1917 Bolshevik attack on the Palace which resulted in their assumption of power.

The pageant was originally conceived as a processional event, moving through the streets of Petrograd with activities staged at designated points along the route. The final scenario, however, was a spectator-engulfing performance on what the directors and designer Yuri P. Annenkov envisioned as five stages surrounding and in the midst of the square (Plate 58). Opposite the Palace was the General Staff Building, a semicircular structure divided by a huge arch. Two immense stages (each about eighteen by sixty yards), the Red Stage and the White Stage, were erected in front of the General Staff and were connected by a bridge which formed a third stage. The result was, in effect, a caliper stage partially surrounding the 100,000 spectators massed in two sections in the center of the square (Plate 57). A corridor was maintained through the crowd, between the General Staff and the Winter Palace, and was also considered a stage area—the fifth stage. The stylized pre-Revolutionary events occurred on the first three stages, while the historical re-enactments utilized Uritzky Square, the Palace, surrounding streets and even the nearby Neva River.

The performance began at ten P.M. and searchlights played on the clouded skies. After a montage-like series of scenes depicting the corruption and collapse of the Kerensky government and the Bolshevik rise to power, a battle took place on the bridge. The performers representing the Provisional government fled through the spectators toward the Palace, followed shortly by Kerensky and some of his ministers in two cars. The several thousand Bolsheviks on the stages prepared to follow as 320 military vehicles of the Red Army poured out of the side streets and through the five entrances into the Square. Singing the "Internationale," the performers moved off the stage and joined the convoys through and around the spectators. Meanwhile, on the Neva, the battleship Aurora fired its cannon. Lights in the sixty-two windows of the Winter Palace facade blinked on and off silhouetting hand-to-hand combat within. Machine-gun fire, artillery and rifles surrounded the audience with a noise that "merged into a deafening symphony of decisive combat."[63] As the battle and spectacle came to an end, the whole Square became an environment of light—as the "Internationale" was being sung by 100,000 people, five-sided red stars were illuminated above the Palace, an enormous red banner was hoisted and a spectacular display of fireworks was set off. "Shafts of golden light were pouring like rain. . . . Thousands of silver fires were flying over the crowd. Bright colorful stars momentarily flickered, then disappeared in the dark background. For a moment it looked as if it were day."[64]

Thus, the performance first surrounded the spectators, then entered into their midst where the two groups—spectators and performers—unified. As the performance changed from dramatic spectacle to celebration, the incorporated area changed from localized space to a more general festival space.

Mass spectacles, as such, had few precedents based on traditional rules—only the festivals of the French Revolution and those of the Medicis provided practical, documented examples. Such spectacles blurred the distinctions between performance and festival and consequently, the distinctions between performer and spectator. Everyone became involved in a celebratory performance. The town became the environment. Men like Kerzhentzev and Evreinov could postulate appropriate theories to allow theatre to conform to Communist principles, but in reality they were doing little more than reviving the pageant and procession for contemporary usage. What was notable about the Soviet mass spectacles was their ability to incorporate at one moment thousands of spectators as active participants in a performance, and then to separate them again into a distinct audience at a play; to transform civic architecture into historical or contemporary settings and in the next scene to transform the same buildings into non-matrixed festival spaces. Such manipulation indicated a sophisticated understanding of the control of environment for performance.

6

Okhlopkov and Tonecki: Environmental Staging in the Thirties

> *Meyerhold is the Moses who has led the theatre to the brink of the promised land, but it may be given to Okhlopkov to be the Joshua who will realize the true* Mass Theatre.

—*Norris Houghton,* Moscow Rehearsals

> *The studies in the modern theatre that we have pursued for the past twenty years have led us to conclude today that the curtained theatre, the alcove theatre, is one of the causes of the immobility of dramatic art: the unique visibility of the actor always in silhouette, his dynamism compromised by the immutable flats, his performance always restricted by the plan of the stage, the entrances and exits always anticipated, endows the stage action with a permanence that crystallizes all dramatic composition. The Theatre of Space transports the stage into the auditorium and thus activates it.*

—*Zygmunt Tonecki*

In the thirties, all the environmental theories of the previous years finally yielded practical results in the Soviet Union and in Poland. Between 1932 and 1934 Meyerhold's pupil, Nikolai Okhlopkov, presented four plays at the Realistic Theatre in Moscow, three of which—*The Start, The Mother,* and *The Iron Flood*—must be considered the first truly environmental theatre productions of the twentieth century. Concurrently, Zygmunt Tonecki, a Polish critic, took the theories and proposals of Apollinaire, Strnad,

Piscator, Gropius, Schlemmer, and Marinetti and proposed an elaborate architecturally integrated theatre. While this was never built, Tonecki's influence led to scattered stage productions—virtually identical to Okhlopkov's—in the mid-thirties. In both instances the performance surrounded the audience on a horizontal and sometimes vertical plane, altered the traditional physical relationships between performers and spectators, and effected, to a greater or lesser degree, a transformation of the whole theatre interior.

Okhlopkov's theatrical career began at the age of twenty-one with the staging of a mass spectacle, *The Struggle Between Labor and Capital*, in his native Irkutsk on May Day, 1921.[1] The performance was not as elaborate technically as the Petrograd spectacles, but it did involve the participation of some 30,000 performers—artillerymen, cavalry, infantry, professional actors, factory workers, students and townspeople. A rectangular platform erected in the city square served as the main stage. At the conclusion of the piece the victorious workers drove around the square in automobiles, waving red banners. As a result of this production Okhlopkov was awarded an acting scholarship and he went to Moscow where he spent the next few years working with Meyerhold.

During the twenties Meyerhold developed the form of stylized acting known as biomechanics. He considered his new pupil, Okhlopkov, the ideal biomechanical actor, but differences began to crop up between the two men, and Okhlopkov quit the Meyerhold studio in 1927. In 1931 he was appointed director of the Realistic Theatre in Moscow (sometimes referred to as the Krasnaya Presnya after the district in which it was located).

As Meyerhold fell from official favor, he claimed that his ideas had been stolen by his former protégé. Okhlopkov, in turn, became one of the more ardent denouncers of his former teacher.[2] It is true, however, that Okhlopkov capitalized on Meyerhold's attempts to fuse the stage and auditorium and on his concepts of the "theatre theatrical"; but he took these ideas further and in a somewhat different direction from that of his mentor. Okhlopkov was not content merely to bring the action into the auditorium, but felt that the constrictions of the stage should be abolished altogether. The entire interior of the theatre should become the performance space.

This attitude, while opening new possibilities in staging, was to be no more strictly adhered to than any other production concept. Each play was to be staged in the most appropriate manner. "The most powerful element of the play is its content, its idea," stated Okhlopkov. "The most precious concept in a production is the organic unity of content and form."[3] Thus, arena, thrust or proscenium productions were as valid as environmental stagings but the more traditional forms were no longer the only possibilities.

What came to determine the organization of space was the emotional and psychological impact desired for the production. Okhlopkov freely mixed naturalistic acting and decor with theatrically stylized performance and effects and with pseudo-Constructivist settings in order to achieve powerful emotional images. By surrounding the spectators with the action, or even incorporating them into the setting, however, he demanded no physical involvement or response in the sense of active participation. Regardless of how completely the setting surrounded or permeated the auditorium, the spectators always sat in conventional theatre seats. No one was asked to catch oranges or move about after the play commenced as in some of Meyerhold's work. Only in one scene in *The Mother* did the performers ever ask the spectators to join in the action. Okhlopkov, in fact, considered a production successful if the audience was so overwhelmed that they could not stir from their places.[4]

Sometimes, however, the emotional involvement achieved by the production resulted in intense physical responses by the spectators. But such reactions were not imposed upon the audience. Okhlopkov described his goal as achieving a "fraternization" between the audience and the performers; that is, the development of a direct emotional bond.[5] He described an incident which helped to shape his ideas:

> One day during the Civil War I stood on a railway station platform. From one direction a troop train drew in and stopped. In a moment another troop train arrived from the opposite direction and halted across the platform. Soldiers poured out to refill their tea kettles, buy a bun, or stretch their legs. Near me one man alighted. From the other train came another soldier. They saw each other, ran forward and embraced, unable to speak for emotion. They were old comrades, dearest friends, whom the war had separated. There on a station platform, as one went one way and the other another, they met for a moment, clasped hands, and parted. In that instant I knew that that was what I wanted my theatre to be—a meeting where two dear friends experience an emotional union, in which for that moment all the rest of the world may be forgotten. Ever since I have worked for that. In my theatre, actor and spectator must clasp hands in fraternity. On my stage, when the mother cries, a dozen in the audience must be ready to spring forward to dry her tears.[6]

Judging by the accounts of spectators, Okhlopkov was extremely successful. As opposed to the passive empathy encouraged by Stanislavsky, Okhlopkov could elicit spontaneous, emotionally inspired physical responses from spectators. This was due in part to altered physical relationships. Rather than the sensation of watching reality through a fourth wall, the spectator felt he was in the same place as the character. Andre van Gyseghem, for instance, in his book, *The Theatre in Soviet Russia*, wrote that a sense of "knowing" the characters in the play existed and that entering the theatre was like walking in on a scene from "life."[7] And Norris Houghton, in

Moscow Rehearsals, noted that although Meyerhold talked *at* the spectator, Okhlopkov talked *with* them; where Reinhardt seemed to shatter illusion every time his actors entered the aisles, Okhlopkov reinforced the theatrical illusion by this same device.[8] One spectator at *The Mother,* for example, was so affected by the surrounding action that he forgot he was at a theatre:

> A military bark—the click of gunlocks. They hesitate, then a pent-up cry is hurled from a strained throat—a mighty surge forward—a volley. Down and back they hurtle—a tumbled heap of grotesque dead and wounded at the foot of the stairs. I start from my seat to their aid—when the blackout reminds me that this is theatre.[9]

While Okhlopkov could claim no carefully evolved theoretical base for his theatre in the manner of, say, Meyerhold or Stanislavsky, he did articulate a set of principles to which he more or less adhered. Although not all of them relate to scenography, and not all are as innovative as he would have us believe, they all express a concern with the relationship of the performance to the spectators.

> First: it [the production] discards the traditional "box" stage and takes the action of the stage to any part of the auditorium that serves the purpose.
>
> Second: in carrying the action into the auditorium we put our stage effects not only in the middle of the hall, with the stage surrounded by the public on all sides on the "arena" principle, but also around and above the audience. Of course, not every production is necessarily staged this way.
>
> Third: we have introduced "montage action." Instead of a simple rotation of scenes and episodes entirely dependent on technical considerations, we have introduced raised montage as a powerful means of affecting the reactions of the audience. In doing this we have not copied cinema montage, though we have carefully studied it together with the montage of the ancient Greek theatre. As a result, the action may be transferred from one of our stage sets to another frequently situated at some distance from the first, not only at the end of one episode and the beginning of another, according to the author's instructions, but at any time within the episode. Breaking up the action in this way permits the regisseur to play with the rhythm and tempo of a production in order to produce a stronger, more vivid and more vital effect on the audience. There must be no break in the action of the performance in connection with the montage.
>
> Fourth: we have introduced music into the drama as a powerful theatrical aid to the regisseur, permitting him to set the atmosphere of the play, reveal its pulse, its respiration. We are placing so much emphasis on the use of music in this way that our theatre may rightly be called a musical drama theatre.
>
> Fifth: in view of the fact that we have discarded the "box" stage, introduced montage and music and other innovations, our actors must adjust themselves to special conditions. The close intercourse between actors and audience in our theatre, involving the maximum nearness of the audience to the points where the action is taking place, is a condition peculiar to our theatre. Such proximity disciplines the actor, leads him to "fine" acting with something of the quality of a water-colour, stimulates him to strive for unusual exactness in his emotional expression. Without this inner "rightness" he would simply be unable to support the fixed gaze of an audience which completely surrounds him. He would not remain on the stage even for a few minutes.

The proximity of the audience permits the actor to make contact with it more quickly, to sense its reactions to the play, its emotions, to feel immediately the "warmth" of the spectators. It stimulates the actor to master the subtleties of acting, to become a virtuoso in subtle pantomime and skilful "sculptured" foreshortenings.

Sixth: we are opposed to naive photographic naturalism with the insistence on all details of the material milieu inherent in it. We are opposed to a protocol-like still life. We have recourse to theatrical conditions, to the language of the genuine theatre, in order not to distract the audience from the contents of the play. We limit ourselves to giving a mere outline of the scene of action, using only what is most essential. At times we content ourselves with a simple—though necessarily clear—suggestion of the place in which the action occurs.

Thus we assert the realism of the theatre through theatrical means, appealing to the imagination of the spectator and at the same time providing it with a powerful stimulus. Thus the audience co-operates with the actors in every performance, so that the actors applaud the audience as well as the audience the actors.[10]

The third principle, especially, should be noted here. Breaking up actions within scenes not only allowed for altered rhythms, but enhanced the sense of environmental action. By fragmenting a single unit and scattering the component parts about the theatre, Okhlopkov approached the illusion of an action occurring simultaneously all around the spectator.

The Realistic Theatre was one of the smallest theatres in the city, seating about 300 people. Okhlopkov's first step was to rip out the existing stage and seats. (There were plans to remove the balcony as well, but that was never done.) Okhlopkov wanted no restrictions on stage and auditorium configurations so that maximum flexibility in production would be possible.[11] In essence he was creating a free-space theatre. Thrust and arena set-ups would be possible—although he tended to avoid those arrangements during the first few years—as well as scattered staging. "We surrounded the audience from all sides," claimed Okhlopkov, "we are in front of the spectator, at his side, above him, and even under him."[12] Despite this statement, Okhlopkov never expressed any interest in, or even any awareness of, the architecturally integrated environment. At his theatre the spectator was enveloped by the performers and the decorative elements. It was thus a predecessor of the modern transformed space. (See Chapter 9.)

The Realistic Theatre operated on the principle of the circus arena—a central platform or ring for the display of scenes—along with what Okhlopkov called an "inverse circus," a peripheral or annular stage.[13] There were basically two types of theatre, explained Pavel V. Tsetnerovich, Okhlopkov's assistant director,

Bourgeois Renaissance stage (picture stage—aims at illusion, machinery, actors as pictures, two-dimensional, the audience sits back in its chairs and watches)—People's theatre (uses a platform stage)—surrounded by the audience—the actor is master and shows off sculpturally—three-dimensionally—this theatre makes an active effect on audience.[14]

The Realistic, of course, was in the latter tradition and in line with those twentieth-century artists who sought a greater plasticity.

Okhlopkov's first production in this theatre was appropriately entitled *The Start* by Vladimir Stavsky. It was designed by Jacob Schtoffer (Plate 59). The play concerned "the years of the great breakthough in collective farming," and the decor created a feeling of a farmyard or arbor.[15] The audience was divided into three sections: the former stage area, the orchestra seating section and the balcony. Separating the first two was a narrow platform spanning the theatre from side wall to side wall. This widened in the center to form a rectangular platform stage with traps jutting into the orchestra section. Steps on either side of this platform connected the former orchestra and stage seating areas. Two narrow platforms at right angles to the central stage ran along both sides of the orchestra seats, and along each of these lateral stages was a fence with two wooden gates that served as entrances for actors. Four more entrances were provided through the curved backdrop that surrounded the former stage area. Circling above the central platform and stage seating area was an oval ramp. Resembling a giant paper-clip, the ends of this ramp rose on an incline from either side of the central stage toward the backdrop. The inclined legs of the ramp crossed behind the seats and curved around at balcony level above the heads of the audience.

Were it not for the decorative elements of the design, this might have been a Constructivist set, gracefully enveloping the audience. But the structural aspects of the set were partially concealed by sunflowers, and, of course, there was the wooden fence and gate motif. In surrounding the audience Okhlopkov had abandoned the abstract, purely utilitarian set of the Constructivists for a suggestive, atmospheric decor.

The action occurred not merely on the platforms and ramps, but in the aisles and anywhere else the performers could go. Okhlopkov had hoped to install swivel chairs in the theatre but never did, and one continuing complaint was that the spectators constantly had to turn their heads. Because he was more concerned with theatrical effect than strict adherence to theory, Okhlopkov attempted to simplify sight-lines and staging in future productions while still maintaining an environmental action.

In February 1933 Tsetnerovich directed an adaptation of scenes from Maxim Gorky's *The Mother*, the story of a peasant woman who becomes involved with and inspired by a group of revolutionaries after her son is arrested for subversive activities. The set was once again designed by Schtoffer (Plate 60). A tiered circular platform of wooden slats occupied the center of the space and two sets of steps fanned out from this arena toward either end of the hall. Curved rows of seats circled the stage in a ripple-like pattern. The spectators, in turn, were surrounded by various steps and platforms lining the walls of the rectangular room. The platforms ranged in height from about two feet along one side to about twelve feet behind the former stage area. From the center of this last platform, a stairway with one long landing extended into the auditorium. The risers on these steps were curved to conform to the curve of the central stage. Stairs also led from other parts of the surrounding stage toward the central platform, and to the balcony.

The decor consisted of a shell of mahogany-colored plywood panels against three walls. Ornate, bronze-painted wreaths, five feet in diameter, with an "M" inscribed on each, were hung at intervals around the shell. Old-fashioned, square street lamps were suspended from curved rods projecting from behind the panels. In addition to these and the usual overhead stage lights, there were lights concealed in the central and peripheral stages. Along the edges of the peripheral platforms were short stone-colored posts supporting what appeared to be a heavy metal link chain. For certain scenes pine trees were inserted in the central stage.

Despite realistic decorative elements, Okhlopkov had no pretensions of creating a total pictorial illusion on the stage. "It is impossible to speak of the presentation of absolute reality," he said, and expressed a strong disapproval of photographic naturalism.[16] Okhlopkov often explained that all the arts could each vividly depict a raging storm but the theatre could not and had to employ stylized, symbolic techniques. But while he often used formalistic or theatricalized devices for the creation of special effects, he utilized realistic detail whenever possible.[17] This is evident in an account of *The Mother*: "Suddenly behind us, the sound of tramping feet and jingling spurs. . . . Heavy boots stamp about. The creaking of leather, clank of accoutrement, the smell of gun-oil, sweat and tobacco."[18]

Perhaps the most memorable scene in the production was that of the Mother setting the table in preparation for the return of her son, Pavel. The table was on the central stage. As she set it she talked to nearby members of the audience about her son, and about boys in general, as she might have talked to neighbors. Having too many objects to hold, she handed a loaf of bread to one spectator while asking another to help her with the table cloth. In so doing she succeeded in incorporating the spectators into the world of the play. "She has told her neighbors about it," van Gyseghem explained, "we share her delight and envy her happiness—those members of the audience that have been actually included in the scene have in some way stretched the veil of illusion to include us all."[19] It remains one of the more remarkable aspects of Okhlopkov's theatre that it created Naturalistic illusions while emphasizing the theatrical aspects of the performance.

Okhlopkov's many critics found *The Mother* the most palatable of his productions because he did not resort to "carnival scenes," which is to say that it was more in the spirit, if not precisely the style, of Socialist Realism—

the realistic production style then encouraged by the government.[20] "The production was founded not on effects but on real feelings," proclaimed a retrospective article in *Teatr*, the Soviet theatre journal.[21]

The next production, *Pierre Patelin* (1933), simplified the set so that it was no longer environmental (Plate 61). The stage was in the shape of a 'T' with a raised rectangular platform running between two facing audience sections, and a narrow stage at right angles to this along the length of one wall. A platform for the orchestra was placed behind one audience section.

The January 1934 production of Aleksandr Serafimovich's *The Iron Flood* did not use overhead scaffolds or annular stages, yet it was perhaps the most successful in creating a total environment, as the whole interior of the theatre was transformed into a setting by Schtoffer. The play concerned a small detachment of soldiers during the post-Revolutionary Civil War who became separated from the main army.

The audience congregated in the lobby before the show.[22] Just prior to the announced curtain time a door from the auditorium burst open and two "soldiers" ran through the foyer with a shout. Then all the doors were opened and the audience was allowed into the auditorium. But instead of entering a traditional theatre, they found themselves in the midst of a revolutionary army camp. There were people preparing a campfire and cutting wood, a woman hanging out wash, another feeding a baby. Two lovers embraced on the ground. Others were repairing trucks or carts, playing instruments, and sitting on boxes and tree stumps. Much of this was spread through the audience area. "When the spectator enters the theatre, he is immediately submerged in the atmosphere of the action," wrote one critic. "He is confronted with the sound of guns, songs and wheels."[23] To reach the seats it was necessary literally to climb over actors, props and the set.[24] (Okhlopkov wanted to replace most of the theatre seats with stumps, boxes and other set pieces, leaving only a few chairs for those who insisted on a conventional view, but space did not permit this approach.)

The set consisted basically of a platform about five feet high along one side of the theatre with three tongue-like protrusions dividing the auditorium (Plate 62). All of this was covered and painted to resemble a mountainous terrain of rocks and earth; the protrusions resembled lava flows. A blue skydrop curved up from behind the embankment and arched across the entire ceiling, thus encompassing the audience as well.

The transition into the play itself was effected by dimming the house lights and bringing up spotlights. As the play progressed, most of the performers who had been "living" in the auditorium aisles repaired to the stage where the bulk of the action occurred. At the conclusion of the play one character sighted the lost army in the distance. Everyone excitedly crowded onto the peninsulas and it became obvious that the lost "comrades" were the audience. The performers jumped off the stage and spread through the auditorium shaking hands and hugging spectators (Plate 63). As forced or trite as this theatrical device might seem in retrospect it was quite effective and the audience inevitably responded with genuine enthusiasm.[25] This reaction was apparently aided by the contact and confrontation with performers prior to the actual commencement of the play. At least one observer felt that such contact allowed him to know these characters as if from life.[26]

For Nikolai Pogodin's *Aristocrats* (1935), which dealt with criminals sent to build the White Sea Canal as part of a social rehabilitation program, the theatre was divided into four sections by V. F. Ryndin's set: two diagonally opposed audience areas, and two tombstone-shaped stages about three feet high, joined in the center of the auditorium where their corners abutted (Plate 64). The result was a mirror image with each audience section surrounded on two sides by stages. One side of the auditorium was covered with three panels on which were designs representing the seasons that changed for each act.

Despite the serious theme of the play, there were many comic scenes and Okhlopkov envisioned the production as a "carnival spectacle" in which the set was an arena for attractions.[27] The only point at which the performers were in the audience was at the beginning when they ran through the house throwing confetti to suggest a snowstorm.

Subsequent sets at the Realistic Theatre were either variants on these plans or else more traditional designs. Schtoffer's concept for the unproduced *The Holy Fool* (1934) consisted of a U-shaped stage with a long bridge bisecting the length of the auditorium (Plate 65). Boris Knoblok designed *Othello* with an "Arabian Nights" flavor in 1935 utilizing a similar ground plan (Plates 66 and 67). The bridge for this production was somewhat shorter than the one in Schtoffer's plan and was used at times to represent a boat. Knoblok also designed the 1936 production of Romain Rolland's *Colas Breugnon* that had a thrust stage, a lateral stage along house left and a long irregularly shaped platform "island" in the midst of the auditorium (Plate 68). Spectators sat on benches placed across barrels. *Dream*, written by a pilot about a flight to the North Pole (and presented on the day he actually accomplished that feat—May 21, 1937), again incorporated a thrust stage above which the front of an airplane protruded from the wall (Plate 69).[28] A much later production, *Hotel Astoria*, done in the mid-fifties, employed a runway from the stage through the center of the auditorium (Plate 70). Okhlopkov referred to it as a "flower path," indicating its derivation from the Japanese hanamichi.[29]

During the 1950s Okhlopkov developed plans for a new theatre which was never built. Designed by I. Maltzin and V. Bikov, and referred to as the "transformable theatre," it was a circular building covered by a retractable dome. The theatre space was a flexible auditorium for 3,000 people that could automatically transform from a thrust to an arena to an annular stage.[30] Maltzin and Bikov also drew up plans for the Leningrad Theatre of Comedy as an annular stage theatre in 1961 (Plate 71).[31]

Okhlopkov, was, above all, a pragmatic person, and his continued success until his death in 1966 was no doubt attributable to his willingness to bend with changing political forces. By 1936 he was renouncing formalism and strongly condemning Meyerhold. An article in *Teatr* magazine in 1937, which may be considered reflective of official policies, was critical of Okhlopkov's abandonment of the conventional stage.[32] But as Okhlopkov retreated from his innovations he seemed systematically to be retracing the steps of earlier and perhaps more officially acceptable experimentation. First there was the reduction to runways and lateral stages from the all-encompassing environment. Then, his 1940 production of *Field Marshall Kutuzov* at the Vakhtangov Theatre utilized a tripartite stage for the first time in the Soviet Union. By the fifties he was back on a proscenium.

In 1929 Zygmunt Tonecki published an essay entitled, "The Theatre of the Future" in which he proposed an elaborate annular stage structure (See Appendix II).[33] As so many other theoreticians of this century, he chastised what he perceived as a stagnated art and called for a revitalization of theatre through innovations in design and architecture.[34] His essay, however, was not an isolated fantasy. As mentioned earlier, he summed up, in this essay, the work of Reinhardt, Piscator, Meyerhold, Leon Schiller, Kiesler, Perret, and Gropius. Tonecki could have been a major catalyst in European scenography had his ideas received wide exposure; he did influence Edouard Autant and Louise Lara and their experimental group, the Theatre of Art and Action.[35] But this group, too, which worked largely with Symbolist ideas, had so little impact that it is virtually ignored in the history books. Tonecki's theories, however, influenced the work of the artist Andrzej Pronaszko and the architect Szymon Syrkus who, in the thirties, produced scattered stage designs strikingly similar to Okhlopkov's.[36]

In "The Theatre of the Future," influenced by Gropius' Totaltheater, Tonecki proposed a rotating annular stage subdivided into smaller individual units. He had advocated the necessity of unifying the stage and auditorium into a physically undivided space and felt that the annular stage did just that.[37] Performers and spectators in his proposed theatre would be separated only by light.[38]

He approached Pronaszko and Syrkus to develop a theatre along these lines and a model was built for the Polish Universal Exposition at Poznan in 1928. These two men were not random choices; both had been working with alternatives to naturalistic settings and the proscenium stage. Pronaszko had been a member of the Formists, a Polish Cubo-Futurist group. Since 1924 he had worked with the director Leon Schiller at the Polski Theatre producing geometrical, multi-level sets. In 1928 Pronaszko and Syrkus designed a set for a production of *The Golem* in Warsaw—it was apparently not built— which was similar in some ways to Lissitzky's project for *I Want A Child.* The set employed an arena stage circled by tiers of seating (Plate 72). Platforms, ramps and steps cut through the arena and jutted into or through the auditorium at three points.

The model they created for Tonecki for the Poznan Exposition was of an 8,000 square meter concrete and glass structure that would stand twelve to fifteen stories tall.[39] The theatre consisted of two concentric annular stages—the inner one wider than the outer—encircling a 3,000 seat amphitheatre-like auditorium (Plates 73, 74, 75). The two ring stages would be able to rotate independently at variable speeds and in opposite directions. Because the audience section was in the form of a raked amphitheatre, scenes would be revolved out of sight behind the spectators. On the two stages, which would be operated by some sort of electro-hydraulic system, were to be circular platforms that could rotate independently as well as rise above or sink below stage level.

For Syrkus, movement was the unifying factor of this form of "total theatre."[40] Like the Futurists he was fascinated by motion. In the proposed theatre, with both rings and all the circular platforms rotating and rising the result would have been somewhat like a Busby Berkeley spectacular. For Pronaszko, simultaneity—which he felt was equivalent to plasticity—was the chief feature of this theatre.[41] In 1933 Pronaszko built a model for a variant of the annular theatre—a "mobile theatre" (*Teatr Ruchomo*) (Plate 76). It, too, had an annular stage but the circular audience section, which sat 300, rotated while the stage remained fixed.[42]

At a series of conferences on the contemporary theatre at Warsaw, Tonecki expanded on his ideas of plasticity and unified space. He referred to his project in a 1936 talk as the "Theatre of Space."

> Modern theatre architecture introduced two ideas to the theatre: acting in space and the *Activation* of the public (in the auditorium). Just as Cubism broke down and expanded the conception of space in Renaissance painting (perspective), so the architectonic theatre of today, that is to say, the Theatre of Space, wants to destroy and abolish the two-dimensional stage. The painting of the Renaissance contemplated reality through a picture frame, just as the conventional theatre wants to contemplate reality through a stage opening. The Theatre of Space seeks to erase this artificial frame; it transports the stage into the auditorium and by this means renders the theatre active.[43]

Because of the usual reasons of economics and practicality the Poznan model was never built. The Irena Solska Theatre at Zolibor, near Warsaw, however, was transformed into a free-space theatre, and at least two scattered stage productions were presented there. In 1933 Syrkus designed and built a scattered stage setting for *Boston*, a drama based on the Sacco and Vanzetti trial. Five stages representing a skyscraper, the street, Sacco's lodgings, the prosecutor's chamber, and the prison were set up in the midst of three seating areas (Plates 77, 78, 79).

Syrkus, working with director Michal Weichart, designed a set for *Krassin*, a documentary drama in fifty-two scenes utilizing a total of fourteen stages that included icebergs, a Moscow apartment, and a ham operator's room at Archangelsk (Plate 80).[44]

Edouard Autant was aware of these experiments at Zolibor and had seen the model of Tonecki's Theatre of Space. He was also familiar with Tonecki's writings. Based on this, he drew up plans in 1937 for his own Theatre of Space. It was partially built for the World's Fair at Paris that year but administrative misunderstandings and red-tape caused it to remain incomplete, although specially devised productions were mounted there.[45] It was torn down at the end of the Fair. The plans for the theatre combined elements of scattered staging, annular staging and open air theatre (Plate 81). The building was a large rectangle about fifty meters in length ("a sort of stadium"). In the center of this space was a smaller rectangle containing various interspersed stage and seating areas that could be rearranged for each presentation. Surrounding this space on three sides was a "panoramic stage"—a platform for mass scenes, choruses, and dance. Flats, screens, or other scenic elements could be placed about this space, and along the floor were outlets for projectors, fixtures for scenery and access for performers. Mirrors were arrranged so that spectators could view scenes otherwise out of their sightlines.

Autant wanted not only a unification of the stage and auditorium but an interplay with the natural environment as well. Thus, suspended above the central area, was a mobile platform which could open like a skylight to effect a transformation of the space into an open air theatre. Furthermore, a "transparent atmospheric belt"—a wall of high windows set above the panoramic stage—admitted natural light and a view of surrounding foliage. Autant felt that this would cause the theatre to "dissolve" into the surrounding environment.[46]

For those spectators who did not wish to be "bathed in the production," as Autant said, there was to be a giant closed-circuit television screen placed outside, above the entrance to the theatre.[47] Spectators could sit on the mall and watch in peace.

Autant believed that the dispersement of performers throughout the audience—the transformation of the theatre into a unified stage—would inevitably affect acting styles. The acting, he felt, would become truer and simpler. The actor, because he would no longer be directly facing the audience at all times, would learn to act with his whole body.[48] Syrkus had expressed this same idea as early as 1934 and, of course, it is similar to the concepts in Okhlopkov's fifth principle above.[49] These ideas, too, sound very much like those Grotowski would express almost thirty years later.

Two types of environmental staging have been seen here: the free-space staging at Zolibor (localized stages scattered through a fragmented audience); and the totally unified space of Okhlopkov (a generalized or specified environment encompassing the total interior of the theatre). These were both motivated by a desire to create a greater sense of reality than was being achieved on the proscenium stage. The audience in both cases was treated as an essentially passive group. Both Okhlopkov and Autant, picking up on the ideas of Tonecki, were aware of the necessity of allowing spectators to remove themselves physically as well as psychologically from the production. Nothing was to be forced upon the audience. It was merely hoped that by surrounding the spectators a more natural style of performing would be forced on the actors and a greater sense of reality would be perceived by the audience. It was, in part, an attempt to capture a certain aspect of events in life—the fact that they occur all around the spectator, not merely in front of him.

During the twenties and thirties much attention was focused on Soviet life because of the Communist Revolution. Consequently, there are many first-hand accounts of Meyerhold, Okhlopkov, and the vast quantity of Russian theatre. During this same time Poland was experiencing an equally unprecedented revitalization of its theatre but it was so totally ignored that Tonecki and Syrkus cannot be found in English language theatre books and Pronaszko appears only briefly as an imaginative designer for Leon Schiller.[50]

48. Plan and model for a Palace of Labor in Moscow by A. and
     L. Vesnin, 1923.

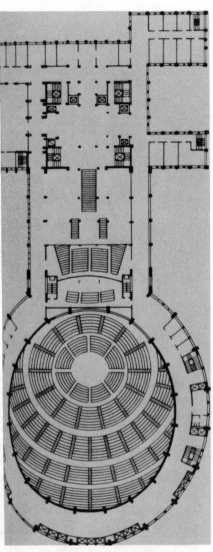

49. Sketch of design by A. V. Khvostenko-Khvostova for a production of Mayakovsky's *Mystery Bouffe* at Kharkov, 1921.

50. Set for open-air production of Tretyakov's *The Earth In Turmoil* designed by Lyubov Popova, 1923.

51. Meyerhold's production of Ostrovsky's *The Forest*, 1924.

52. Meyerhold's production of Alexei Faiko's *Bubus the Teacher*.

53. Model of Lissitzky's set for Tretyakov's *I Want A Child*, 1926–30.

54. Plan of proposed Meyerhold Theatre by Mikhail Barkhin and Sergei Vakhtangov, 1932.

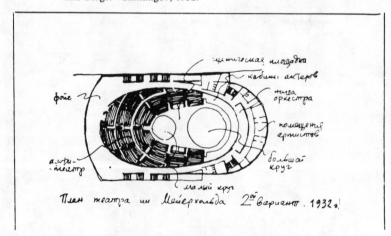

55. Sergei Eisenstein's production of Tretyakov's *Gas Masks* in a Moscow gas plant, 1924.

56. Eisenstein's production of *Gas Masks*.

57. Sketch by Yuri Annenkov of the stages and audience for
     The Storming of the Winter Palace.

58. Plan of Uritzky Square for *The Storming of the Winter
     Palace*, 1920. The Winter Palace is at the bottom of the
     photograph, the Red Stage is the curved section in the upper
     left center, the White Stage upper right center. The shaded
     areas in the center are the spectators.

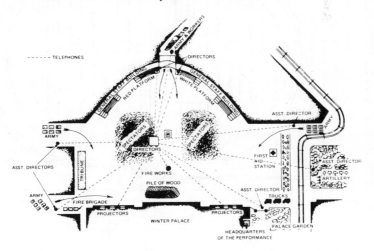

59. Plan of Okhlopkov's production of *The Start*, 1931.

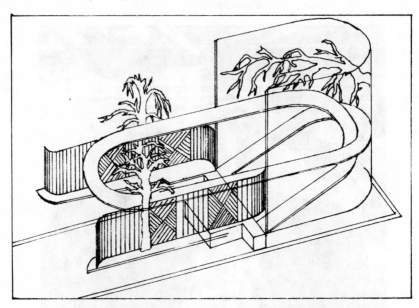

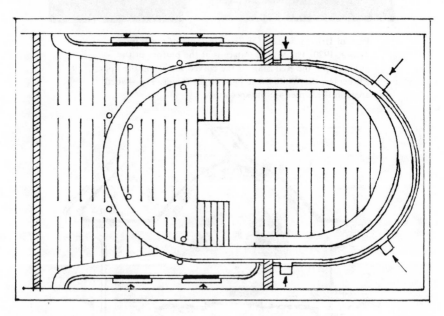

60. Plan of Okhlopkov's production of
   The Mother, 1932.

61. Plan of Okhlopkov's production of *Pierre Patelin*, 1933.

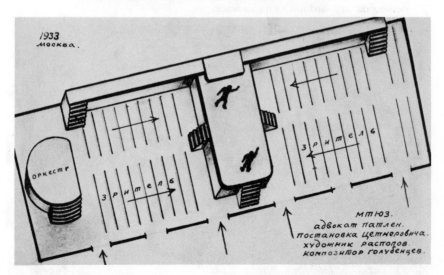

62. Plan of Okhlopkov's production of
     The Iron Flood, 1933.

63. Final scene from *The Iron Flood* showing performers
     leaving the stage and joining the audience.

64. Plan of Okhlopkov's production
of *Aristocrats*, 1934.

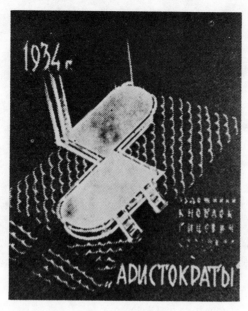

65. Plan of Okhlopkov's production of *The Holy Fool*, 1934
(unproduced).

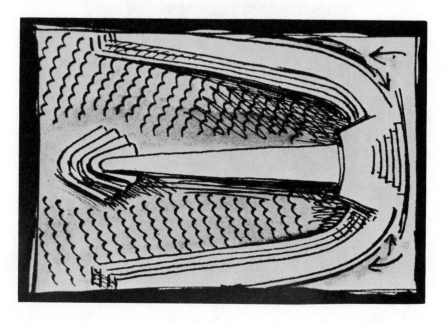

66. Design for Okhlopkov's production of *Othello*, 1935.

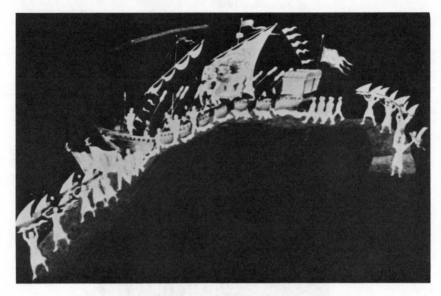

67. Groundplan for Okhlopkov's production of *Othello*, 1935.

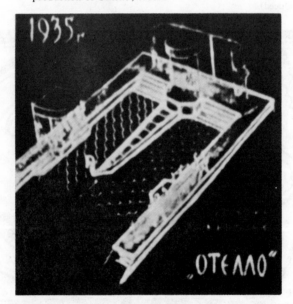

68. Plan for Okhlopkov's production
     of *Colas Breugnon*, 1936.

69. Okhlopkov's production of *Dream*, 1937.

70.   Design for Okhlopkov's production of *Hotel Astoria*, 1953.

71.   Plan for the proposed Leningrad Comedy
      Theatre by Maltzin and Bikov, 1961.

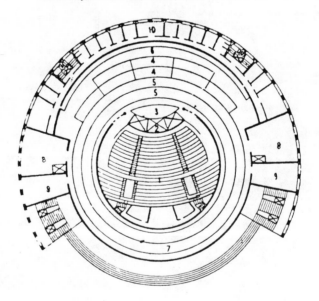

72. Plan for a production of *The Golem* by Andrzej Pronaszko and Szymon Syrkus, 1928.

73. Plan and elevation of the Theatre of the Future (Simultaneous Theatre) by Pronaszko and Syrkus, 1928–29.

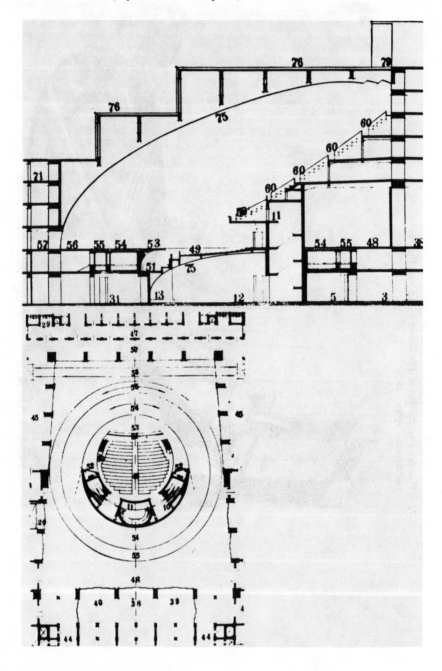

74. Model of the Theatre of the
     Future (exterior).

75. Model of the Theatre of the
     Future (interior).

76. Model of Mobile Theatre (Teatr
     Ruchomo) by Andrzej
     Pronaszko, 1933–34.

77. View of the performance area for *Boston* in Warsaw, 1933,
     by Szymon Syrkus.

78. Ground plan for *Boston* in Warsaw.

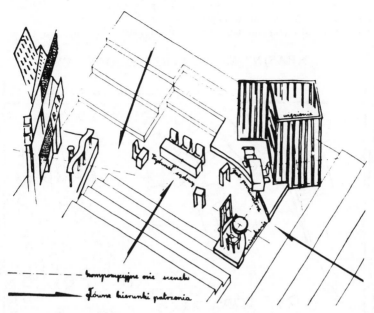

79. Performance area of *Boston* showing prosecutor's office at
left and Sacco's lodgings at right.

80. Plan of production of *Krassin* by Pronaszko and Syrkus.
Key: 1) Icebergs; 2) Moscow; 3) "Krassin"; 4) Apartment of
Professor Samoilovicky; 5) Ham operator's room at
Archangelsk; 6) Ham radio stations of different countries.

„KRASIN" W „TEATRZE MŁODYCH".

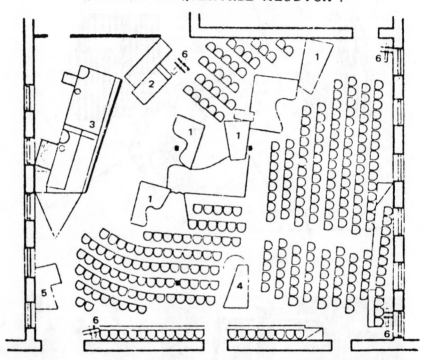

81. Plan of Edouard Autant's Theatre of Space, 1937. Key:
A) "Transparent atmospheric belt (open to the outside);
C) Counterweight system for the sliding ceiling; D) Grooves
for scenery; E) Marquee; F) Spectator seats; L) Sliding ceil-
ing (to act as a skylight and protection against weather);
O) Orchestra pit; P) Panoramic stage; R) Mirror; V) Lobby.

THEATRE DE L'ESPACE
Plan et Coupe

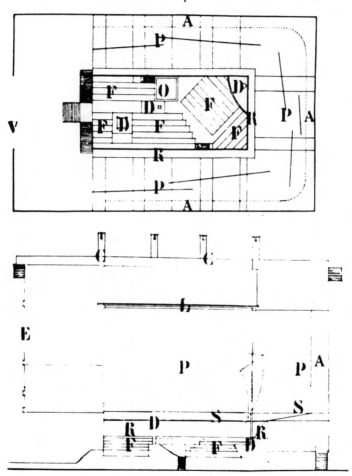

7

Environments and Happenings

*Overwhelmed by the enormous stage set of life,
what can the artist who aspires to conquer his
public do? He has only one chance left to take: to
rise to the plane of beauty by considering everything that surrounds him as raw material; to
select the plastic and theatrical values possible
from the whirlpool that swirls under his eyes; to
interpret them in terms of spectacle; to attain
theatrical unity and dominate it at any price.*

—*Fernand Léger, 1924*

Politics and depression put an end to most theatrical experimentation in
Europe by the mid 1930s and with the onset of World War II virtually all
artistic innovation ceased. The forces that were stifling European art,
however, also encouraged an emigration of artists to the United States. The
Bauhaus, for instance, was closed by Hitler in 1933 and most of its members
found their way to America; Marcel Duchamp, who had first visited this
country in 1915, settled here in 1942, designing an environment for the
Surrealist exhibition in New York that year. It may be argued that the new
Bauhaus founded by refugee members in Chicago lacked the cohesiveness
and inspiration of the original, that Duchamp produced little art after
settling in this country, and even that earlier emigrés such as Kiesler had
minimal visible influence, but it is undeniable that by the close of the War
the well-spring of much avant-garde art was centered in the United States.
Primary sources were thus available to developing American artists, and it
was from this confluence of forces that new forms of theatre were to
develop.

During the post-War period three art forms emerged which had a direct
bearing on environmental theatre and which had historical precedents in the

first half of the century. These are environments, action painting and Happenings, the last of which, like much Futurist and Dadaist art, combined art and performance. It is to these art forms that we must turn for the immediate roots of contemporary environmental performance.

American scenography between the wars had developed primarily in response to the esthetics of the New Stagecraft under the leadership of such designers as Robert Edmond Jones, Normal Bel Geddes and Lee Simonson. While there was some tendency toward a unification of stage and auditorium in their work, only Geddes' set for Reinhardt's *Miracle* could be considered in any way environmental. Perhaps the only significant alternative to proscenium staging in this country was offered by a production of Irwin Shaw's *Bury the Dead* in 1939. Staged at Black Mountain College in North Carolina by Robert Wunsch and designed by George Hendrickson, the setting surrounded the audience.[1] Apparently this experimental form of staging was based not so much on any theatrical theory as on the fact that the tiny stage of the university dining hall provided insufficient space. The grave scenes occurred onstage but other actions were placed on platforms around the auditorium. The scenes with the businessmen and the prostitutes, for example, were played behind the spectators. Loudspeakers were also placed around the audience and were suspended from the ceiling. "At the end of the play," noted a contemporary account,

> the montage effect, the powerless ravages of the church, the failure of the mothers, wives and sweethearts to persuade the corpses to "lie down," the demands of voices from the audience, from loudspeakers, from all sides for "somebody to do something" create a mounting hysteria as the corpses slowly rise out of their graves and walk toward the audience.[2]

The production was almost certainly a unique occurrence without ostensible influence. It was not until the fifties and Happenings that environmental staging began to flourish in this country.

Happenings opened a new world of scenographic possibilities.[3] It is important to note, however, that while most of them consciously attempted to alter spectator-presentation relationships, an environmental approach was not necessarily an integral aspect of Happenings.[4] Not all Happenings were environmental, but because of their exploration of spectator-performance relationships, there is a strong association between unconventional staging and the esthetics of the Happening. Many Happening artists, especially those developing more or less independently in Europe and Japan in the late fifties did, in fact, consider environment as an inseparable aspect of the performance. Jean-Jacques Lebel, a leading French Happenings artist, considered such performances to be active attacks on conventional scenography and theatre in general. For him, "environment [was] the essential element of any Happening."[5]

Art must literally "go down the street," come out of its cultural zoo, to enrich itself with what Hegel, and without humor, called "*the contamination of the casual*". . . . We hope to do other things in a station, a stadium, an airplane. To be elsewhere. To be radar. To be there. The conventional theatre, the art shop or gallery, are no longer (and perhaps never have been) sacred places, so why shut ourselves up in them?[6]

Lebel was obviously interested in the potential of found environments, especially as an alternative to the proscenium stage, but most early Happenings utilized a created environment. Combinations of the two, as well as processional forms, began to evolve. Most Happening artists were concerned to some degree or other with the spectators' perceptions, and this frequently manifested itself in the manipulation of space or the manipulation of spectators into specific environments. We are concerned here with those Happenings in which such spatial considerations are most apparent.

The development of the created environment is usually traced back to the collages and assemblages of the early part of the century. Painting, of course, is two-dimensional; it exists on a flat surface. (Any perception of three-dimensional space is an illusion, the result of perspective.) In 1912, Picasso pasted a piece of oilcloth to a painting, surrounded the canvas with a piece of rope, and collage was invented.[7] This accomplished two things: it introduced "foreign" (i.e., non-paint) elements into painting so that henceforth any item could conceivably be included; and the actual space of the picture now projected out from the surface plane. (This latter trend was prefigured by Van Gogh's use of thick slabs of paint on the canvas.) Whereas perspective painting created an illusion of infinite space behind the picture surface plane, collage created a potential for unlimited projection into actual space. The limits of the frame would now be transcended.

Sculpture, likewise, began to expand its particular frame. Although sculpture has, of course, always been three-dimensional, it was, until the twentieth century, a concentrated mass which organized space about itself— it did not generally incorporate or envelop space. It was, rather, a center to which the spectator oriented himself and was thus analogous, in a way, to theatre-in-the-round. The spectator, while perceiving the three-dimensionality, was forced to remain outside the object—beyond the frame as it were. Christian Norberg-Schulz, a Norwegian architect, terms this centricity or focusing aspect "concentration":

The ability of a mass to serve as a 'centre,' could be described by the term 'concentration.' Concentration is a function of the main shape, as well as the treatment of details. In general it is strengthened by a continuous bounding surface and by symmetry. . . . Concentration is also enhanced by isolation: when a mass is lifted up in relation to its surroundings, a vertical axis is implied, around which space is organized. . . . In general, the mass is a symbolic or ideal centre, rather than a real place or activity. It puts a stop to the horizontal extension of man's environment, and makes his need for fixed points visible.[8]

Norberg-Schulz is referring not merely to sculpture but to any mass. Sculpture, however, has the ability to incorporate space, thereby shaping the environment rather than merely focusing it. As early as 1912 Umberto Boccioni, in his "Technical Manifesto of Futurist Sculpture," stated: "There can be no renovation if not through a SCULPTURE OF ENVIRONMENT, for through this, plasticity will be developed and, continuing, will be able to MODEL THE ATMOSPHERE that surrounds things."[9] Plasticity had to come from a manipulation of the environment, not merely from the form itself. Boccioni was aiming for an influence on the spectators' perceptions by an incorporation of spectator space.

Earlier chapters have outlined similar theories and experiments by the Russian Suprematists and Constructivists: Naum Gabo, for example, had proposed the idea of space as a sculptural element.[10] Space, he felt, formed an envelope which could be penetrated by a sculptural object, thus becoming a bounded entity in relation to sculpture.[11] If space is an envelope, then it may conceivably include the spectator. In the Realistic Manifesto of 1920, Gabo and his brother Anton Pevsner noted that time and space were a part of life and should thus be a part of sculpture.[12] At about the same time El Lissitzky was working on his concept of the room as an environment—a six-sided enclosure which would affect a person's perceptions through varying treatments of the room's planar surfaces.[13]

Meanwhile, the Dutch painter Piet Mondrian had declared, in 1919, that "the abstract-realist picture will disappear as soon as we can transfer its plastic beauty to the space around us," thus adding still another call for a physically encompassing art.[14] In sculpture, some of these ideas began to be realized in the thirties by Henry Moore who became fascinated by the tensions created between voids and solids. His sculptures often included voids or spaces.

Perhaps the ultimate manifestation of this progression of ideas was Kurt Schwitters' *Merzbau* (1925). Schwitters transformed his house in Hanover, Germany into a mammoth collage—an environment. Merz was the generic title Schwitters gave to his work, taken from the word "kommerz" which was glued to one of his collages. In the Hanover *Merzbau*, constructions of cardboard, iron, wood, broken furniture and other "junk" jutted out from ceilings and walls.

> There were cave-like openings hidden in the abstract structure, with secret doors of colored blocks. . . . There was a Murderer's Cave, with a broken plaster cast of a female nude, stained bloody with lipstick or paint; there was a caricature abode of the Niebelungen in miniature; in one of the caves a small bottle of urine was solemnly displayed.[15]

The structure kept evolving until its destruction by bombs in 1943. Schwitters apparently manipulated the objects in the house for his friends, putting on a sort of performance, thus nearly completing, as Kirby suggests, the transition from collage to Happening.[16] A similar, ongoing, labyrinthian environment was carved out of a mount near Woodstock, New York in the 1930s by Clarence Schmidt. In both cases the environments were not created by mere alteration of surface planes, they involved a total transformation or creation of space. They sculpted space, penetrated space, and used space as an envelope and thus as a means of manipulating perceptions.[17]

In 1938 Marcel Duchamp designed an environment for the International Exposition of Surrealism at the Galerie Beaux Arts in Paris. Calvin Tomkins described it as a "subterranean cave."[18] Twelve hundred coal sacks were hung from the ceiling. Around a pool was a carpet of grass and four beds. There were paintings on the walls. Flashlights were given to the visitors to view the paintings (Duchamp had wanted electric-eye stimulated lights), although conventional lighting was installed after the flashlights had been stolen. The smell of roasting coffee filled the air.[19]

For the 1942 Surrealist exhibition in New York Duchamp strung miles of string through the gallery.[20] The tradition of environments was continued at the 1947 Surrealist exhibition at Paris' Galerie Maeght, although without the participation of Duchamp. There was a room carpeted in artificial grass in which there was a constant rainfall. The 1960 exhibition, also in Paris, contained several individual environments—rooms with different colors, forms, textures, sounds and activities.

These precedents seemed to pave the way for environmental sculpture— sculpture which surrounds the spectator on all sides. It is always difficult to say who did what first, but once again, Frederick Kiesler seems to have been a pioneer. His architecture, of course, had always been concerned with environments, but in the late forties he began creating environmental sculptures.[21] His most famous was perhaps *The Last Judgement* (1955–59), a room containing sculptural objects and forms in niches and on alter-like tables. It has been described as a "somber and somehow menacing chapel."[22] In 1949 Italian sculptor Lucio Fontana ws creating "spatial environments with free forms and black light."[23] By the fifties, environments became a major creative form.

Allan Kaprow, who coined the word "Happenings," believes that the form descends directly from collage and summed up the history, as he saw it, very succinctly:

> With the breakdown of the classical harmonies following the introduction of "irrational" or nonharmonic juxtapositions, the Cubists tacitly opened up a path to infinity. Once foreign matter was introduced into the picture in the form of paper, it was only a matter of time before everything else foreign to paint and canvas would be allowed to get into the creative act, including real space. Simplifying the history of the ensuing evolution into a flashback, this is what happened: the pieces of paper curled up off the canvas, were removed from the surface to exist on their own, became more solid as they grew

into other materials and, reaching out further into the room, finally filled it entirely. Suddenly there were jungles, crowded streets, littered alleys, dream spaces of science fiction, rooms of madness, and junk filled attics of the mind. . . .[24]

It is interesting that in Kaprow's simplified progression he seems to include the found and created as part of one continuum.

While this has become a fairly accepted version of the history of the environment, several other factors must be taken into account in considering the evolution of Happenings. Foremost is the work of the composer John Cage. The performance now considered to be the first Happening was devised by Cage at Black Mountain College in 1952, using various concepts with which he was working at the time. From Oriental philosophy came Huang Po's "Doctrine of the Universal Mind" which, as Martin Duberman explains, is "the postulate that centricity within each event is not dependent on other events."[25] (This is the concept that Michael Kirby would later define as "compartmentalization.") Cage had also been introduced by the composer Pierre Boulez in 1948 to the writings of Artaud, whose ideas held great attraction for him. Finally, Cage was fascinated with Duchamp's concept that the work of art is completed by the individual observer. According to Cage, these "all fused together into the possibility of making a theatrical event in which the things that took place were not causally related to one another—but in which there is a penetration, anything that happened after that happened in the observer himself."[26]

Apparently various observers completed the first Happening in very individual ways because Martin Duberman relates five conflicting eye-witness accounts of the event. This is Cage's own description:

> The seating arrangement was a square composed of four triangles with the apexes of the triangles merging toward the center, but not meeting. The center was a larger space that could take movement, and the aisles between these four triangles also admitted of movement. The audience could see itself, which is of course the advantage of any theatre in the round. The larger part of the action took place *outside* of that square. In each one of the seats was a cup, and it wasn't explained to the audience what to do with this cup—some used it as an ashtray—but the performance was concluded by a kind of ritual of pouring coffee into each cup.[27]

Suspended above the audience were Robert Rauschenberg's white paintings. A movie was projected at one end of the rectangular hall and slides at the other. The performers included M. C. Richards, Charles Olson, David Tudor, Rauschenberg, Merce Cunningham and, unintentionally, a stray dog that began to follow Cunningham around the space. During designated time periods the performers were "free within limitations . . . compartments which they didn't have to fill . . . Until this compartment began, they were not free to act, but once it had begun they could act as long as they wanted to during it."[28]

Cage was on a ladder delivering a lecture that included silences. Richards and Olson climbed another ladder at different times and read poetry. (One account claims that Olson passed out parts of a poem that were to be read by individual spectators.[29]) Rauschenberg played an old-fashioned phonograph and Tudor played the piano. Cunningham and other dancers moved through the space.

Cage has defined theatre as "something which engages both the eye and the ear."[30] Consequently, in his view, "theatre takes place all the time wherever one is, and art simply facilitates persuading one [that] this is the case."[31] This idea, together with Artaud's concepts of staging, was a primary impulse behind staging the piece all around the audience—it made it more like the experience of life. Cage explained that this surrounding concept was just as true of music. Electronic music, for example, as currently performed must flood the concert hall from just a few speakers.

> But in our everyday life sounds are popping up, just as visual things and moving things are popping up, everywhere around us. I would like to imitate that—to present fantastic architectural and technological problems. That's how theatre will be . . . so that sounds can move or appear to come from any point in space. . . . I would also like it to appear, as I think it will with transistor means, in the center of the space."[32]

When Cage's use of silence in composition is considered, the theoretical basis for Happenings becomes nearly complete. Cage uses silence much in the way Henry Moore used space. Cage abandoned harmony as the basic principle of music. He felt that any sound was acceptable as music and the only property common to all sounds is duration. Silence, because it also has duration, is likewise acceptable in music. Furthermore, there is no such thing as absolute silence—a silent duration is filled with "found" nosies. In some cases the auditors provide the sound; in other cases the performance merely aids the auditor in the perception of the sounds. If any sound or lack of sound is acceptable, then visual elements can also become acceptable elements. In some cases, the playing of various instruments invented by Cage (such as the water gong) became specific acts of performance. In other cases he added physical or visual components to his compositions.

Cage represents the final catalyst in the destruction of artistic boundaries and categories. After his work art, music, and theatre can admit of any element, all can be aspects of performance. They can be presented to the spectator in a fashion analogous to life—both randomly and spatially encompassing. Unlike many environmental productions of the twenties and thirties which essentially tried to intensify the effect of the performance by surrounding the audience, Cage's idea was to produce an art that mimicked life as perceived by what he terms the public senses: hearing and seeing. The specific elements one perceived in a Cage piece might be unlike anything encountered in the everyday world, but the perception of them would be the same.

Allan Kaprow took a course from Cage at the New School for Social Research in New York during the mid-fifties and the influence was undoubtedly a primary factor in the development of Happenings.[33] Kaprow coined the term in 1956 in an article on Jackson Pollock, the action painter. (The article was not published until 1958 in *Art News*.) In it he reiterated the idea of including all elements of the real world in painting:

> Objects of every sort are materials for the new art: paint, chairs, food, electric and neon lights, smoke, water, old socks, a dog, movies, a thousand other things which will be discovered by the present generation of artists. Not only will these bold creators show us, as if for the first time, the world we have always had about us, but ignored, but they will disclose entirely unheard of happenings and events, found in garbage cans, police files, hotel lobbies, seen in store windows and on the streets, and sensed in dreams and horrible accidents.[34]

The inclusion of non-painterly elements in art seemed to lead inevitably to performance and the next use of the word Happening was in 1959 in a descriptive title for a suggested theatre piece: "Something to take place: a happening."[35] For this event Kaprow proposed a massive environment—a space about 500 feet by 350 feet by 20 feet high. There would be colored bands on the floor and colored chairs, a "cubic framework covered with transparent plastic film," changing lights and various activities occurring in the space.[36] He suggested "fourteen groups of chairs—random—in rows circles rectangles and singly—spotted here and there over the floor of this area. . . . People will sit in the chairs whose arrangement causes them to face in different directions."[37] The spectators would be asked to change seats from time to time according to the numbers on their tickets of admission.

Aside from Cage, Kaprow acknowledged the influence of Duchamp and of Mondrian, about whom he wrote his master's thesis. But above all he was strongly influenced by the action painting of Jackson Pollock. He admired the way Pollock was a part of his own work during the process of painting, and Kaprow wanted to continue that active quality into the finished product. "I wanted above all to be literally part of the work. I further desired something of my social world to be part of whatever art I did."[38]

This led him, in 1957, to begin creating environments. The first one was a sort of maze of overlapping, hanging sheets of plastic onto which were sewn and glued various materials. The spectators could be partially seen through the plastic as they moved about the space and they thus became "diaphanous parts of the Environment."[39] Sound was played from tape recorders. At first Kaprow tried giving two "performances" a day but he became disturbed, not only by the performance aspect and its implications— theatrical elements in which he had no interest began to dominate—but also because "it wasn't as constant as the physical parts of the environment."[40] Rather than trying to produce a prearranged program of sounds with the environment, he subsequently presented a continuous "random distribution" of taped and mechanical sounds.

One of Kaprow's insights while working on environments was that visitors became an integral aspect of the piece. This was significantly different from the environmental theatre which had preceded it. With the presentation of a play, no matter how much the spectators were physically incorporated into the setting or even encouraged to participate, they could never coalesce with the time, place and character matrices created by the performers. The spectators at Okhlopkov's Realistic Theatre were not actually in the Mother's kitchen or at the Russian front any more than the spectators at *The Miracle* were in a Gothic cathedral. The sensory impact of environmental settings or performer activity may intensify the experience and aid in the suspension of disbelief, but it is difficult for the spectator to maintain the illusion for long. It is easily shattered by an awareness of oneself and fellow spectators. If a performance does not create these standard matrices, however, then it becomes easier for a spectator to become part of the whole. This is generally the case in environments. "Inasmuch as people visiting such environments are moving, colored shapes too, and are counted 'in,'" explained Kaprow,

> mechanically moving parts could be added, and parts of the created surroundings could then be rearranged like furniture at the artist's and visitors' discretion. And, logically, since the visitor could and did speak, sound and speech, mechanical and recorded, were also soon to be in order. Odors followed.[41].

On October 4, 1959 a piece entitled *18 Happenings in 6 Parts* was presented by Kaprow at the Reuben gallery in New York. It was the first Happening identified as such and was a partial realization, with variations, of the earlier proposal. The gallery was divided into three rooms by plastic partitions. A collage covered one wall and there were projections. Various activities and events occurred while the audience, in various combinations, moved from one to another of the rooms at designated points within the performance. Listed among the "Cast of Participants" were "The visitors— who sit in various chairs."[42] The spectators were not not only in the midst of the environment, they were integral parts of it.

Through his continuing performance of Happenings, Kaprow developed a series of axioms. His chief aim was to eliminate conventional theatrical associations and performer-spectator divisions—the "side show" quality—that he felt still accrued to Happenings. Among these axioms were:

> *The performance of a Happening should take place over several widely spaced, sometimes moving and changing locales. . . .*
>
> Time *which follows closely on space considerations, should be variable and discontinuous.* It is only natural that if these are multiple spaces in which occurrences are scheduled, in sequence or even at random, time or "pacing" will acquire an order that is determined more by the character of movements within environments than by a fixed concept of regular development and conclusion. . . .
>
> *It follows that audience should be eliminated entirely.* All the elements—people, space, the particular materials and character of the environment, time—can in this way be integrated.[43]

Obviously, not all Happenings subscribed to these axioms. Each artist drew from his own background, influences and particular intentions. There were Happenings presented in fairly conventional proscenium fashion, Happenings presented in a single environment, and Happenings that maintained a definite separation between spectator and presentation. But for Kaprow, who perceived a direct evolution of the form from collage, these conclusions were inevitable. In his discussions of the development of Happenings Kaprow echoed the theories and concepts of Boccioni and Mondrian:

> The whole work begins to actively engulf the air around it, giving it shape, dividing it into parts, weighing it, allowing it to interact with the solids at such a rate or in such a strange manner that one now cannot help noticing the shape and feel of the gallery which, like some radar signal, sends back its shape to contend with the work of art.[44]

Happenings had succeeded in accomplishing what other theatrical environments had not done—effecting a total transformation or incorporation of space. In those Happenings in which the manipulation of space was a desired end, the spectator was not merely surrounded by an environment—he was a *part* of the environment, acutely sensitive to its dynamics and changes.

The subsequent burgeoning of Happenings in the early sixties in a sense recapitulated the history of environmental scenography. There were created and found environments as well as processional Happenings. Created environments were basically of two types: a single transformed space; and multispace environments. Found environments, on the other hand, capitalized on the qualities of their surroundings, although occasionally altering them in some way—as through the introduction of various scenographic elements. There were also combined forms in which the piece would occur in several places, sometimes widely separated, either simultaneously or sequentially, and in which there would be both found and created environments.

Processional Happenings caused the spectators to move in some sequential fashion, usually through found environments, during which time they would perceive or experience the environment along with various programmed activities or merely decorative elements. An example of a processional Happening was Jean-Jacques Lebel's "Funeral Ceremony of the Anti-Procès" performed in Venice in 1960.[45] One hundred fifty guests were invited to a cocktail party at a palazzo. They were told to come in formal dress and bring white flowers. From the cocktail party they proceeded to a large funeral hall in which a draped "body" lay. After the body was "killed" and other ceremonial events were performed, a cortege was formed to take the body to a waiting gondola. A procession of gondolas and speed boats advanced up the Grand Canal and after a formal ceremony the body (a Jean Tinguely sculpture) was dumped into the water (Plate 82).

Wolf Vostell has also presented many processional Happenings. "You: A Decollage Happening for Bob and Rhett Brown" was done by him at King's Point, New York in 1964 (Plate 83).[46] Guests had to pass along a narrow path, one at a time, then through woods and an orchard, across various obstacles, over a tennis court, through a stable and finally a pool. The environments, like the spectator-guests, were employed for their own qualities.

The varying uses of a created environment may be seen in a comparison of two outwardly similar Happening environments. The space for Allan Kaprow's "Eat" is a generalized environment of a cave (Plate 84). Within it, however, are more or less defined areas in which specific activities take place or "themes" are emphasized. A visitor might wander from one localized area to another but will be continually enclosed by the single, unified environment. Paul Sills' "Monster Model Funhouse" (Plate 85) seems to have certain similarities to "Eat" at first glance, but it is segmented into discrete environmental compartments. Each compartment, as in "18 Happenings," is connected physically and by the activities which make up the event, yet they are essentially autonomous units.[47]

Inherent in the concept of Happenings is not so much the idea of environment but of altering or manipulating spectator perceptions. There is a clear desire on the part of the artists to provide alternatives to conventional theatrical viewing habits. Thus, in some cases, such as Robert Whitman's *Prune Flat* (1965) or Red Grooms' *The Burning Building* (1961), conventional proscenium or frontal settings were considered desirable to create particular effects; but most Happenings have, in some way or other, consciously controlled the spectators' environment as well. The audience at Whitman's *American Moon* spent more than half the performance viewing activities from within a circle of small "caves" made of paper and chicken wire. In Kaprow's *Spring Happening* the spectators were herded into a narrow tunnel-like construction. At the conclusion of the piece they were forced out of the tunnel by a roaring lawnmower pushed directly at them. In some Happenings, such as Claes Oldenburg's *World's Fair II*, there was no created environment, as such, yet spectators were tickled or touched or had their shoelaces untied.[48]

In this last example may be seen one of the most important contributions of Happenings to environmental theatre. By its lack of time, place and character matrices a Happening can create or at least suggest a totally shared performance space. There is, in such cases, no clear frame around the performance and the performance space thus extends indefinitely, thereby including the spectator. There is none of the inevitable tension created by the interaction of character and spectator at certain types of environmental performances in which more or less realistic characters attempt to interact with spectators. Ultimately, Happenings, as other environmental forms, may be considered on a continuum. At one end are those performed in a totally encompassing environment (either found or created), and on the other end are those performed in fairly conventional ways. In between fall those which perhaps do not employ an environment but which incorporate the spectator into the action in some way.

The impulse which led to the environmental aspects of Happenings also lay behind much earlier environmental theatre—an attempt to create a more true to life experience. For the Happening artists this did not mean an attempt to recreate the familiar emotions or experiences of life as usually seen on the stage, but rather, to bring elements of the everyday world into the realm of performance and to present them physically as they might occur in life—that is, non-frontally and multi-focused. For many performers in the sixties who had been influenced by Happenings, it seemed logical, then, to turn to the natural environments themselves as performance spaces. The next chapter surveys the use of these found environments.

8

Found Environments

The liberation of the theatre from the dictator-
ship of architects will result from the increasing
mobility and versatility of man, means, and
material. One step towards independence would
be to abandon theatre architecture entirely and
mount productions in "profane" situations and
locations. Such superimposed or provisional
theatres could be on top of towers and sky-
scrapers, in abandoned churches, in mines or
other subterranean spaces, in defunct factories, in
armories(!), in elevators, trucks, trains, boats,
stadiums, water basins, dead ends, planetaria, on
highways, in trees. . . .

—*Otto Piene*
The Theatre That Moves *(1967)*

As indicated in the first chapter, a found environment is any given space
used in its existing state for performance. While this serves as a workable
definition, a few qualifications might be added. A found space ordinarily
implies an area not originally intended for a performance. A production on
the stage of a theatre—even if the stage is used in its "existing state"—is
nonetheless in a space created for such performance. The Living Theatre's
use of the Brooklyn Academy of Music (or the Yale Theatre) in *Paradise
Now*, however, incorporated, as we shall see, the auditorium, lobby, and
eventually the street into the performance space. The Living Theatre was
thus using a building and its environs as a found space and not as a theatre,
per se. Had the performers remained primarily on the stage, venturing into
the auditorium only occasionally, as in previous productions, the theatre
could not be considered a found space.

This raises an interesting question: the auditorium of a theatre is not
intended for performance although it is sometimes used for that purpose—at

what point, then, does the use of the auditorium cease to be an extension of the stage and become a found space in its own right? When Meyerhold or Reinhardt sent their performers down the aisles they in no way altered actual audience space; they employed the aisles as extensions of the stage to surround the spectators. The Living Theatre, however, treated the auditorium as a found environment. The performance of *Paradise Now* consciously strove to obliterate any distinction between stage and audience space; the entire interior of the theatre was considered a valid performance area. The conventional placement of the spectators was disrupted so as to alter their perception of the space.

Most conventional performance occurs in theatres with clearly designated and fairly fixed audience areas. A found environment, of course, has no pre-ordained spectator space. While such space is usually determined prior to the performance, there are many instances in which the respective audience and performance areas are determined by an interaction of spectators and performers, this arrangement often changing throughout the production. Richard Schechner refers to this process as "negotiation." "One negotiates with an environment," stated Schechner in the third of his "Six Axioms for Environmental Theatre," "engaging in a scenic dialogue with a space. . . . in a negotiated environment a more fluid situation leads sometimes to the performance being controlled by the spectator."[1] In much street theatre and in such performances as the Bread and Puppet's *Domestic Resurrection Fair and Circus*, a negotiation of this sort occurs—the displacement of performers and spectators is not so much predetermined but arrived at by topography and action. It may constantly shift.

Finally we should note that there are very few performances that actually occur in a truly found environment—the given space is usually transformed in some way. The incidental decorative elements of a parade—banners hung from street lamps, for instance—effect a minor transformation of space. The Bread and Puppet Theatre often uses banners and signs, as well as placing free-standing dolls and puppets in a space. Robert Wilson, in *KA MOUNTAIN AND GUARDenia TERRACE* (1972), placed cardboard cut-outs and even some scaffolding on the side of Haft Tan Mountain. But in all these cases the found environment (the street, meadow, mountain) predominated. The physical nature of the space remained basically unchanged, although the perception of it may have altered. We must conclude that there is a continuum of environments that includes found at one end and transformed at the other. At some point the transformation of an environment rather than its natural qualities begins to dominate.

The street has been one of the most popular found environments for performance, especially among the political theatre groups of the sixties. But street performance, as with outdoor performance in general, is not inherently environmental. Many performers, through the use of simple booth or platform stages, or their own disregard of their surroundings, create traditional and conventional audience-performance relationships.[2] In those cases the physical surroundings become incorporated into the setting just as they do in outdoor productions discussed in the first chapter. It is a perceived environment. Other performances, of course, quite consciously capitalize on the milieu of the street. This was the case, for example, with the anti-Vietnam War agit-props staged by Richard Schechner's Performance Group in the late sixties.

Schechner first began using found environments in 1961 in Provincetown, Massachusetts. Spending the summer there, he staged two productions: Euripides' *Philoctetes* in the sand dunes along the Atlantic, and Ibsen's *When We Dead Awaken* in the local town hall where the audience moved about with the performers.[3] Schechner claims that there was no theory involved in these choices and that he was not aware of historical precedents, although he had just read Artaud.[4] It just seemed logical, at least in the case of *Philoctetes*, to present the play in as close an approximation to its natural setting as possible. In *Philoctetes* performers even arrived by boat. Schechner later wrote a play based on some events in Provincetown called *The Blessing of the Fleet* and this was staged in New Orleans in 1963 in an actual bar, which is where the action of the play occurs.[5]

Later in the sixties Schechner's Performance Group occasionally took to the streets, as did other groups, to present performances or actions with political messages. In October 1967 members of the group and others participated in a piece of "guerilla" street theatre called *Guerilla Warfare* based on Robert Head's *Kill Viet Cong*.[6] This occurred in various locations around New York City including Grand Central Station and the Port Authority Bus Terminal.[7] The play itself was quite simple: the performers would suddenly materialize in some public place. Some would mime dive-bombers on a raid while others chanted, "Kill Viet Cong"; a performer in black pajamas would be displayed as a captured "Viet Cong" while another performer gave a speech about the War and patriotism. Finally a bystander would be handed a toy gun and asked to shoot the prisoner, after which the performers would rapidly disperse. The whole event took no more than a few minutes. The performance was repeated by various groups at different locations around the city.

This sort of presentation was typical of the genre of street performance now known as "guerilla theatre," which has its roots in the agit-prop theatre of the thirties.

> Guerilla/street theatre is a radical political theatre performed in the streets, in the schools, in shopping centers, outside of plant gates—anywhere people gather. . . . The very conditions of performance . . . as well as the politics of most of the participants, insure that these groups retain a nonprofessional character.[8]

Like guerilla warfare, from which it takes its name, there is a kind of hit-and-run approach to staging. Inherent in these productions is both an incorporation *and* a rejection of found space. On the one hand, the performers purposely choose the streets (or parks, or public buildings) because it places them in the midst of the audience they wish to reach—"go where the people are," admonished R. G. Davis of the San Francisco Mime Troupe.[9] The people on the street, in essence, become a "found audience" whose expectations and cultural and social associations with the street (whether they are affluent shoppers or ghetto children) are as important to the performers as the surrounding architecture or topography. The attitude of a "found audience" is inherently different from that of an audience at a conventional theatre and the performers have learned to play in direct opposition to audience attitudes or to re-enforce them to convey their message.

An example of this can be seen in the Pageant Players' *Laundromat Play* which was performed in an actual laundromat.[10] The performers waited until there was an empty washing machine, then one of them went in and began to do laundry. The other performers entered—some were musicians— marched around the space to attract attention, and began to fight over possession of the wash in an allegorical play about the Vietnam War. The performers were playing to an essentially captive audience which was caught unawares because of the performers' manipulation of a found space and a social environment. In guerilla/street theatre, the primary found environmental element is not so much the physical surroundings but the people, who often form an unsuspecting audience.

On the other hand, the performers sometimes ignore the physical aspects of the environment. In *Kill Viet Cong*, for example, the specific physical characteristics of Grand Central Station, Paley Park, or the United Nations did not significantly inform the performances in any way. This is not to say that the found environment is unimportant—it is essential—but its effect is more social and psychological than physical.

One of the difficulties of street theatre in a city like New York is the complaisance with which most city dwellers react to street events. Unusual occurrences may provoke mild curiosity but rarely political action. Success in this form requires a strong understanding of the environment and the ability to manipulate it—to negotiate with it. Schechner warns that "you must know the differences among *friendly*, *neutral*, *unfriendly*, and *hostile* places/audiences."[11] If, indeed, the people on the street are a prime environmental factor, then Schechner's warning translates as a dictum to choose an environment carefully and understand it well. What type of people are found in each space? What are their expectations, associations, and patterns of behavior? What is it that will focus their attention on the message of the performance? (That is, how can their perception of that given space be altered?) In an evaluation of the day's performances of *Guerilla Warfare*, Schechner commented,

> We must learn to negotiate with the environments, to deal swiftly and efficiently with them. . . . look at the environment . . . get through the verbal stuff swiftly and get on to the gestural point. . . . Gesture [is] stronger than words in public places. . . . the notion of flooding even a city of this size [New York] with simultaneous performance is a good one: it gives you the feeling that the total environment is controllable, that you have your hands on it, can feel it, use it, transform it.[12]

The Bread and Puppet Theatre, founded in 1961 by Peter Schumann, although not solely an environmental group, has dealt more effectively with found environments than any other group of the past two decades. Its plays have often been political in content and religious in spirit. The masked performers, the dolls and puppets—some as much as eighteen feet tall—have been found in peace parades, the streets of Harlem and the Bronx, an old theatre at Coney Island, and a meadow in Vermont. The Bread and Puppet Theatre performs indoors as well as outdoors, although generally avoiding conventional theatrical spaces. But no matter what the surroundings, the group demonstrates a keen awareness of space and the performers' relationship to a given audience. "Some of our shows are in the street and some are inside. The inside shows are meant for the Insides; the outside shows are meant to be as big and loud as possible."[13]

From the beginning Peter Schumann has been aware of the need to negotiate with the environment, even if he does not express it in those terms. Perhaps more than other similar artists, he is aware of the subtle differences between indoor and outdoor performances. He knows the quality of the street, the necessary techniques of performance in a non-theatrical and competitive atmosphere, and the methods for manipulating space. Inside, the group almost always performs in a frontal arrangement; nonetheless they try to incorporate the space into the performance. "We do a show for a particular space—the space we happen to be in," claims Schumann. "The one space we reject is that of the traditional theatre. . . . When you use the space you happen to be in you use it all—the stairs, the windows, the streets, the doors."[14] The nature of the performance changes with the nature of the space, there is generally no imposed setting. This flexibility was concisely noted in an article by Stefan Brecht: "Schumann's practice suggests that the norm should be plastic, undefined, broken space, not enclosed by sets but fragmentarily defined by mobile decor, so that the action is not between or within but around."[15]

In their outdoor performances, at least, the Bread and Puppet Theatre pays little attention to spatial boundaries. Although it is not interested in the incorporation of spectators into the action of a performance, the group is concerned about incorporating them within the performance space. Many of the indoor performances commence with a ceremony of breaking bread and passing it among the spectators. This has the effect of creating a communal atmosphere—everyone, both performers and spectators, are made a part of the performance. In parks or parades, on the other hand, a Chinese dragon-like puppet may weave in and out of the crowd, encircling and incorporating everyone within the environment. But even when the performers merely march in a parade, the huge, towering puppets seem to hover over the crowds and include them as part of a unified mass. There is an almost medieval quality, a religious stateliness, to the Bread and Puppet in these processions; they are processional performances and as such they are environmental.

Perhaps the most difficult aspect of performing in found environments is the achievement and maintenance of focus. Indoor spaces provide at least minimal focus through the physical boundaries of walls, floors, and ceilings which constitute a frame of sorts. But such boundaries frequently do not exist in outdoor environments; skylines, the horizon, or the physical limits of vision may make up the only restricting frame. In city streets there is often much activity leading to a distracting, multi-focus environment involving the random movement of people, cars, and perhaps overhead aircraft, and sometimes oppressive noise. It is difficult to achieve any sustained focus in such an environment.[16] Schumann feels that puppets are ideal for such a situation: "Puppets and masks should be played in the street. They are louder than the traffic."[17] The large moving sculptures of the Bread and Puppet centralize focus, they reshape the space of the street around themselves. The simple gestures of the puppets stand out in contrast to the finite detail of street activity. But it is more than that, for the same plays—and puppets—are often used both indoors and out.

It is an understanding of the difference in space in each case that has allowed Schumann's puppets to function so successfully:

> We've had our best performances in the streets. Sometimes you make your point because your point is simply to be there in the street. It stops people in their tracks—to see those large puppets, to see something theatrical outside of a theatre. They can't take the attitude that they've paid money to go into a theatre to "see something." Suddenly there is this thing in front of them, confronting them. . . . Indoors you can get by with technique . . . but on the street you come across only if you have your mind on What Has To Be Done. Everything will become awkward and lame if your guts aren't in what you're saying.[18]

Since the Bread and Puppet Theatre moved to Vermont in 1970 it has staged an annual summer event entitled the *Domestic Resurrection Fair and Circus* in a vast meadow near Goddard College. Puppeteers who have worked with Schumann in the past, members of the troupe, students from the college, and others all gather to participate in the event. During July 1974, for instance, approximately fifty performances and exhibits were presented for two days. "Every inch of land was used as a stage. . . ." noted one observer. "There were puppets in rivers, up trees, on cliffs, and even in the chicken coop."[19] One of the major performances was entitled "War and Peace." Armies of red and white puppets roamed over the meadow attacking one another while most of the audience watched from the top of a hill. For another piece, "Jephte," the audience sat at the base of a cliff which was covered with masks mounted on sticks. In the 1976 version Schumann added a "Bicentennial Circus" which began with a display of popular entertainments in a natural arena at the foot of a hill.[20] Afterwards the spectators could wander through a midway section. There were also performances staged throughout the meadow and in an adjacent pine forest (Plate 86).[21]

For each performance some sort of frontal arrangement was usually established for viewing but this seems to have been a result more of mutual agreement than design. The placement of puppets and masks as sculptural elements throughout the farm and meadow turned the area into a total environment much like one of Kiesler's or Kaprow's environments. The spectator was constantly surrounded by elements of performance; the entire meadow became a shared space in which focus was constantly shifting as a result of the actions of spatial manipulations of the performers.

The Living Theatre has been theatrically innovative for most of its thirty and more years. Ironically, it began to work in street theatre at about the time most other groups were abandoning the idea, but the street work evolved as a logical part of its political and theatrical progression.[22] The group's first major venture into non-frontal staging was Jack Gelber's *The Connection* (1959). Although the play had no ostensible political overtones, the production style and intent were similar to much work by Meyerhold and Okhlopkov, or perhaps more significantly, to Piscator with whom Judith Malina had studied in the forties. During the theatre's first decade she and her husband Julian Beck, the group's founders and guiding spirits, constantly sought to destroy the falsity they perceived in commercial play production and to create a more immediate reality for the audience. This frequently manifested itself in Pirandellian productions which questioned not only the stage reality but the audience's own reality as well. With *The Connection* the Becks felt that they had finally destroyed the false illusion of the theatre.[23]

The characters in the play are supposed to be drug addicts, among them jazz musicians, who have been brought to the theatre to do some improvisations for a documentary film crew. They are to be paid in heroin and the characters are waiting for their "connection." The Living Theatre led the audience to believe that the performers were real junkies. (The musicians, although performing in the play, *were* real musicians.) When the supposed "author" of the play—actually another performer—introduced himself at the beginning of the performance he invariably got applause, indicating that theatrical illusionism was still functioning.[24] The performers were onstage when the audience entered, the "author" and "producer" came up from the back of the house, the two photographers were frequently in the aisles, and various characters would break out of their roles of the play-within-the-play and address the audience as "themselves." At intermission the performers could be found in the lobby talking to the spectators and asking for handouts. The character and situation matrices were so strongly created that the audience maintained its belief in the illusion even when the performers were separated from the stage. The entire theatre had become the environment for the performance.

Despite the success of that production, the Becks abandoned the style as being too deceitful because it tricked the audience into believing the performance to be something it was not. "Very early we were concerned with the problem of recognizing the presence of the audience," said Beck.

> Then we took it to the next level with Pirandello, Jack Gelber, William Carlos Williams—where you pretend that you're rehearsing a play or you pretend that this is the performance and something else is happening. And then we got a little distrustful about that because we kept talking all the time about being honest on the stage and we felt that you can't really lie to an audience that way. . . .[25]

The Living Theatre, like other groups at about the same time, began moving toward the idea of performance-as-performance. In this new approach, the environment was not used as a tool to bolster theatrical illusion; rather, the environment emphasized the fact that the performers shared the same reality as the audience. The performers were themselves and the stage was not some fictitious place but a stage in a theatre.

Although *The Brig*, the Living Theatre's final production before voluntary exile in 1963 established very definite boundaries between auditorium and stage (in many ways it was their most illusionistic proscenium-style production), true environmental elements began to occur in *Mysteries and Smaller Pieces* (1964), its first piece created in Europe. The play originally evolved as a sort of pastiche of improvisations and segments from earlier productions. *Mysteries* began with an adaptation of the cleaning sequence from *The Brig*, but now the performers entered the stage from the back of the auditorium, through the audience. While *The Brig* sequence was being mimed onstage, other performers recited John Harriman's "Dollar Poem" from scattered points throughout the house.[26]

Part 3 of *Mysteries* was entitled "Odiferie," and was adapted from a Happening of the same name by Nicola Cernovich.[27] In this section performers would move through the auditorium, among the spectators, with burning incense, thus suffusing the space with various odors. Near the end of the play certain performers supposedly suffering from the plague would "die" in the aisles. Their bodies would stiffen and other performers would carry them onto a body pile on the stage (Plate 87). Sometimes members of the audience would also join in the dying and if their bodies stiffened when lifted they, too, would be carried onto the stage. A similar ritual occurred in *Frankenstein* (1965) in which "victims," and at one point, the monster, would be chased through the aisles, captured, and "executed." In these cases the auditorium became an extension of the stage which enabled the action to surround the audience. The physical proximity of the dying actors to the audience was apparently more provocative than it might have been if it had merely occurred onstage. In some of the European performances of *Mysteries* Judith Malina as a corpse was kicked, tickled, poked and even had her hair set on fire in an attempt to get her to move; in Amsterdam members of the troupe were carried out of the theatre toward a canal.[28]

In the 1967 production of Brecht's *Antigone*, however, the auditorium became not merely an extension of the stage but another acting area and the audience implicitly became performers. Lights remained on the stage and house throughout. The stage represented Thebes and the auditorium Argos and the spectators thus became Argives.[29] Since the Thebans were at war with Argos the performers demonstrated a hostile attitude toward the audience.[30] Before the first lines of the play were spoken there was a mimed battle scene in which the Thebans descended into the auditorium and Eteocles and Polyneices were killed.[31] The two were carried back onto the stage in a procession through the aisles. Megaros remained in the auditorium throughout the performance. The performers entered the auditorium twice more during the play. In the fifth scene all the Thebans except Antigone, Creon, and the guard descended into the auditorium, their arms outstretched, chanting choral verses about hate and the ingenuity and monstrosity of man. And finally, at the death of Megaros, they moved through the house, echoing cries and a "rumbling, hollow sound." In the sense that the performers paraded and crawled through the aisles, *Antigone* was little different from *Frankenstein* or *Mysteries*. But because the Living Theatre treated the house as a place in essence no different from the stage, it became fully a part of the performance space—an implied environment.

Despite these forays into the auditorium, the Living Theatre was still operating with an essentially conventional scenography. There was always a frontal stage and no matter how the audience might be implicated, surrounded, or threatened they still remained an entity safe in their paid seats.

With *Paradise Now* (1968), however, the entire theatre became a found environment and was dealt with accordingly. Preconceptions about space and roles were challenged and destroyed as the Living Theatre strove to disrupt the physical as well as psychological complacency of the spectators. Performance occurred in the house and the audience was encouraged to come up on the stage. At the end, when any sense of boundary or delineation was sufficiently destroyed and the theatre had become a homogenized performing space, the audience was encouraged to continue the performance—of which they were now a part—into the street.

Paradise Now was composed of eight acts or "rungs" of three sections each. In the first sequence, "The Rite of Guerilla Theatre," members of the company circulated among the audience, confronting them with statements about the restrictions of society: "I am not allowed to travel without a passport"; "I am not allowed to take my clothes off."[32] This often provoked verbal and physical responses from the spectators, although the performers would never react directly to a spectator's response. During the third segment of the first run, entitled "New York City," it was intended that some of the audience would join the performers on the stage.[33] Accordingly, actors throughout the auditorium and onstage began to engage individual spectators in discussion. Rung II dealt mainly with concepts of non-violent change, and by the end of that rung there were generally many spectators on the stage engaged in discussions about relevant topics. No time limit was set for discussions.[34] By this point in the performance, it was obvious that standard notions of defined audience space and stage space did not apply. Both performers and spectators shared a common space. It was up to each to deal with that space in a way that would be comfortable—in other words, to negotiate with the environment. The length, shape, and style of the performance varied significantly with each audience and with each performance space.

The first sequence of Rung IV, "The Rite of Universal Intercourse," was the most notorious part of *Paradise Now*. The performers would lie on the floor of the stage and caress the persons nearest to them—frequently spectators, who often joined the pile on the floor. They then split up into couples. By now few spectators were left in their seats, some were naked, many were embracing. Conventional order had disappeared.[35] Audience participation continued in the "Paris" section of Rung V where a call for the non-violent destruction of current political systems often resulted in the burning of money. Finally, in Rung VIII, the spectators, who had supposedly been shown the way to "Paradise"—the Anarchistic society—were led to the doors of the theatre and formed a procession into the street—to extend the environment, as it were—with the exhortation: "Theatre is in the street. The street belongs to the people. Free the theatre. Free the street."[36]

Although the Living Theatre continued its repertoire through 1970, they then abandoned the confines of the conventional theatre for a cycle of 150 plays they called *The Legacy of Cain*. Most of these plays (perhaps twenty have been completed to date) are street theatre and "*The Legacy of Cain* is a street spectacle. It was conceived to take place in all different areas of an entire city over a period of two or three weeks."[37] Parts of this cycle have been created and performed in cities in Brazil and in Pittsburgh. In all cases the company has tried to use the topography of the city as well as its cultural characteristics to shape the performances. In Pittsburgh, for instance, plays were created to take place outside factory gates and capture the attention of workers leaving the plants. In a city in Brazil which was comprised of several streets leading to a central square they created a partially processional performance. The play performed there, *Visions, Rites and Transformations*, began with several simultaneous processions down different streets toward the square, a process which took about an hour and a half. Upon reaching the square the actual play was staged in a more-or-less arena fashion.[38] As in the medieval tradition, the production used the town as a performance environment. Most of the contemporary street performance which has not adopted the hit-and-run tactics of guerilla theatre tends to be at least partially processional—employing the form natural to the found environment of the street. Among the major street theatres of the sixties and seventies, the Bread and Puppet, the San Francisco Mime Troupe, and the Teatro Campesino all have bands, and in the best medieval tradition they generally parade through streets or parks prior to a performance to "drum up" an audience.

For the second Festival of Experimental Theatre at the University of Michigan in May 1975, the Living Theatre created a perambulatory performance entitled *Six Public Acts*.[39] Although the theme was purely political, the physical structure of the performance was that of a mumming. It was staged at six locations on the campus and in Ann Arbor, with processions between each site (Plate 88). Each location was chosen so as to be readily adaptable to an allegorical significance. Beginning at Waterman Gymnasium it moved to the lawn outside the Engineering Building ("House of Death"), the flagpole at the center of the campus ("House of State"), a local bank ("House of Money"), the University administration building ("House of Property"), the lawn outside the ROTC building ("House of War"), and concluded in the park around the Power Center ("House of Love"). Within scenes they employed their technique of engaging the audience in discussion and, at times, encouraged the spectators to join in certain actions. The spectators generally followed the processions between stations and there were elements of active performance during the processions. But once again, boundaries of spectator-performer space were constantly being destroyed and reshaped and the town and campus were used as a performance environment.

In the politically oriented performances of the Living Theatre, the Bread and Puppet Theatre, and others, the found environment is most often used because the street or other public place is seen as a more effective background for revolutionary themes than the inside of a theatre, and because the "found audience" of the street has different sensibilities from the one that pays for a good seat. But, as in the case of the *Domestic Resurrection Fair and Circus*, there are theatre artists working in experimental and avant-garde modes who turn to found environments for their esthetic qualities, their effect on the performers and performances themselves, and for the effect these environments might have on audience perceptions.

One of the more spectacular productions of this sort was Peter Brooks' *Orghast*, done with performers of the International Center for Theatre Research at the Festival of Shiraz in Iran in 1971. Although ideas for *Orghast* began to take shape months in advance, the final style and form of the piece was ultimately determined by the environment in which it was performed: the tomb of Artaxerxes II and Naqsh-i-Rustam on a mountainside at Persepolis.[40]

The selection of the site was partially accidental. Brook had seen the tombs at Persepolis and was intrigued with their dramatic potential. Although he wanted to do a performance for that space, the original plan was for a created environment. The designer, Jean Monod, proposed a huge steel-framed, open-topped movable box.[41] It was to be fifty feet high with cranes atop each corner for flying performers, props, and scenery. There was even provision for a train to run through. Inside, the audience would be seated on scaffold-like galleries which could detach from the walls and roll through the space.[42] But a combination of restrictions by the Iranian government and the practicalities and economics of such a set made it impractical. Instead, Brook began inspecting the site and conceiving ways to use its natural characteristics. He wanted to create a performance for that specific place. "As soon as we found three places of stone, simple surfaces against which movement can be dynamic and speech resonant," said Brook, "the idea of a specially built set became an excresence that just dropped away."[43] Creating a performance for that space would subject the performers to the particular influences of the environment.

> We aimed at every level to put ourselves as closely in tune with the place, to tune our work, as one tunes a musical instrument, with the very special, remarkable situation; remarkable practically, remarkable through its acoustics, and remarkable for all its extraordinary overtones.[44]

After exploring the mountainside, testing the acoustics and the light, Brook decided to do the piece in two parts, one to take place at dusk and the other at dawn, rather than perform it at night. This plan not only utilized the dramatic quality of the light at those two times, but meant that there was no need for an electric generator. In the final form three weak spotlights, as well as firelight in the first part, were used. The first part of the performance employed a relatively conventional arrangement of audience and stage. A platform was set up at the base of the tombs and the audience sat in three rows on two sides of the platform.[45] But the performers worked not only on the stage but on the cliffside and the top of the cliff as well. The second part of the performance—dawn at Naqsh-i-Rustam—took place in an open space at the base of the cliff in which are located the tombs of Darius II and Artaxerxes III. The space is about 80 by 300 yards.[46] Part of the found environment here included some scaffolding erected by archeologists around a temple and it was used by the performers. The spectators moved about the plain with the performers who descended from the cliff or came charging up behind the audience in a reenactment of the Persian defeat by the Greeks. At the conclusion a herdsman led a cow into the distance toward the rising sun. The spectators were thus fully incorporated into a performance space that extended to the horizon.

A year later Robert Wilson likewise performed a piece on a mountainside for the Festival of Shiraz. The piece, *KA MOUNTAIN AND GUARDenia TERRACE*, began at the base of Haft Tan Mountain and over a period of seven days (without interruption) proceeded to the top.[47] Cardboard cutouts, props, and set pieces were erected up the mountain side. These included bearded old men, Noah's Ark, flamingoes, a "suburb" of fifty cardboard houses (in which the actors performed), the Acropolis, and so on. The opening section, "Overture," at the base of the mountain used a proscenium-like stage but the rear of it had been left open so that spectators would have a view of the whole mountain (Plate 89). Although Wilson originally wanted to blow up the mountain top at the conclusion, he had to settle for burning an emblemetic Chinese pagoda.[48] Not only was there a perambulatory quality to Wilson's piece, but like *Orghast* it extended the viewing process over a great length of time so that the process of leaving the performance space, returning home, and then travelling back to a different or altered space became incorporated into the performance. Normally, performance is seen as occupying a small period of time in daily life. Rarely does performance surround daily life in time. If one fully accepts the incorporation of daily life into the performance then all space encountered and all activities of each individual spectator might be considered an aspect of the performance.

Perhaps the area of performance that consistently has made the most varied use of found environments is post-modern dance. Originally developed primarily by choreographers who came together in the Judson Dance Theatre in the early 1960s the movement was strongly influenced by the ideas of John Cage and by Happenings. The choreography thus reflects, among other things, ideas on the use of space found in Happenings (or at least a sense of freedom from preconceived notions of space). Despite characteristics which make post-modern dance a cohesive movement there has been no conscious or consistent body of theory among the various practitioners. In regard to space, for example, Ann Halprin grew frustrated with the spatial limitations of the stage, Trisha Brown wanted to expand visual boundaries, and Joan Jonas wanted to experiment with perceptions of space. What follows is a limited survey of some significant post-modern dances which use found space.

In the early 1960s Ann Halprin, director of the Dancers' Workshop of San Francisco, was creating pieces whose movements were often determined by tasks assigned to the dancers. In *Five-Legged Stool* (1961), for instance, tasks included crawling up a board which was leaning diagonally against a ceiling beam and then sliding down head first, moving forty wine bottles, changing clothes, and pouring water. It was in the process of developing this piece that Halprin grew frustrated with the imposed limitations of a stage. "Up until then," she stated,

> we had been content with using the space that we had. But I got discouraged with having to be up there in that relationship to an audience. I began to look at the lobby, the aisles, the ceilings, the floor. Suddenly I thought: "Who says we have to stay on that stage, this is a whole building."[49]

She began to explore the possibility of using the whole space of the theatre for performance. In its final form *Five-Legged Stool* was performed all around the spectators who were placed at the center of the space. Vertical as well as horizontal space was used and noise drifting in from the street was considered a valid part of the performance. Such an audience-performer relationship was unusual at the time and it resulted in a great deal of spectator disorientation which often manifested itself in hostile forms of audience participation: shoes were thrown at performers on occasion and there was almost always loud talking.[50] Halprin continued working with environments and some of her other pieces will be considered in the next chapter on created spaces.

Elaine Summers is another choreographer whose work falls midway on the continuum between found and created space. In February 1964 she did a piece called *Fantastic Gardens* in the sanctuary of Judson Memorial Church.

The audience was seated on chairs scattered throughout the space and sculptural objects were set among them. During the performance the audience was repositioned.[51]

Robert Morris, an artist and, for a time, a choreographer, created a somewhat similar piece called *Check* in October 1964 for the Moderna Museet in Stockholm. The piece as described by Morris

> had no central focus, climax, dramatic intensity, continuity or action . . . nor did it even demand continuous attention from an audience. In a room some 100 by 300 feet (the central gallery at the Moderna Museet, Stockholm) seven to eight hundred chairs were placed at random in the center area, leaving aisles around the perimeter. Various actions by individual performers occurred in these aisles. Forty other performers . . . "wandered" through the entire space; totally at random and as individuals.[52]

At one point in the performance the company of forty split into two groups and action occurred simultaneously at opposite sides of the space. Because of the arrangement of the 700 spectators, no action was ever visible to the entire audience. (Morris noted that a later performance of *Check* for a smaller audience in a smaller space "failed totally as the action did not have a chance to disappear."[53])

None of these performances, of course, occurs in a truly found space. In all of them the definition of the performing space is being expanded and the audience and performers are sharing the same total space. On the other hand, despite physical arrangements that facilitate multiple or random focus, there is control over spectator focus and, to a degree, spectator activity. The sharing of space is not a result of negotiation but of design. Furthermore, the arrangement of chairs in the Morris and Summers pieces (and the sculpture in the latter) creates a sense of environmental sculpture. The random arrangement of 800 chairs, for instance, alters the focus and perception of what would otherwise be a found environment even before the performance begins.

Joan Jonas, who does a great deal of outdoor performance, is an example of someone working in truly found environments. In her work she plays with the perception of space primarily through the use of physical distance—placing spectators as much as a quarter of a mile from the action and framing an action with natural features of the terrain. Writing about her work Jonas has said, "My own thinking and production has focused on issues of space—ways of dislocating it, attenuating it, flattening it, turning it inside out, always attempting to explore it without ever giving to myself or to others the permission to penetrate it.[54]

Her first outdoor piece was *Sound Delay* at New York's Jones Beach in 1970 and its intention was to study the effect of distance on perception.[55]

Performed on "a large mud flat with intermittent and surrounding dunes," the audience was placed a quarter of a mile down the beach.[56]

> A performer stood in the far space, one in the middle space, and a third next to the audience, clapping blocks of wood together repeatedly in-and-out of unison, making a sound that rippled across the quarter-mile expanse. In the far space, the act of hitting the blocks of wood was perceived before the sound was heard—distending the distance that separates the two perceptual fields of sight and sound. The gap between the visual and auditory image was narrowed as the sound was transmitted closer and closer to the audience. The effect of the piece was to measure the speed of sound through the air. As well, the work projected illusionism into the actual space scape. Distance flattens space, erases or alters sound, and modifies scale. Performers were given simple patterns to run: perpendicular and parallel to the audience and curvilinear and circular. Movements tend to become two-dimensional due to the illusion of the depth of field. As a way of pointing to the reduction of complex patterns to univocal effect of a signal, and as a way of cutting directly and immediately through the depth of the space, I sat behind the performers on top of a ladder holding a mirror through which I could reflect the sun's rays directly into the audience's eyes.[57]

A sequel to this was *Beach Piece II* in Nova Scotia in 1971.[58] The performers were located on a fairly narrow beach at the base of a cliff while the audience viewed the piece from above, looking between two slopes of the cliff that formed a "V" shaped frame around the performance (Plate 90).

Delay Delay (1971), performed on streets and vacant lots on the lower west side of Manhattan, used the same principles.[59] The audience was situated on the roof of a five-story building and the thirteen performers were scattered around the rubble-strewn landscape below. At least one performer was hidden from view at the beginning. The only addition to the found environment were placards bearing numbers indicating the distance in paces from the placard to the audience building. The greatest distance was 610 paces to a Hudson River pier. The only limits to the space, however, were the skyline and horizon. Jonas conceived of the space as a flat plane on which a moving drawing was superimposed and which, because of the distortion caused by distance, would be perceived as a film-like image.[60] Jonas noted that "people in the space are flattened and dream-like in that their movement is silent. One has the feeling of non-reality because the [kinetic] connection is lost over a distance, and they are self-contained; they do not relate to the audience."[61] The piece began with the clapping together of wood blocks at various distances. Other actions included identical movements by performers at different distances from the audience and the rolling of a performer placed inside a hoop down the street. All the actions related to the perception of space.

From one point of view, all of these pieces are little more than experiments in elementary physics. Jonas, however, has specifically chosen found environments with virtually unlimited visibility in which to perform. While the viewers are distinctly separated from the performers and are viewing in a frontal relationship to the piece, the performance space has no boundaries; it includes the audience. The spectators are asked to notice how their own space differs (or seems to differ) from space at varying distances from them.

Mention must be made here of Trisha Brown, whose *Roof Piece* (1971 and 1973) was similar in certain ways to Jonas' work.[62] For the first public performance of this work (June 1973) fifteen dancers were placed on rooftops over a nine block area of New York's Soho district. The audience was placed on two other roofs in the area (Plate 91). Brown noted that there was also a "found" audience of people who might look out a window and see part of the performance. The piece consisted of each performer in turn executing a series of movements which was then repeated by the nearest performer who in turn "sent" the movements on to the next performer and so on. Like Jonas, Brown was trying to eliminate the artificial constrictions of interior spaces and to deal with "real distance." "Distance in an interior space," she says,

> is stopped or held by the walls of the room or curtains of the stage unless through illusion the boundaries of the given area are transcended. The *Roof Piece* occupies real distance and the boundaries transcended are those of the viewers eye. It is understood, though not seen in its entirety, that the dance started some other place, passed by the audience, and ended up in still some other place.[63]

Brown has also used found environments in other works, although in a somewhat more incidental fashion. One of her so-called "Primary Accumulations" was performed on rafts on a lake in Minneapolis. *Man Walking Down the Side of a Building* (1969) used the facade of a seven-story building as the audience watched from a courtyard.[64] Unlike *Roof Piece*, however, the structure or organizing principle of these last two was more important than the use of environment.

It seems appropriate to conclude this chapter with a discussion of the work of Meredith Monk because her pieces, which fall somewhere between dance and theatre, often employ both found and created spaces in a single performance. She creates much of her work for "specific sites," that is, pre-existing spaces or environments.[65] As such, these performances, like Brook's *Orghast*, can exist only in that space. To recreate them elsewhere, if possible at all, changes the form.

The first of her specific-site pieces was *Blueprint* (1967). The audience was seated in front of a building and the performance was glimpsed through doors and windows. Three specific-site pieces were created in 1969. *Tour: Dedicated to Dinosaurs* occurred in the halls and rotunda of the Smithsonian Natural History Museum. *Tour 2: Barbershop* was performed in three galleries of the Chicago Museum of Contemporary Art. As of now she has produced five *Blueprints* and eight *Tours*. *Juice* took place at three consecutive sites: the ramps, galleries, and stairwells of the Guggenheim Museum; the Minor Latham Playhouse at Barnard College; and Monk's loft on lower Broadway. Each space was proportionately smaller. As the audience waited to enter the museum a woman rode back and forth outside on a white horse. Inside, the audience was placed at the center of the atrium and the performance took place all along the spiral ramp that ascends to the top of the museum. Near the end of the piece the performers formed tableaux in the niches and stairwells of the museum and the spectators wandered about observing them. On a given cue the performers ran down the ramp into the space formerly occupied by the audience.[66] Each succeeding section of the performance at the other sites seemed to be a reduction and fragmentation of the piece into its component parts. The second section occurred three weeks after the first and the third a week after that. As with *Orghast* and *Ka Mountain*, time and daily life were being incorporated into the performance.

Vessel (1971), like *Juice*, was performed at three sites, this time over the course of two days. The sites were her loft, the Performing Garage, and a parking lot down the street from the Garage. Both the loft and the parking lot are what Monk calls "reality space" since they provide a "grounding" or "counterpoint" to fantasy images.[67] They are, in other words, found environments with non-theatrical functions and associations. In both the loft and the parking lot there was a manipulation of audience. In the first part the audience was placed at one end of the loft looking, through a basically empty space about twenty feet long, at Monk's living room. Even though the performance was occurring in a found space, Monk framed it in such a way as to create the kind of physical and psychological distance associated with a proscenium. "The irony of the situation," she noted,

> is that this section of the performance, which could be the most personal since it's my own house, was actually the most remote. Instead of becoming the most intimate part of the piece, it's the least intimate because I'm putting a bracket around my living situation by making it so that you are looking into a real room, but from a great distance away.[68]

Like Jonas, Monk was playing with depth perception in the loft. Furthermore, focus was being controlled by lighting.

At the parking lot, where the third section occurred, the audience was placed on bleachers along one side of the lot. But while this was a frontal arrangement the action was strongly horizontal, necessitating a constant shifting of focus. Spectators also became aware of activity beyond the brick walls which surrounded the space and at first seemed to limit perception. A church, visible above the wall to the left of the audience, was lit up and action took place in front of it. "It's like expanding the environment," said Monk, "until you're aware of more and more and more in that parking lot. When you think you've got to the limits of the parking lot, the two brick walls, your eye moves across the street, expanding even more."[69] Just as Peter Brook wanted an environment whose characteristics would influence the performance, Monk chose the lot because she wanted an "outdoor space that had a specific New York ambience."[70]

The second part of *Vessel* took place in Schechner's *Performing Garage*, in the scaffolding environment constructed for the Performance Group's *Commune*, although Monk draped the towers with muslin to create a "handmade mountain." Here, although there was a created environment to work in, Monk set up a basically frontal performance space and, other than using the Garage's vertical space, did not attempt to use the environment as such.

Aside from the qualities of the three spaces, *Vessel* is environmental for its essentially perambulatory nature. Monk thought of the piece as an "epic." The audience was transported from the loft to the Garage by a bus. Monk considered having performers stationed along the route but decided that the found activity of New York Streets was more than sufficient.

> I called *Vessel* an epic because of the sense of journeying in the whole piece. Not only did I want the content of *Vessel* to be a journey, but the point of having the audience move from one place to another in one evening is that the audience is also on an epic. . . .[71]

Bringing up the epic should remind us that the use of found environments is not new; indeed it is probably the original form of theatre. From what little information survives, it is possible to picture the Greeks seeking out an appropriate space at the foot of a hillside, with a view of the sea framed in the background. There the spectators would come and sit from dawn to dusk over a period of several days. Considered in this light, Peter Brook, Joan Jonas, and Robert Wilson do not seem very far removed from the classical origins of the theatre.

9

Transformed Spaces

In the created environment the performance in some sense engineers the arrangement and behavior of the spectators . . . There is no bifurcation of space, no segregation of scenery . . . From the Bauhaus and men like Kiesler, the environmental theatre learned to reject conventional space and to seek in the event itself an organic and dynamic definition of space.

—*Richard Schechner*
"6 Axioms for Environmental Theatre"

Transformed space is simply a pre-existing space that has been altered scenically to create a unified theatrical environment for both the performer and the audience. Unlike created environments—the "total theatres" of Chapter 4—which are architectural structures, transformed environments shape and delimit space through the arrangement of decorative elements, stage areas, seating units, and so on, within an already existing area. Transformations tend to be relatively temporary and flexible, much as traditional stage settings are; they can be changed for each production, thereby altering not only physical arrangements but mood as well. While a transformed environment could conceivably be an outdoor space, most often it is an interior space: a loft, garage, storefront, and even, occasionally, a traditional theatre.

In surveying the use of transformed spaces in post-World War II performance, there seems to be a wave of influence that arises in Europe in the fifties, flows to the United States in the sixties, and returns to Europe in the seventies. This apparent chain of development is chronologically provable but actual influence, unfortunately, cannot be easily established. The directors of the various theatres discussed in this chapter acknowledge sources for their methods of actor training or performance style, but few will admit to any scenographic predecessors. Most claim that their particular use of space developed out of a confrontation with specific and unique problems.

Jerzy Grotowski, for instance, has been directing in Poland since 1956. He is well read and has travelled widely, and it might be expected, therefore, that he would be aware of the work of Tonecki and Syrkus in the thirties. But if this is the case he does not acknowledge it. Although he speaks of Meyerhold in relation to acting, he does not mention him in relation to scenography, nor does he mention Okhlopkov, to whom he is frequently compared.[1]

Grotowski and Ludwig Flaszen, a literary and theatre critic, founded the Polish Laboratory Theatre (known at first as the Theatre Laboratory 13 Rzedow) in Opole in 1959. Concerned primarily with methods of actor training, the Laboratory Theatre also explored the relationship of the performer to the spectator. It was this exploration that informed the scenographic aspects of the Laboratory's work. "If the particularity of the theatre resides in the actor-spectator relationship," wrote Grotowski in 1966,

> the role of scenic space is to modify this relationship in accordance with the structure of the play in hand. There is no need to build new theatres for this purpose: an empty hall in which the respective places of the actors and spectators are distributed afresh for each new play is amply sufficient.[2]

As will be seen, this simple tenet—to transform the space according to the needs of the play—is echoed by most subsequent environmental designers. "The essential concern," reiterated Grotowski, "is finding the proper spectator-actor relationship for each type of show and embodying the decision in physical arrangements."[3]

The experimentation with space was a result, in part, of Grotowski's reaction against the technology that he felt should be left to film and television. Film and television are two-dimensional media, but a unique aspect of theatre is the ability of the performers to speak directly to the audience and to occupy the whole space of the theatre.[4] By exploiting theatrical space in this manner, the immediacy of the event—the performance-as-performance—was emphasized. Grotowski noted that in such a situation "the action of the production takes place at the same time as that of the performance. The theatre is literally where it happens."[5]

In each of the eleven productions presented by the Laboratory Theatre since 1959, most of them designed by Jerzy Gurawski, the spectators have become passive participants. They have never participated directly in the stage action (except in *Forefather's Eve*), nor were they always included physically within the set, although they have always been implicated in some way in the action of the play. In *Cain* (1960), for instance, the spectators were treated as Cain's descendants.[6] In the words of Grotowski's disciple, Eugenio Barba, the spectator/ancestors "are present but remote and difficult to approach."[7] The staging of this early production was primarily frontal but performers at times moved off the stage, down the central aisle of the auditorium and into the audience (Plate 92). At certain points the performers even spoke to the audience. They did so not as characters but as themselves.[8] This marked the beginnings of the style for which Grotowski later became famous.

In *Shakuntala* (1960) the spectators were supposed to represent a crowd of monks and courtiers.[9] The staging was reminiscent of Okhlopkov: a platform stage spanned the width of the theatre at the center and action also occurred in a central aisle along the length of the theatre, as well as behind the spectators at each end (Plate 92).

For Mickiewicz's *Forefather's Eve* (1961) the spectators were seated on chairs scattered throughout the entire space of the theatre (Plate 92); this gave the impression of random or haphazard design but was, in fact, carefully arranged. The play was

> treated as a ritual drama. The audience is a collective group participating in the action. Spectators and actors are scattered through the whole room. The actors speak to everyone who is there. They treat the audience as fellow actors and even invite them to become active participants.[10]

The spectators were asked to participate in the harvest ritual; they became the chorus and an actor became the chorus leader.[11]

Slowacki's *Kordian* (1962) was set in an insane asylum and, again, spectators were scattered throughout the entire space, this time an environment made up of institutional beds representing a mental ward. Spectators could sit on chairs set at various places or on the beds themselves with the performers.[12] For Wyspianski's *Akropolis* (1962, 64, 67) Gurawski and Josef Szajna created an environment of wire and stovepipes to represent the concentration camp at Auschwitz (Plate 93). In this case the performers, who represented the dead, ignored the spectators, who were the living.[13] The performance began in a more or less arena set-up with most of the pipes and the few simple props piled in the center. But the "architecture of the action," in Grotowski's words, spread outward, engulfing the audience and subjecting them to "a sense of the pressure and congestion and limitation of space."[14] Elsewhere, Grotowski has described this expanding environment: "At the start, the room was empty (except for the pile of pipes) and there was a seating arrangement for the audience. By the end of the production the entire room was filled, oppressed by the metal."[15]

With the production of Marlowe's *Doctor Faustus* the group returned to a more direct incorporation of the spectators into the performance. The setting consisted of two long wooden tables running the length of the room and a smaller table at one end. The audience was limited to the number that could be seated at the long tables and they thus became Faustus' guests. He greets them and asks them to be seated as he sits at the head table "like the prior in a refectory. The feeling is that of a medieval monastery."[16] Some actors were also seated at the tables and action occurred on top of the tables as well. By this inclusion of the audience claimed Grotowski, "the dramatic function of the spectators and the function of spectator as spectator were the same."[17]

In 1968 Grotowski commented: "I am always ready to be a traitor to an absolute rule. It is not essential that actors and spectators be mixed. The important thing is that the relation between the actors and the spectators in space be a significant one."[18] *The Constant Prince* (1965, 68), for example, located the spectators in a true arena arrangement—surrounding the action—although they were forced to view the performance by standing on benches and looking over a wooden partition like voyeurs or, as Grotowski put it, "as medical students observe an operation."[19] By the time of the production of *Apocalypsis Cum Figuris* (1968) even this degree of participation no longer existed. The audience of thirty sat on benches around the edge of the space.

Unlike his predecessors such as Tonecki or Okhlopkov, who seemed to have little immediate impact on design, Grotowski has been a major scenographic force since his work became known in the mid-sixties. Even today, most directors or scenographers working environmentally either acknowledge Grotowski's influence or else feel compelled to deny similarities.[20]

Grotowski's major disciple was undoubtedly Eugenio Barba. An Italian actor and director, Barba spent three years as Grotowski's assistant at Opole and then went to Denmark where he founded the Odin Teatret at Holstebro in 1964. While all of his work shows the influence of the Polish Lab Theatre, two of Barba's productions in particular, *Kaspariana* (1967) and *Feraï* (1969), demonstrate singularly Grotowski-like staging techniques.

Barba employed an arena-style setting for *Kaspariana*. Approximately eighty seats were arranged in double rows around a central playing space, leaving about a three-foot aisle around the outside. The room was completely black.[21] Six raked, white lattice-work benches were placed symmetrically between sections of seats, radiating out from the central space like the points of a star (Plate 94). These platforms were about two feet wide and two feet high at their apex. A rectangular black box was placed in the center of the space. These benches were referred to as "mansions," thus emphasizing a certain medieval quality to the staging.[22] Action could occur in the arena, on the benches (which were occasionally stood on end) and around and behind the spectators. Thus, despite the arena set-up, the spectators were placed virtually in the center of the performance. Barba, like Grotowski, intended, however, that they remain passive. In this case, he felt that the spectators would acquire the anonymity of people in a city—surrounded but ignored.[23]

The environment for *Feraï* was even simpler. Two rows of spectators faced each other along the length of the theatre (Plate 95); action occurred between them and around them. One critic described the configuration of the action as two concentric ellipses—one between the rows and one encompassing the rows, with major actions occurring at the foci, i.e., at either end.[24] For this production the audience was treated somewhat more directly. During the course of the play, which combines Euripides' *Alcestis* with Scandinavian mythology, the King and Queen asked the spectators for help. The chorus, on the other hand, treated the audience as if it were dead and hid behind it.[25] A 1972 production, *House of the Father*, based on stories by Dostoevski, used a similar arena-environmental setting (Plate 96).

More recently, Barba and the Odin Teatret have been in the countryside of southern Italy working in isolation and sometimes performing in small towns. Their performances have frequently been in found spaces, often in market squares or fields, and parades through the towns have become an integral feature of their work.[26] Interestingly, some of Grotowski's recent work—his so-called paratheatrical experiments—have also been in found spaces.[27] The Living Theatre has also recently (since 1979) been creating processional performances in small Italian towns.

Jacques Polieri has been directing and designing since the fifties, apparently quite independently of his contemporaries. Aside from his previously discussed created environments, such as the Total Movement Theatre, Polieri has presented several transformed-space productions as well as turning out a fairly large body of theory and proposals. In a 1959 essay entitled "Systematization of Scenographic Space," he worked out, with mathematical precision, all the possible arrangements of performer-spectator relationships in a rectangular, circular, cubic, and spherical theatre.[28] In the first two this includes, of course, frontal, alley (stage between two sections of seating), thrust, and arena staging, as well as the environmental modes: annular and scatter staging (the latter having two possibilities—the audience occupying the greater area or the performance occupying the greater area). The cubic and spherical theatres, aside from containing these possibilities, lead to total environments through the use of vertical space: performance above and/or below the spectators, spectators on a central shaft viewing a performance on the interior surface of the cube or sphere, and vice versa. Thus, by 1959, all the possibilities had been stated for anyone who cared to employ them.

Polieri's own progression toward environmental work can probably be dated from 1954 and his production of *March of the Jugglers*, which combined film and projections with live action. Although this in itself was not environmental, it was a short jump from this to placing projection screens around the spectators. This was done in 1959 at the Théâtre de l'Alliance Française in Paris with his production of Mallarmé's *Cast of the Dice*. Elements of decor were likewise placed in the auditorium. In a 1964 interview he described this use of space:

> I began to use the diagonal points of the theatre, that is, the auditorium and the stage at the same time—by projecting images and film clips, diffusing sound, and by adding actors and plastic elements to these to form the action—these diagonal points of the theatre were joined together by unforseen relationships creating a kind of scenic axiometrics . . . It was a mobile theatre without mobility.
>
> When I presented *Cast of the Dice* by Mallarmé, to better represent the typographic pagination of the poem, I put my actors and lights onstage and in the house at the same time, creating a type of stereophonic and "polyvisual" action that was very faithful to the idea Mallarmé stated in his preface. The production was nearly identical for *Mobile* by Michel Butor, that I presented at the Teatro Reale in Liegi, except that the very different subject also called for the projection of film in cinemascope and multiple projections throughout the entire hall.[29]

Scale of 7 was first presented at the Théâtre Gérard Philipe in 1964 and again in 1967 at the Salle du Rond-Point des Champs-Elysées. Polieri referred to it as a "ballet-play," and it combined closed circuit televison images with fourteen live performers who executed relatively abstract gestures and sounds in a multi-stage environment.[30]

The 1964 version utilized three primary stages: one "Italian" or traditional stage (10 meters by 9 meters by 8 meters high) in front of the audience, and two rectangular stages (4 meters by 14 meters by 1.10 meters high) on either side of the audience (Plate 97). There were also five other stages or areas constructed of glass and metal tubing: one on each lateral stage at stage level near the front, two raised platforms (3 meters by 3 meters by 4 meters high)—one on each lateral stage at the rear—and one large scaffold-like stage (4 meters by 11 meters by 10 meters high) jutting out over the auditorium above the Italian stage. At the rear of the audience was a platform for television cameras. A huge television screen hung over the front stage above the scaffold (in the 1967 production this screen was placed behind the house-left lateral stage). The glass platforms allowed spectators to view the performers from beneath. "The general structure of the action," said Polieri, "commands the gestual signs, which progress from simple to multiple spatial perspective and finally attain the three-dimensional: a sort of conquest of space."[31]

In 1967 Polieri also presented *The Book of Mallarmé* at the Salle du Rond Point using the same basic environment. The intention was to achieve spatially certain concepts set forth by the French writer Mallarmé.[32] The auditorium was divided into quarters, with the audience on two raked seating platforms in opposite corners facing center. The two other quarters contained two stages each—one at floor level and the other raised as in *Scale of 7*. Actors circulated on all sides of the audience (Plates 98 and 99). "Faithful to the spirit of The Book," explained Polieri, "the scenographic principle adopted establishes maximum fluidity. Circulation of actors, lighting, and the counterpoint of television projection constitute the mobile elements of the staging."[33]

One other Polieri production that merits attention is *L'Oeil-Oiseau* presented at the Foundation Maeght in 1968 in conjunction with Joan Miró, Joseph Lazzini, Jacques Dupin, and Patrice Mestral.[34] Aside from the collaboration of important artists, it was significant for its combination of found and transformed space and perambulatory performance. For this three-part production, stages, seating platforms, and decorative elements were set up in the gardens and courtyards of the Foundation (Plate 100). Polieri had originally conceived of the three parts occurring simultaneously, but they were performed sequentially. Part 1, the "Garden," was performed on the entrance lawn of the Foundation. There were three asymmetrically shaped seating "shells"—more or less fan-shaped galleries that facilitated a multi-focus view for the audience—three oval stages, and various sculptures by the contributing artists (Plate 101). Action occurred not only on the stages but around the seating areas as well.

Part 2, the "Labyrinthe," was presented in a section of the Foundation's garden consisting of winding paths and stairways that had been decorated by Miró with frescoes and sculptures. Spectators stood along the undulating walls and followed the action from point to point, moving with it. There were four "stages" in the Labyrinthe. The Labyrinthe led to the Giacometti Courtyard where there were two large oval seating platforms, two smaller oval stages, and two platform stages at either end of the courtyard. Roofs and terraces around the courtyard were used for performances as well (Plate 102). For the mixed-media effects incorporated in the performance there were twenty-one loudspeakers and twenty-nine screens and projectors. Despite such novel productions, Polieri has received little attention in the United States and consequently has had little, if any influence.

Another little known group is the Victory of February Theatre in Hradec Králové, Czechoslovakia. Since 1958 this group has experimented with alterations of the performer-spectator relationship with an attempt to counter the illusionism of the theatre.[35] Early experiments led to the alteration of their theatre from proscenium to arena and thrust arrangements. But beginning in the early sixties, through 1967, more environmental techniques were used. A modern Czech drama, *Zpěněný kůň* combined overhead projection screens with a central revolving platform. At times house lights were turned on and the audience was engaged in discussions. *Romeo and Juliet* was staged on five oval stages placed throughout the auditorium. In this arrangement, the balcony scene was staged on two separate platforms.[36] Scatter staging has been used on several occasions. Perhaps what appealed most to the Victory of February Theatre was the awareness spectators had of each other in these configurations and the resultant change in their perceptions of the performance. Director Milan Pásek felt that the spectator would realize that "he himself is part of the scenic picture ... Questions on the necessity of the actor's veracity of performance are posed anew ... The spectator feels qualitatively different emotions, the theatre suddenly changes into a law court."[37]

Tadeusz Kantor is a Polish designer and director who has been working in theatre since 1945. Since 1955 he has worked with the experimental Cricot 2 Theatre of Cracow and is closely associated with the plays of Witkiewicz. In his early designs he wanted the stage to represent the "inner space" of a character's mind—"Not architectonic. Not concrete. But a space that could contain the ideas, the thoughts, the spiritual conflicts, the psychic tensions and an interior model of the drama."[38] Since his 1958 production of Witkiewicz's *In A Small Country House*, Kantor has been creating what he calls "abstract theatre" (which is not necessarily environmental).[39] In 1965 he produced his first Happening and his theatrical performances since then have tended to resemble Happenings more than conventional plays. Kantor has defined a Happening as "a situating of a work of art in the realities of life" and many of his Happenings have occurred in found environments.[40] The *Sea Happening* and *The Raft of The Medusa*, for instance, both occurred on beaches, while many of his early performances took place in cafes.

His production of Witkiewicz's *Water Hen* in 1967 was directly influenced by his work in Happenings.[41] The audience sat about on boxes, planks, mattresses and on the floor. The impression was of a chaotic arrangement, but it was carefully laid out to allow the movement of performers throughout the space, although most activity occurred in a central area (Plate 103).[42] Kantor presented Witkiewicz's *Lovelies and Dowdies* at the 1973 Edinburgh Festival and it was fairly typical of his approach.[43] Some of the spectators were asked to hand over their outer garments, others were given signs on poles which they were asked to hold. The first row of spectators was wrapped in canvas. Audience members who had volunteered to participate prior to the show were placed together in one section of seats and did take part in the performance.

While Kantor's sets are frequently striking, he tends to be more of an eclectic than an innovator—absorbing much new theatre but influencing it little, at least in the treatment of space.

Whether as a result of the work of these performers and directors or the sense of general scenographic freedom introduced by Happenings, or through sheer coincidence, more and more environmental productions appeared during the mid-sixties. In 1965, for instance, the Dramatiska Teatern of Stockholm presented an environmental *Marat/Sade*. Unlike the famous Peter Brook production which merely acknowledged and implicated the audience, this production, designed by Gunilla Palmstierna-Weiss, literally surrounded the spectators. The decor extended from the stage around the auditorium.[44] Another proto-environmental work was a production of Arrabal's *Automobile Graveyard*, presented in 1966 by Joseph Dunn and the 2 Bleecker Street Workshop in a New York City loft. Though not, strictly speaking, an environmental production—the audience was seated against the walls around the perimeter of the space—the design gave the impression of a total environment and was one of the first such designs, other than Happenings, to be seen in New York. A sculpture of automobile parts filled the central space and flashing lights intermittently brightened the dark space as spectators entered one by one.[45] It was not unlike entering a Kaprow environment.

In the same year the Argentinian director Victor Garcia staged a montage of four Arrabal plays in Paris (where he had been living since 1961) under the general title *Automobile Graveyard*, which was one of the four. The three other plays were *Oration*, *The Two Executioners*, and *The Solemn Communion*.[46] During the preparation for the production at a festival at Dijon he happened upon a hangar housing the International Gastronomic Fair. Large storage tanks hanging from the ceiling seemed to delineate areas and create spaces in the vast hangar and it was this image that shaped the scenography of his production.[47] In the theatre space, automobile "carcasses" hung from the ceiling over the performance area (Plate 104) which was divided into six "zones" placed among and around the spectators. "I was not trying to make the public participate, as in a Happening," claimed Garcia, "but I wanted to further integrate them into the action."[48]

Zone 1 was a central platform, a sort of thrust stage; Zone 2 was a ramp from backstage to Zone 1 which provided access for a car in *The Two Executioners* section. Partially surrounding these platforms on three sides were sections of swivel chairs for the audience. Zones 3, 4, and 5 were essentially a series of ascending ramps behind the swivel chairs with fixed audience seating between the walls and Zones 3 and 4. The musicians were placed in Zone 4. Zone 6, to one side of the central stage,was a steeply raked platform. This plan was more or less recreated for a production at the Théâtre des Arts in Paris in 1968.

In December, 1969, Garcia directed a production of Genet's *The Balcony* in São Paulo, Brazil, in a vertical, cone-shaped environment created by Wladimir Pereira Cardosa.[49] Cardosa, who claims to have been influenced by the ideas of Walter Gropius, ripped out part of the interior of the Ruth Escobar Theatre to build an eighty-foot cone of metal scaffolding.[50] The audience of about 250 sat on platforms that encircled the central shaft at five levels (Plate 105). The main action occurred on elevator platforms of metal and clear acrylic along the shaftway, as well as on spiral ramps, platforms, and cages of metal grill-work which were lowered into the shaft by cranes.

The interior of the same theatre was gutted again in 1972 to create a multi-level environment for a production called *The Voyage*.[51] The play was based on a sixteenth-century allegorical epic poem about the voyage of Vasco da Gama. The setting, designed by Helio Eichbauer, established four ascending levels through which the audience followed the performers. It began in the theatre basement, decorated to represent the Middle Ages, and ascended through the sea and the ship, the African coast, and Olympus (Plate 106). On the first level the audience was surrounded by the action, but the viewing in the other levels was frontal.

Most environmental Post-Modern Dance, as already noted, has employed found spaces; Ann Halprin, however, has been one of the few choreographers to work in transformed environments as well. *Exposizione*, created for the 1964 Venice Biennale, involved carrying assorted objects through the aisles of the Venice Opera House, onto the stage, and up a huge cargo net strung across the proscenium. A nine-year-old girl swung over the heads of the audience on a rope. The only part of the space that was actually transformed was the proscenium itself. The use of the cargo net was an attempt to employ the vertical space of the vast stage. "That dance evolved out of a spacial idea, an environmental idea," said Halprin. "We said our theatre was our environment and we were going to move through the theatre."[52]

Later that year Halprin's workshop presented *A Series of Compositions for an Audience*, several events exploring audience-performer relationships, primarily the power an audience has in a performance. In one of the events a sculptor, Chuck Ross, carried through the audience objects, including weather balloons, which seemed to surround and engulf the spectators. According to Halprin, "The whole place was full of sound, action, and props. When we did it outdoors in Fresno it was like a gigantic three-ring circus . . . But when we did it in a closed arena, it was always terrifying."[53]

By now it is clear that the work of Richard Schechner has not been especially innovative; however, his significance lies in the creation of a body of general theory and criticism. By giving a disparate collection of theatre work a focus (and a name) he turned it into a "movement" and was responsible, more than anyone else, for the dissemination of information that would influence and inform much of the scenography of the late sixties and seventies. The work of The Performance Group (founded in 1967) is generally taken as the primary example of contemporary environmental theatre.

Schechner is an eclectic and readily admits the influence of Kaprow, Cage, and Grotowski, noting, for example, that the term "environmental theatre" was taken from Kaprow's discussion of environments.[54] He is also one of the few to acknowledge the important work of Kiesler.[55] As early as 1960 Schechner had thoughts about incorporating the spectator into the world of the play and of using the vertical space of the theatre.[56] It was not until 1966, however, with a Happening entitled *4/66* that he actually worked in a transformed space. *4/66* was staged by The New Orleans Group in an open, L-shaped loft about forty feet square.[57] Chairs for spectators were arranged in varying configurations, but as the piece progressed these arrangements changed and disappeared.[58] Schechner claimed that this "was the first time I had ever asked a spectator to do anything in the theatre except buy a ticket, sit still, laugh in the middle, and applaud at the end."[59]

Employing many of the concepts and techniques learned in that Happening, the Group next staged an environmental version of Ionesco's *Victims of Duty*.[60] Many of the practical examples which support Schechner's "6 Axioms" come from this production. Jerry Rojo, one of the designers of *Victims* and the principal designer of most of Schechner's work, has stated that the scenography of Happenings was an early influence on much of his own work.[61] In this production Choubert's living room and dining room ranged over the entire performance space—a large open room of Le Petit Théâtre du Vieux Carré in New Orleans. The lobby and the outside of the theatre were incorporated as well (Plate 107). The original space had a small proscenium stage at one end. As Schechner describes it:

> We built the room up with a series of platforms so that the stage disappeared as a separate part of the space. On the former stage was a TV set (with a closed-circuit system), stairways that led to a blank wall, and a table and couch and cupboards filled with hundreds of cups. In the main space (where the audience would be for a proscenium show) was a dining table, an easy chair and a lamp, and many risers. These risers filled the space making a terrain which we covered with rugs. To one side was a spiral tower of chairs . . . On the other side a pair of large doors opened directly onto the street. At the back was the door leading to the lobby which had a complicated display including film, tape recordings, collage, and hangings . . . All over the walls were slogans and graffiti . . .

There is a scene where Choubert goes up a stairway and disappears. You hear him running in a room above—and he is actually over the audience in the room above. There is a scene where he goes to the bottom of the ocean: he dives underneath the platforms (there were lots of trapdoors in the platforms), and he emerges first in one place and then another—dislodging spectators as he pushes up the traps.[62]

The audience had the option of sitting anywhere in the space; not all spectators could see or hear the entire performance. There were even scenes in which performers would whisper to individual spectators (a device repeated in *Dionysus In 69*). "We found that the audience would crowd in during the intense scenes and move away when the action became broad or violent," said Schechner; "they usually gave way willingly to the performers and reoccupied areas after the action had passed by."[63] Most of the elements found in *Victims*—the surrounding decor, mobile audience, shared space, multiple and random focus, private spaces—are typical of Schechner's style of environmental theatre and occur in varying degrees in his later work with The Performance Group in New York. The major characteristics are dealt with in some detail in his "6 Axioms."

Schechner's theory of environmental theatre is not entirely a physical or scenographic one, although it is founded on a basic design concept:

> I call the theatre environmental theatre because its first scenic principle is *to create and use whole spaces*—literally spheres of spaces—which contain, or envelop, or reach out into all the areas where the audience is or the performers move. *All the spaces* in the theatre are actively involved in all aspects *of the performance.*[64]

Aside from this one tenet, however, his criteria are more involved with the creative process than the setting itself. "When you talk about environmentalism," he says,

> you talk about an ongoing process among the performers, in other words, the creation of an ensemble or a group, and also an ongoing fragmented process between the performers as a group and the spectators as a group. So it is not a question of space only, but the sharing of the space—how the space is shared. A proscenium could be highly environmentalized if the lights in the house were on.[65]

In Schechner's broad definition the distinction between environmental and ensemble theatre fades and a group like The Open Theatre becomes environmental because of its working process.[66]

The creation of an environment is one of the more significant aspects of The Performance Group's work. Their environments are generally the end result of a process of "negotiation" in which, according to Schechner, the performers are "the chief designers."[67] "Articulating a space," he says, "means letting the space have *its* say. That is, looking at a space, and exploring it, not as a means of doing what you want to do in it, but of doing what the space encourages you to do in it."[68] The environment of *Dionysus In 69*, the first production of The Performance Group, for example, evolved in part in that manner. The two dominant towers evolved from a design suggested by Michael Kirby, and Schechner had a vague concept of a place of warmth that would give a womb-like feeling. But the actual environment built by Rojo grew out of the process of transforming the recently acquired Garage into a performing space (Plate 108).

> Here was no mere set construction or even the building of an environment within an already articulated space. Rather, we found a space, made it ours through work and slowly squeezed out the *Dionysus* environment by our labor. There is no better way to know a ceiling than to paint it, or feel a floor than to scrub it.[69]

The environment for Sam Shepard's *The Tooth of Crime* (1973)—an asymmetrical bridge of modular units and platforms in the center of the space—was achieved through a relatively conventional design process, but its relationship to the audience was a result of chance or negotiation (Plate 109).[70] The original idea was to have the audience clustered around the set peering into the "house" through cut-out windows. In early performances at the University of British Columbia, however, the audience, which wanted a better view, began moving about.[71] This idea of moving from point to point was kept when the Group returned to New York. Mobile spectators, of course, were not new to The Performance Group. The audience had been encouraged to move in *Dionysus* and were told they could follow the action in *Makbeth* (1969), provided they did not disrupt it. Even in the more recent *Marilyn Project* (1975), an ostensibly arena-style production, the audience was encouraged to move about the edges of the space.

In the Rojo-designed sets, at least, the relationship of the audience to the performance space is determined largely by the nature of the play. "One should try to find a spatial metaphor for the play itself," claims Rojo, unconsciously echoing Grotowski.[72] Thus, in *Makbeth*, a play about manipulation, the audience space was carefully manipulated, while in *The Tooth of Crime* the spectators were made to compete for space. In almost all of the Group's productions, however, the spectators have a choice of seating that will allow them varying degrees of physical involvement—whether to be in the midst of the action or placed on some high perch observing the whole scene.

Part of Schechner's approach to design and direction is an awareness of vertical space. This entails, on the one hand, the use of towers, scaffolding, and bridges to place the performers and spectators on several levels, and also directing scenes to be viewed from above such as the duel in *Tooth* or the murder in *Commune*.[73]

Because of Schechner's eclecticism, it is not surprising that his work frequently seems to recapitulate the environmental work of many other groups (the taking of *Dionysus* into the streets à la *Paradise Now*, and the *Doctor Faustus*-like banquet in *Makbeth* spring to mind) but Schechner takes from the popular tradition as well. The *Makbeth* audience had to negotiate a dark, carnival maze designed by Brooks McNamara on the second floor of the theatre in order to descend into the bright, first-floor performance space. The maze used mirrors, dim lights, and a collage of materials referring to both the present and past productions of *Macbeth*. McNamara, a historian of popular entertainments, based his design on Mme. Tussaud's Chamber of Horrors and a typical amusement park hall of mirrors.[74]

Writing in 1971, Schechner proposed "Six Principles of Environmental Design" which, although less well known than his "6 Axioms," are more succinct and cogent from the standpoint of physical theatre:

1. For each production the whole space is designed. This includes performing space, audience space, technical space. To begin his design the environmentalist asks first of all what the orientations of the space fields are. There is no presumption of rectangularity or single focus, or of a static audience.

2. The human body is the source of the environment. Space can be designed from the primal cavity or other body spaces. The environment must maintain a scale consistent with the human body.

3. All space senses are to be included in planning an environment. Separate space maps must be drawn for visual, acoustic, olfactory, tactile, thermal, and tasting senses. Questions concerning these spaces must be put as precisely as those asked about stress, weight, volume, and safety.

4. All parts of the environment are functional. This is not only a safety matter but a prime element of environmental theory—environmental design is actively anti-illusionistic.

5. The performer is the touchstone of all designs. His work reveals to the environmentalist what the design is about, and how it can be organized. Performers are included at all phases of design and construction, even if this means more over-all time spent. As workshops and rehearsals continue, the performer explores and articulates the various space fields and space senses. He is the one who determines if the space is to be sharp or soft, easy to move through or difficult, etc. The environment, like the rest of the production, is collective.

6. The space evolves with the play it embodies. Just as there is no pre-existent play to be "realized" so there is no pre-existent design to be built. At each phase of design and construction changes may occur. The environment is not finished when the play opens. The line between rehearsal and performance dissolves, as does the line between an unfinished and finished environment. Safety must obtain at all phases of development. The environment is a process.[75]

Since about 1970, more and more environmental sets have been appearing off and off-off-Broadway, in regional theatre, and even on

Broadway itself. Jerry Rojo has done many designs outside The Performance Group, creating, among others, environments for the Manhattan
Project's *Endgame* (1973)—a hexagonal audience environment surrounding
a performing arena (Plate 110)—and The Shaliko Company's *Ghosts* (1975)
at the New York Public Theatre in which the audience occupied "rooms"
and niches of a Victorian environment.[76]

Eugene Lee was the resident designer of the Trinity Square Repertory
Company in Providence, Rhode Island, from 1967 to 1970, a period when
that group felt a need to experiment with audience-performer relationships.
"We got very frustrated with the proscenium set up," explained Lee, "and we
started extending out further and further, wrapping around the side wall,
putting holes in the ceiling, and hanging things."[77] Lee feels that he must
have been influenced by seeing Grotowski's work at the 1968 Edinburgh
Festival.[78] In 1969 Lee designed Le Roi Jones' *Slaveship* for the Chelsea
Theatre Center at the Brooklyn Academy of Music. The raked seating area
of the theatre was platformed over to create a level playing space. Five
platforms of varying heights were erected around the edge of the space while
a two-level platform and runway in the center of the space represented the
slave ship itself. The audience sat on wooden benches around this section so
that action could surround them and come from several different points in
the room (Plate 111). Appropriate sounds and smells permeated the space.
In 1973 Eugene Lee designed a scattered-stage setting for the Chelsea
Theatre Center's revival of *Candide*. The production moved to Broadway in
1974 thus becoming the first environmental design in the modern commercial theatre.

In Milan, in the summer of 1969, Italian director Luca Ronconi created
an environmental spectacle called *Orlando Furioso*. Based on the sixteenth-
century story by Ludovico Ariosto, the production consciously combined
the ideas of Schechner with medieval staging.[79] Until this time most
environmental productions had been relatively static, the audiences seden-
tary. Processional and perambulatory performances, and the like, and even
Schechner's mobile productions, moved with sufficient slowness so that
spectators had no trouble following. But with *Orlando*, designed by Uberto
Bertacca, audiences were literally plunged into the midst of battle and had to
learn to move rapidly or run the risk of injury from moving scenery.
Reviewing the New York production, done in an inflated bubble structure in
Bryant Park, John Lahr noted that "theatre becomes sport. The audience,
themselves transformed into a new community of seekers, rushes to meet the
action wherever the stories unfold around them. They learn quickly how to
dodge the dangerous 20-foot steel horses caroming around the floor."[80]

The production was designed for a space with a minimum floor area of 120 by 45 feet. This was to be a neutral space in which the spectators could stand, with a proscenium stage at either end.[81] Action that did not occur on these stages took place on rolling platforms or floats (and at least one "flying horse" mounted on a crane-like construction) that were pushed, often at great speed, by performers through the spectator-filled space. Simultaneous scenes added to the general disorientation. "The Siege of Paris," which was "the most perilous for the audience," provides a sense of the production:

> The curtains of the two stages rise at the same time. On one of them is Charlemagne's fortress, symbolized by a wooden tower with small turrets, the king at the top. On the second stage the legions of the enemy army, armed with long wooden lances, ride on horseback, each horse on its own float. Charlemagne's tower is moved to one side of the stage area; the three groups of enemy knights fan out in front of it, touch the city-tower with their lances and make it revolve. Next is the attack by Rodomonte, who leaps from his horse onto the fortress next to Charlemagne. The battle is finally decided by Rinaldo and his band of English knights who arrive to liberate the city. At this point the audience is pushed to the edges of the stage area, while in the center performers abandon their floats and the battle develops on the level of the audience. Barefoot actors play the rout of the Moors. At the end the space is strewn with dead soldiers, piously attended by the others.[82]

This was truly a shared space in Schechner's sense. Other than the two proscenium stages, there was no distinction between performer and spectator space, a concept which was emphasized in the program notes.[83] As with Schechner's production, the spectators could place themselves in the center of the action and even participate—some spectators helped push the floats at times—or they could remain as passive observers around the edges. No one could see or hear everything. Aside from the use of simultaneity, the fact that the audience was standing on a level surface precluded a clear view across the space. Performers in the more intimate scenes often spoke softly and used small gestures.[84]

At the conclusion of the performance much of the audience was engulfed in a labyrinth (Plate 112):

> As Orlando's floats move away, a double complex of plywood and gauze cages moves from the two ends of the stage area along the ground toward the center of the space and joins together, forming a single labyrinth that occupies almost all of the stage area, shutting in part of the audience with the actors. In each of the open cages, in which the audience can walk around, are the principal actors of the spectacle (and of the poem) who recite monologues and reenact their deeds. Meanwhile, on the four sides of the stage area, in four niches, four novellas are recited . . . Each is recited by five or six actors, who are practically on top of each other since the space is so small. More than ten actions are going on at once. At this point the language is most explosive and Babel-like, and the dialogue between actors and audience most complete. Astolfo rises on the hippogriff over the stage area in the center, to search for Orlando's senses on the moon. His invocation brings the spectacle to a close.[85]

Ronconi's next production, *XX* (1971), was a multi-space performance that seemed to evolve from this idea of labyrinthean entrapment. A two-story "house"—a construction of twenty cubicles and hallways—was built in the auditorium of the Odéon Theatre in Paris.[86] The rooms, ten on each floor, could hold about twenty spectators each and were connected to one another and to the corridors by doors. The second floor rooms had windows; there was no ceiling. Upon entering the theatre spectators were given instructions about remaining in the rooms in which they were placed; then ushers took each spectator to the house and performers and led them, one by one, to the individual rooms where they were to remain. A reviewer aptly referred to this as "Ronconi's Luna Park funhouse."[87]

During the first part of the performance three solo scenes were played in each room as the actors circulated from one to another. Because each of the twenty actors played a different character (a World War I colonel, a transvestite, a maître d'hotel, etc.), the spectators in any one room saw only a fraction of the total performance. Ronconi felt that in a sense this was a reflection of the real world in which it is impossible to know everything that is happening.[88] In an account of the production in *The Drama Review* (T52), Colette Godard described three different "versions" of the play based on three separate viewings. This is something quite different from viewing a frontal performance from different areas of the auditorium or even the simultaneous action of something like *Orlando Furioso* in which a general sense of the total action is experienced. In *XX* the environment fragments and therefore manipulates perception: a total performance is known to exist, but it is unknowable.

In the second section more information was provided. Certain partitions were raised to join pairs of adjoining rooms so that there were ten rooms with a single scene being played in each. Three more rooms were then combined in Part Three so that there were five rooms and an equivalent number of scenes. Finally all the spectators were in one room watching one scene. "When the lights come up," wrote Godard, "there are no longer any actors. The spectators find themselves alone and powerless in a set that has become a trap."[89] Unlike *Orlando*, to which most people reacted enthusiastically, *XX* seemed sinister and disturbing.

In 1972 Ronconi staged Kleist's *Kätchen von Heillbronn* on a lake in Zurich. Using techniques reminiscent of Polieri and the theatre at Tampere, Finland, Ronconi planned to seat the audience on the lake on three barges which would be rotated to face the different scenes unfolding on the water and on the land. Unfortunately local authorities forbade the mobile amphitheatre and the performance was finally given frontally to a stationary audience.[90]

Although Ronconi's productions since then have been equally theatrical and spectacular, only *Utopia* (1975), a montage of Aristophanes' scripts, was in any way environmental. Creating, in essence, a very long alley stage, the characters and props (including buses and airplanes) were slowly paraded between the spectators.[91]

The work of Ariane Mnouchkine and the Théâtre du Soleil of France—especially their productions of *1789* and *1793*—has frequently been compared to *Orlando Furioso*. Mnouchkine protests vigorously. Aside from ideological differences, she feels that scenographically, Ronconi is trapped by the physical theatre whereas her work has a greater freedom. Describing *1789* she commented:

> Placed at the center of the performance, the spectators can sit or stand about. If I add: "as in *Orlando Furioso*," everyone admiringly agrees: "Oh yes, *Orlando Furioso*." But it was necessary for Ronconi to show his production somewhere and then everyone followed. Here they still refuse something so simple. And these are people of the theatre! I am not talking about a secretary at the town hall or others of that type. I am talking about theatre people, damn it! They have agreed to be prisoners of their own space . . . I don't accept this. Even greater than the advantages are the inconveniences of their prison.[92]

The Théâtre du Soleil was founded by Mnouchkine in 1964, and since the late sixties has been devoted to politically oriented themes and bringing these themes to working-class audiences. Both *1789* and *1793* dealt with periods of the French Revolution from the viewpoint of the oppressed classes, using performance styles adapted from *commedia dell'arte*, fairground entertainment, and other popular forms. Since 1970 the group has used the Cartoucherie, an old cartridge factory near Paris, as its theatre, and it is there that *1789* played during 1970–71. (The play premiered in Milan in the summer of 1970 only a few months after *Orlando* and this undoubtedly fostered comparisons.)

For *1789* the vast space was divided into two rectangular sections, one becoming a lobby and storage area, and the other, larger area, serving as the performing space.[93] In this second area a grandstand about thirty meters long was placed against the wall which backed the lobby, facing the performance space. Five platforms, each about five feet high, were arranged in a rectangular configuration in this space and each was accessible by at least two sets of stairs. Runways connected these platforms and the other two (Plate 113). Spectators, of course, filled the grandstand but could also stand in the midst of the platform area. "Our first intention," explained Mnouchkine,

> was that the audience be freer—which doesn't happen, of course, because there are usually too many people. But at the first few performances in Milan, when we had only about six-hundred people, it was incredible to see how they moved around, in order to get closer.[94]

Mnouchkine tried to recreate the atmosphere of the fairground, "a form which is simple and popular, which existed at that time [the Revolution], and before and after that time."[95] Action moved from stage to stage with great rapidity, reproducing the multi-focus disorientation of the fairground. Mnouchkine was also quite aware of the different perspectives possible at medieval market fairs—from the midst of the crowd or observing from the upper window of one of the surrounding houses.[96] The group's technical director Guy-Claude François compared the staging to basketball. The playing area was roughly equivalent to that of a basketball court. "Basketball," noted François, "is a sport that needs to be watched from close [up] because the individual player's moves are interesting to follow, while still demanding a certain distance so that the overall strategy can be appreciated."[97]

The design for *1793*, by Roberto Moscosco, was based on the same principles although the specifics varied somewhat. The performance space was divided longitudinally by a curtain (each section was 45 by 18 meters). The first area, next to the lobby, contained a large movable platform (15 by 4 meters) for the "parade"—the pre-show entertainment once used to attract audiences at fairground booths—by the performers. At the conclusion of this section, the curtain rose so that everyone could enter the second space. The curtain closed when everyone had entered. This area contained three platforms placed as if at three points of a triangle and facing a two-tiered gallery for spectators along the far wall (Plate 114). Spectators also stood among the platforms.[98]

After this the Cartoucherie was remodelled for the 1975 production of *The Golden Age*. The partitions were removed to make it a unified space, and four "craters" were formed in the earthen floor. François explained that they were attempting to create an "open space without definite architecture . . . a sort of agora, a *place of encounter*."[99] This, of course, sounds something like Grotowski's desire for the spectator to "meet" the performance. The four spaces allowed intimacy when experienced individually, and vastness when taken as a whole. The decor, claimed François, was created by the performers themselves, who played on the crests and bases of the craters as the audience sat on the slopes.[100] Like Ronconi, François felt that simultaneous action in different quarters would not be distracting but would, as Cage suggested, simulate the multi-focus environment of everyday life.[101]

It should be noted that while Mnouchkine's productions physically incorporate the spectators, they do not allow for participation. Comparing herself to Grotowski she noted: "Without sharing his ideas as a whole, nevertheless I think the same as Grotowski—that the public should not change the spectacle. If it is changed, afterwards there is very little chance to make it better."[102]

There are many people today working, at least in part, environmentally. Peter Stein of Germany, Terayama of Japan, Memé Perlini of Italy, and Andrei Serban and Snake Theatre in this country are some of the better known directors and groups who have worked with non-frontal staging.[103] It is indicative of the success of this style of theatre that a production staged in this manner is no longer newsworthy and reviewers use the term "environmental theatre" with as much ease as they use "naturalism" or "absurdism." This term may be Richard Schechner's legacy to theatre history.

82. Sequence from Jean-Jacques Lebel's *Funeral Ceremony of the Anti-Procès*, Venice, 1960.

83. A map (sketch) for Wolf Vostell's *You: A Decollage Happening for Bob and Rhett Brown*, Kings Point, N.Y., 1964.

84. Plan of Allan Kaprow's *Eat*, 1964.

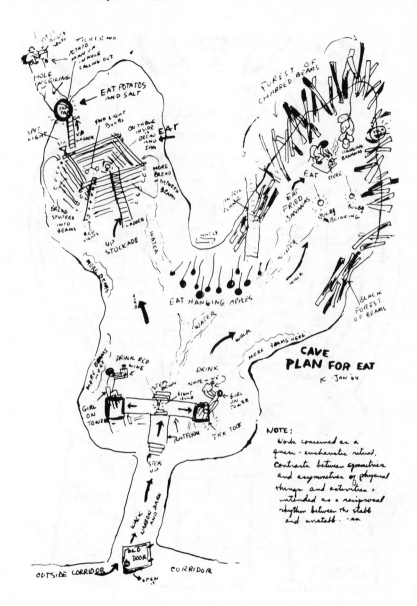

85. Plan of Paul Sills's *Monster Model Funhouse*, 1965.

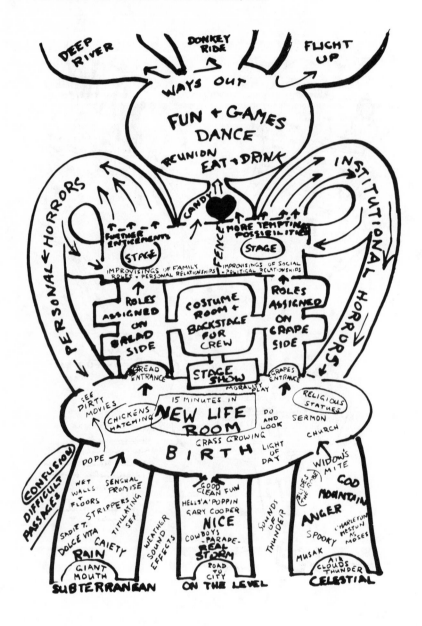

86. Scene from the Bread and Puppet Theatre's *Anti-Bicentennial Circus* as originally done at Davis, California, 1975.

87. Carrying a "plague victim" back to the stage in The Living Theatre's *Mysteries and Smaller Pieces*, 1965.

88. Scene from The Living Theatre's *Six Public Acts*, Ann Arbor, Michigan, 1975.

89. Stage for final night of performance of Robert Wilson's *KA MOUNTAIN and GUARDenia TERRACE*, Iran, 1972.

90. Joan Jonas's *Beach Piece II*, Nova Scotia, 1971.

91. View of Trisha Brown's *Roof Piece*, New York, 1973. Six performers and one spectator are visible in the near and middle distance.

92. Plans of Jerzy Grotowski's productions of *Cain* (1960),
Shakuntala (1960), and *Forefather's Eve*, 1961.

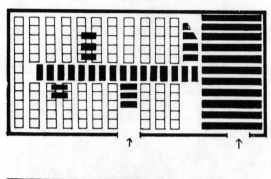

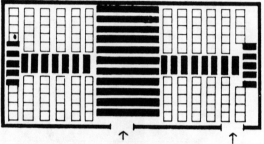

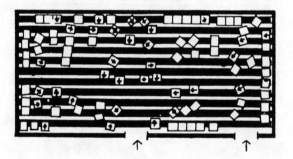

93. Plan of Grotowski's production of *Akropolis* (1962, 1964, 1967) and sketch showing growth of environment.

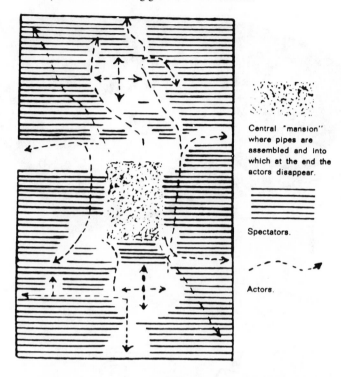

Central "mansion" where pipes are assembled and into which at the end the actors disappear.

Spectators.

Actors.

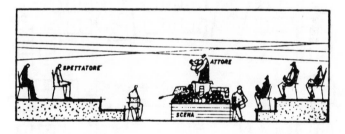

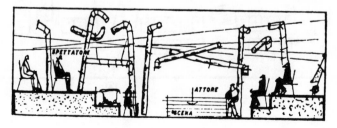

94. Sketch and plan of Eugenio Barba's *Kaspariana*, 1967.

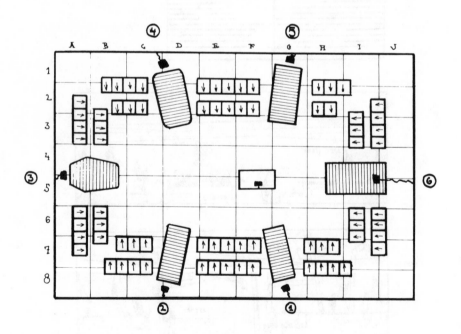

95. Plan of Barba's *Feraï*, 1969.

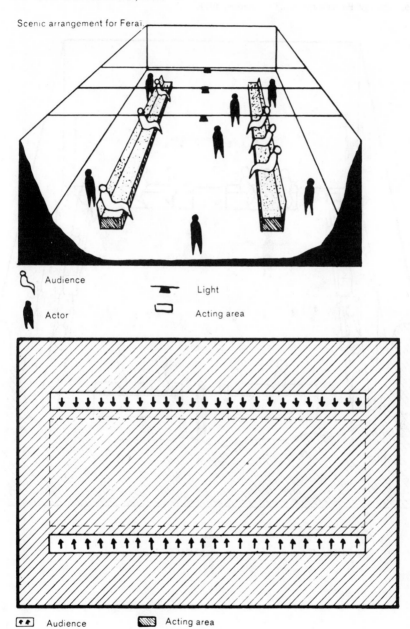

Scenic arrangement for Feraï

Audience

Actor

Light

Acting area

Audience

Acting area

96. Plan of Barba's *House of the Father*, 1971.

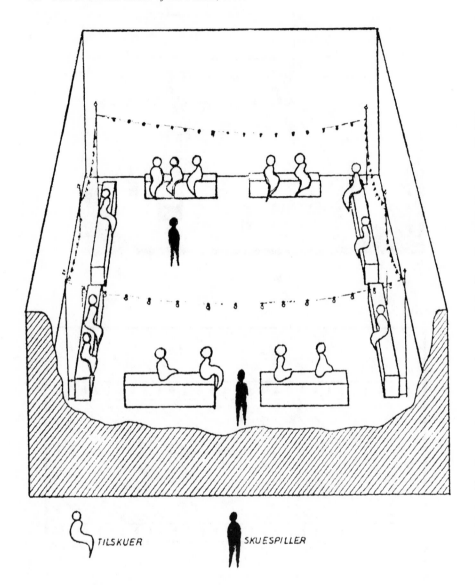

97. Plan of Jacques Polieri's *Scale of Seven*, 1964.

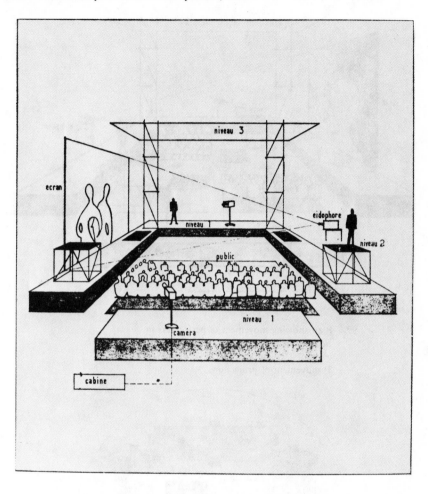

98. Plan of Polieri's *Book of Mallarmé*, 1967.

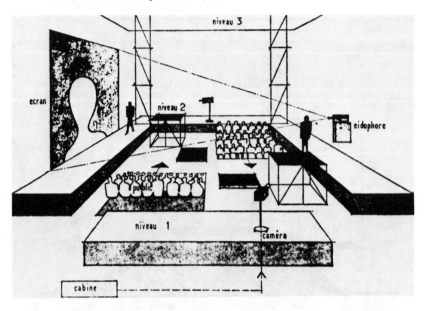

99. Plan showing movement of performers in
Book of Mallarmé. Key: 1) Exterior movement
of actors; 2) interior movement of actors;
3) movement of projections.

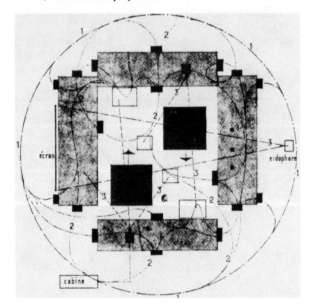

100. General plan for Polieri's *L'Oeil-Oiseau* at the Foundation
     Maeght, 1968. Key: P) Seating areas or movement patterns
     of the spectators; OE) Scenery.

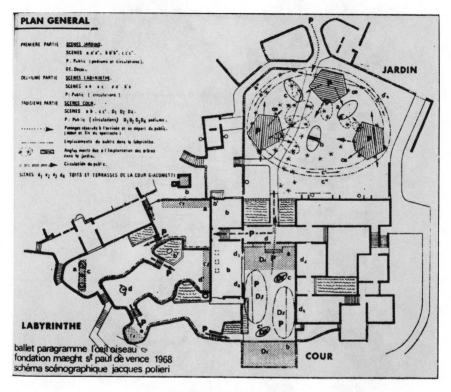

101. Sketch of setting for *L'Oeil-Oiseau*, Part I.

JARDIN

ballet paragramme l'oeil oiseau
fondation maeght st paul de vence. 1968
schéma scénographique Jacques polieri.

102. Sketch of setting for *L'Oeil-Oiseau*, Part III.

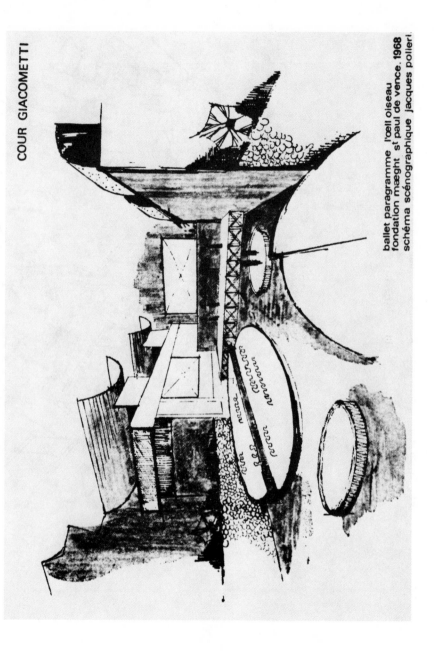

COUR GIACOMETTI

ballet paragramme l'œil oiseau
fondation maeght s^t paul de vence. 1968
schéma scénographique jacques polieri.

103. Sketch of setting for Tadeusz Kantor's production of *The Water Hen*, 1968.

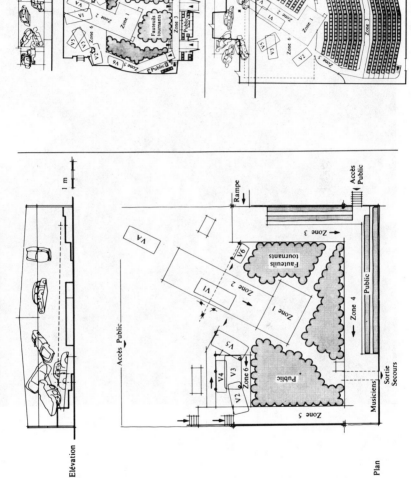

104. Plans for Victor Garcia's production of *Automobile Graveyard* at Dijon, Paris, and Belgrade, 1966 and 1968.

105. Scene from Garcia's production of *The Balcony* at São
Paulo, Brazil, 1969.

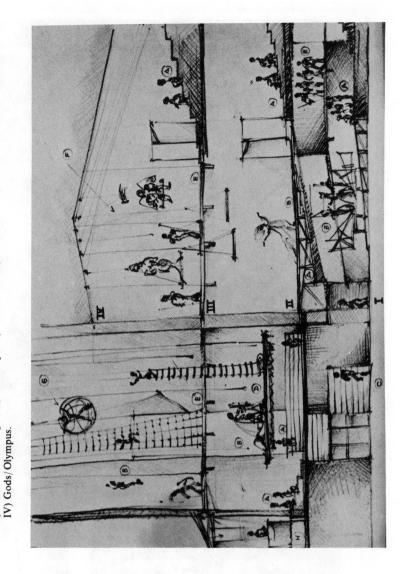

106. Sketch of Helio Eichbauer's design for *The Voyage*, São Paulo, Brazil, 1972. Key: A) Public; B) Actors; C) The Way Up; D) Ship (Elevator); E) Bridges; F) God Machine; G) World Machine; H) Indian Mirror Palace. I) Underground—Middle Ages; II) Sea-Ship; III) African Coast; IV) Gods/Olympus.

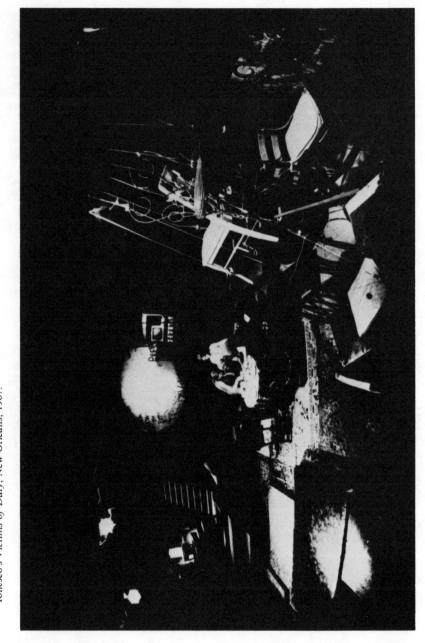

107. Environment for Richard Schechner's production of Ionesco's *Victims of Duty*, New Orleans, 1967.

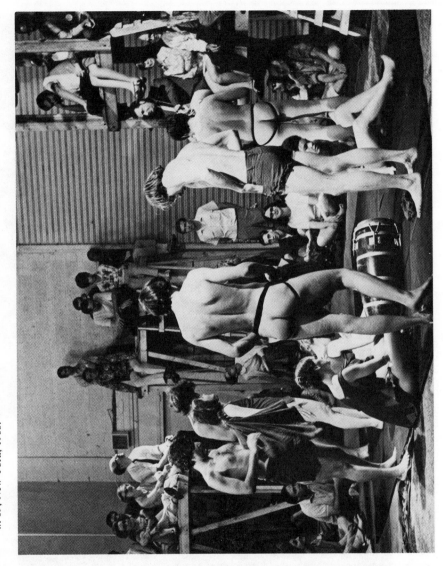

108. View of part of the environment for Schechner's *Dionysus in 69*, New York, 1968.

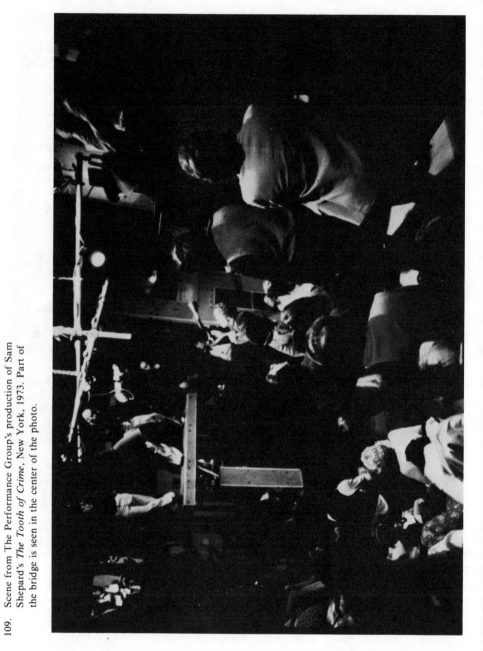

109. Scene from The Performance Group's production of Sam Shepard's *The Tooth of Crime*, New York, 1973. Part of the bridge is seen in the center of the photo.

110. Sketch of *Endgame* environment designed by Jerry Rojo, 1973.

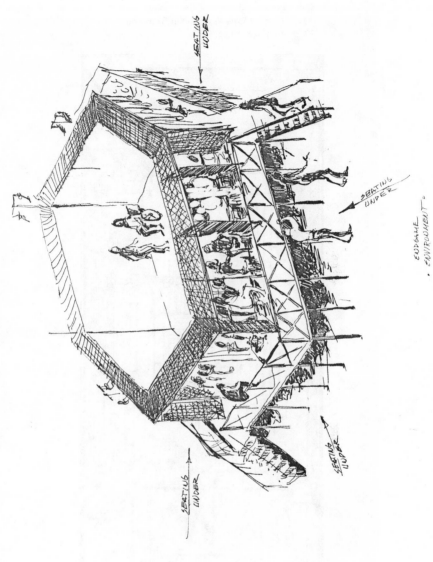

111. Plan of *Slaveship* as seen from above,
by Eugene Lee, 1969.

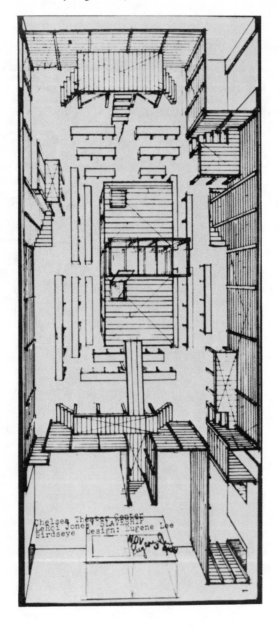

112. Scene from Luca Ronconi's *Orlando Furioso*; New York production, 1970.

113. Plan of Ariane Mnouchkine's *1789*, 1970.

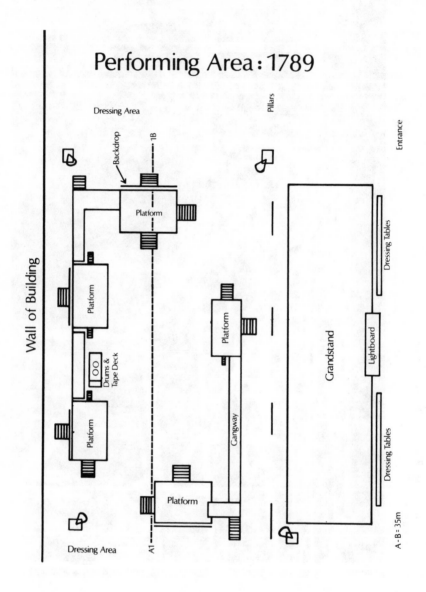

Performing Area : 1789

114. Plan and sketch of Mnouchkine's *1793*, 1972.

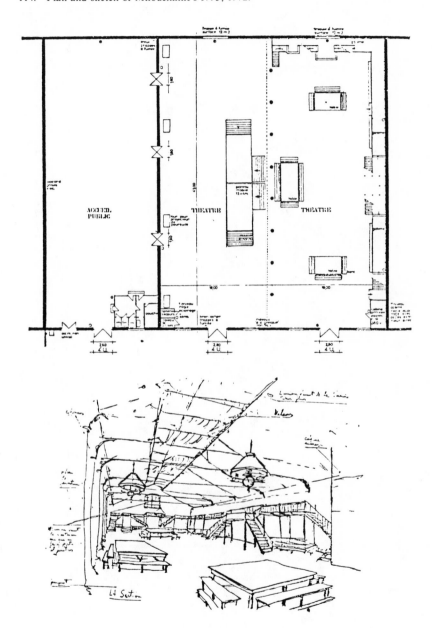

Appendix I

"A Propos d'un Théâtre Nunique"[1]

by Pierre Albert-Birot

The intimate theatre, the theatre of manners, the psychological theatre, is a dead theatre; it no longer relates to our sensibilities. It has no more life than a portrait by Bonnat.

In a time when science is placing the whole world in the hands of each man, minds cannot do less than broaden their horizons and ambitions: today, more than ever, man, and above all, the artist must speak: *nihil humanum* . . . The whole world is his studio, the whole world is his study, the whole world is his model and he must aspire to what could be termed globalism or universalism.

Artists have resolutely embarked on this path, the poets as well; the theatre will inevitably follow. The first step, of course, is the abolition of the three unities.

The principal action will be of little more importance than the other actions or fragments of action of which it will be composed; one must not be put off by any contrast, any diversity, any unexpectedness, acrobatics, songs, clowning, tragedy, comedy, buffoonery, film projections, pantomimes. The *théâtre nunique* must be a grand, simultaneous ensemble containing all the means and all the emotions capable of communicating an intense and intoxicating life to the spectators. To add still more to this intensity, the multiple actions will unfold on the stage and in the auditorium. To attain a more profound realism, certain characters will be split so as to show acts and thoughts, so frequently in contradiction.

The play having neither unity of place nor unity of time—that is to say, having before us simultaneously scenes in Paris, in New York, in Tokyo, in a house, on the sea, underground, in the sky, in prehistoric times, in the middle ages, in 1916, in the year 2000—decor is out of the question: light alone must be the paint of this theatre. A whole palette of colored projections will create the mood. Certain objects will constitute indispensible representations such as projections of the country, monuments, inscriptions.

As for the playhouse, it is no more than a circus in which the public will occupy the center, while on a peripheral, turning platform, most of the performance will unfold, still connected to the audience by actors scattered throughout the theatre.

—translated by Arnold Aronson

Appendix II

Technology—Forerunner of Dramatic Creativity: The Theatre of the Future[1]

by Zygmunt Tonecki

To date, heightened efforts in the field of set design and modern set architecture have been evoked by the experiments of a galaxy of theatre reformers whose revolutionary productional imagination was overly hampered by the three-walled "box stage," which is insufficient in many respects.

Hatred for this cramped and uncomfortable *"Guckkastenbühne"* [peek-box stage], as the Germans have christened it, forced Reinhardt to make his exodus from the theatre to the circus, and later to transform the circus arena in an open-air theatre (the Salzburg festival).

Meyerhold, renouncing the traditional stage with its ever-present curtain, builds his own (for Tretyakov's *Zjemlja dybom* [*The Earth In Turmoil*], Erdman's *Mandat* [*The Warrant*], etc.), but even this does not satisfy him, as he feels heavily restrained despite the interesting results he has achieved.

Piscator's eruptive directorial talent strives to achieve complete scenic expression by force, building six to eight smaller stages vertically on a normal one. Connected at the center by a screen, as was done in Toller's play *Hoppla, wir leben!* [*Hurrah, We Live!*], they facilitate complete continuity of action. This is the most thorough exploitation of the ordinary set to date.

Schiller also took full advantage of it in Langer's *Przedmieście* [*The Suburb*] and especially in *Dzieje grzechu* [*The History of Sin*]. But his production overestimated both the possibilties of the revolving stage (which Piscator, for example, did not have) and a rich array of technical accessories; intending to avoid scenery and visual hypertrophy, it forsook the use of the screen. Because of this the Żeromski story which was being dramatized, cut up into individual fragments, lost those bonds which would undoubtedly have turned the action into a film.

Theatre technology in the productions mentioned, which are characteristic against the backdrop of modern theatrical trends, played into the hands of daring directorial ideas.

Having won their way into the theatre and having become such an important factor, such new trains of thought, timid at first, did not dare to attack the traditional stage; however, they soon began to propose a compromise and, in their desire to provoke the theatre reformers with their impressive artistic record, took their place with them at the starting line in a race for conceptual boldness.

The embodiment of advances in theatrical technology and construction was the Vienna exhibit of 1924.[2]

Among the array of plans, prototypes, and models, in which disturbing, almost apocalyptic imagination went hand in hand with refined diligence, one basic theme reverberated: the struggle against previous forms of stage, auditorium, and theatre building.

Innovators of the Russian theatre had, in their revolutionary zeal, already done away with the curtain. After this operation the visibly aging, faded muse was rejuvenated, grew in verve and will to live, and began anew to entice and illuminate the masses with fresh charms.

It is not surprising, then, that the Russian example proved to be contagious—its success with the curtain provoked the elimination of the stage.

At the Vienna exhibition many who had produced sensational models had already disowned both curtain and footlights, that line of demarcation which divides set from auditorium, and already disliked seeing anything on stage which was completely detached from the viewers and foreign to the audience; hence, their byword was the unification of these two previously separate parts, erasing the formal division of the theatre into stage and auditorium.[3]

In Kiesler's so-called "Railwaytheater" the auditorium, nothing less than a carousel, turns around a fixed "spacial stage," whereas Dr. Strnad's model has a round stage which, together with the numerous independent smaller stages on it, encircles the audience.

Here the stage and auditorium appear completely unified and interpenetrate each other. But exaggerated technical virtuosity went hand in hand with abstraction, hence the Viennese models had little hope of realization and practical use.

Following years brought to theatre architecture the Theatre of Decorative Art Display, the project of Perret and Grant (a three-part stage) as well as Gropius' model, specially constructed for Piscator (a mobile arena with three sets).[4]

Although equally bold in their construction of building and stage, these experiments were already more mature and realistic than their predecessors.

The Theatre of the Future, by Andrzej Pronaszko and Szymon Syrkus (with the cooperation of Zygmunt Leski), built by order of the city of Warsaw for the National Exhibition in Poznań, not only documents the modernity of Poland in the field of theatre technology and construction, but also happily crowns previous efforts. Who knows if it may not be the real solution to the essential problems of modern theatrical art?

Extraordinary simplicity, a lack of any kind of ornamentation, and harmony liken the Theatre of the Future to classical Greek and Japanese models. It is artistically constructed of heavy masses with large glass surfaces, based on a steel and reinforced-concrete foundation.

Its dimensions are impressive: in its entirety it occupies 8,000 sq. meters, its façade reaches a height of 50 meters, equalling 13 to 16 stories.

A large number of exits, staircases, elevators, and escalators facilitate quick evacuation of the building in case of fire.

Out of concern for public comfort, the most modern conveniences have been installed on the premises: cloakrooms, buffets, cafés, restaurants, etc.

The auditorium is designed for 3,000 viewers, i.e., as many as can be seated amphitheatrically, while the same dome embraces both the auditorium and the stage, creating as it were a gigantic clamshell whose curvature was determined by precise acoustic calculations (according to Lyon's method, which was incorporated into the new Pleyel Hall in Paris).

But the creative genius of its authors is most clearly visible in the Theatre of the Future's stage construction.

This consists of two fixed and two movable stages (circular ring-stages).

The round movable ring-stages, which are fairly wide and encircle the auditorium, rotate in the same or different directions (not around their own axes, as with the revolving stage). The rate of rotation may be controlled at the director's discretion depending on the demands of a given spectacle.

The huge stage unfolds before the viewer's eye. On this the above-mentioned movable rings come forward, only to disappear again under the amphitheatrical auditorium where a series of set changes can be accomplished, allowing the action to continue without interruption.

If we remember that these movable rings possess smaller revolving stages and trap doors we will understand to what a great extent the Theatre of the Future's designers have provided the director with the possibility of capitalizing on the motions of actors, supernumeraries, and scenery in all possible directions.

This raises only one question: What kind of director will succeed in mastering the dynamics, acoustics, and lighting of such a stage, and fuse this synchrono-synoptic and simultaneous amalgam into one artistic whole?

When the powerful motors set the circular rings in motion and the reflectors begin to illuminate individual fragments of the stage, not only is it possible to achieve continuity of action, but also instantaneous scenery changes rivaling, for dynamism, even film; the theatre, whose death film enthusiasts have been preaching, becomes . . . a talking movie, moreover, three-dimensional and in color.

It would, however, be erroneous and an insult to the creators of the Theatre of the Future were we to see in their creation only a competitor for the movies. For even if the Theatre of the Future approaches film with respect to its technology and dynamism, the artistic concepts from which it arose and on which it is based are foreign to film and lie on a wholly different plane.

The technology of the Theatre of the Future, outdistancing contemporary dramatic creativity, aims at encouraging the latter to emulate it; it does this by calling attention to wide horizons and paths of development.

Pronaszko and Syrkus's enterprise yearns to be the prod which will stimulate dramatic creativity from out of its current chronic torpor, caused, among other things, by necessary dependence on the possibilities of today's stage.

For the ruler against which the Theatre of the Future's range of application can be measured is of hitherto unheard of length. Complete utilization of its technical installations can produce frankly phenomenal results, but this will remain tomorrow's song for some time to come, since such an achievement calls for a single theatre person who will embody the genius of a director and a playwright at once.

The Theatre of the Future of Pronaszko and Syrkus, despite its great modernity, will not lose contact with reality, as happened with its predecessors, but opens wide the field of productional possibilities and in so doing reveals wonderful new perspectives to the producers of the future great mass spectacles for which it is above all destined.

—translated by Thomas Malionek, September, 1977

Notes

Chapter 1

1. Richard Schechner, "6 Axioms for Environmental Theatre," *The Drama Review* 12 (Spring 1968): 41–64.

2. Allan Kaprow provides an excellent example of framing in his book *Assemblage, Environments, and Happenings* (New York: Harry N. Abrams, Inc., 1966), pp. 155–57.

3. An example of the way in which found surroundings impose themselves on outdoor performances is seen in a review of *Threepenny Opera* which was moved from the Vivian Beaumont Theatre to the Delacorte Theatre in Central Park in the summer of 1977: "Of far greater magnitude, however, is the change which occurs by putting the show outdoors .... When the back wall moves in Central Park, it reveals Belvedere Castle, so that space, rather than being transformed, is revealed." (Terry Curtis Fox, "Does Mack the Knife Belong Outdoors?" *Village Voice*, July 18, 1977, p. 63.)

4. This is demonstrated by Part Two of Meredith Monk's *Vessel*. Although staged in the Performing Garage in the *Commune* "environment," it was presented as a frontal performance without any significant alteration of space.

5. The stage house of a proscenium theatre, of course, is usually part of the same architectural space as the auditorium. The audience, however, generally perceives it as a separate unit. An interesting interpretation of this separation of space can be found in Donald M. Kaplan, "Theatre Architecture: A Derivation of the Primal Cavity," *The Drama Review* 12 (Spring 1968): 105–116.

6. This is taken from E. K. Chambers' so-called "normalized" text. See Chambers, *The English Folk Play* (Oxford: Oxford University Press, 1933), p. 6.

7. Chambers, *The Medieval Stage* (Oxford: Oxford University Press, 1903), Vol. 1, p. 216.

8. There are, of course, mummings that utilize the entire room. See, for instance, Raymond Pentzell, "A Hungarian Christmas Mummers' Play in Toledo, Ohio," *Educational Theatre Journal* 29 (May 1977): 178–98.

9. John Cage has commented that theatre is "something which engages both the eye and the ear" and consequently performance is independently structured by "each person in the audience." Asked in an interview if he thought the activity at a beach, for instance, could be classified as theatre he replied: "If a person assumes that the beach is theatre and experiences it in those terms I don't see that there's much difference. It is possible for him [the spectator] to take that attitude." ("Interview with John Cage," *Tulane Drama*

Review 10 [Winter, 1965]: 55.) Basically, found environment performance encourages spectators to view everyday space as performance space.

10. Michael Kirby, in his essay, "The Activity: A New Art Form," defines an Activity as a work of art that causes the spectator to focus in on his own actions. "This work of art can only be seen by one person, and it can only be viewed from within." (In *The Art of Time: Essays on the Avant-Garde* [New York: E. P. Dutton & Co., Inc., 1969], pp. 153–69.) Since there is no separate performer and spectator the Activity is technically not theatre.

11. See Michael Kirby, "Marta Minujin's *Simultaneity*," *The Drama Review* 12 (Spring 1968): 149–52.

12. An excellent discussion of the use of space in mummings can be found in Alan Brody, *The English Mummers and Their Plays* (Philadelphia: University of Pennsylvania Press, 1970); and Herbert Halpert, "A Typology of Mumming," in *Christmas Mumming in Newfoundland*, ed. Halpert and G. M. Story (Toronto: University of Toronto Press, 1969), pp. 34–61.

13. Brody, p. 15; Schechner, personal files.

14. See Bill Simmer, "The Theatrical Style of Tom O'Horgan," *The Drama Review* 21 (June 1977): 65–66.

15. Erika Munk, "The Price is the Mind and the Spirit," review of *Fefu and Her Frinds* in *Village Voice*, May 19, 1977.

16. Brooks McNamara, Jerry Rojo, and Richard Schechner, *Theatres, Spaces, Environments: Eighteen Projects* (New York: Drama Book Specialists, 1976), pp. 2–3.

Chapter 2

1. Among those who have noted historical influences are Firmin Gémier and Ariane Mnouchkine (see Chapters 3 and 4).

2. See, for instance, Glynne Wickham, *Early English Stages*, 2 vols. (New York: Columbia University Press, 1959); Alan Brody, *The English Mummers and Their Plays* (Philadelphia: University of Pennsylvania Press, 1970); Herbert Halpert and G. M. Story, eds., *Christmas Mumming In Newfoundland* (Toronto: University of Toronto Press, 1969).

3. Suresh Awasthi, "The Scenography of the Traditional Theatre of India," *The Drama Review* 18 (December 1974): 43–44.

4. For a classification of these performances see E. C. Cawte, Alex Helm, et al., *English Ritual Drama* (London: 1967).

5. See Halpert and Story, pp. 34–61 passim.

6. Halpert and Story, p. 36.

7. Richard Southern, *The Seven Ages of the Theatre* (New York: Hill and Wang, 1961), pp. 37–38.

8. Ibid.

9. See Marjorie Young, "Performance in Polish Villages," *The Drama Review* 18 (December 1974): 16–21.

10. Ibid., p. 17.

11. Ibid., p. 18.

12. Raymond Pentzell, "A Hungarian Christmas Mummers' Play in Toledo, Ohio," *Educational Theatre Journal* 29 (May 1977): 184.

13. Young, p. 6.

14. Awasthi, pp. 40–41.

15. Richard Schechner, "Selective Inattention," *Performing Arts Journal* 1 (Spring 1976): 8–20.

16. See Wickham, vol. 1, pp. 55–58.

17. Sheldon Cheney, "Renaissance Entries," *Theatre Arts Monthly* 13 (August 1929): 611.

18. See Wickham, vol. 1, p. 59.

19. Jacques-Louis David, quoted in David Lloyd Dowd, *Pageant Master of the Republic* (Lincoln, Nebraska: University of Nebraska Press, 1948), p. 66.

20. Marvin Carlson, *The Theatre of the French Revolution* (Ithaca, N.Y.: Cornell University Press, 1966), p. 43.

21. Dowd, pp. 60–61.

22. Ibid.

23. Marquis de Villette, cited in Dowd, p. 50.

24. Awasthi, pp. 39–40.

25. For a detailed survey of the development of European market fairs see André Allix, "The Geography of Fairs," *Geographical Review* 12 (1922): 532–69; and for an interesting theory of pre-Christian origins see T. F. G. Dexter, *The Pagan Origin of Fairs* (Cornwall: New Knowledge Press, n.d.).

26. Allix, passim.

27. Cornelius Walford, *Fairs Past and Present* (1883; reprint ed., New York: A. M. Kelley, 1968), p. 206.

28. E. E. Cummings, "Coney Island," *Vanity Fair*, June 1926.

29. David Braithwaite, *Fairground Architecture* (New York: Frederick A. Praeger, Inc., 1968), p. 22.

30. Ibid., pp. 24–25.

31. Cummings.

32. Douglas Haskell, "To-Morrow and the World's Fair," *Architectural Record* 88 (August 1940): 67.

33. Kenneth Lindley, *Seaside Architecture* (London: Hugh Evelyn, 1973), p. 75.

34. Ibid., p. 68.

Chapter 3

1. Kenneth Macgowan and Robert Edmond Jones, *Continental Stagecraft* (New York: Harcourt, Brace and Company, 1922), p. 157.

2. Sheldon Cheney, *The Open Air Theatre* (1918; reprint ed., New York: Kraus Reprint Co., 1971), p. 1.

3. Thomas Herbert Dickinson, *The Case of American Drama* (Boston: Houghton, Mifflin Co., 1915), p. 126.

4. Ibid.

5. Johnston Forbes-Robertson, *A Player Under Three Reigns* (Boston: Little, Brown, and Co., 1925), p. 101.

6. Ibid.

7. David James Fisher, "Romain Rolland and the French People's Theatre," *The Drama Review* 21 (March 1977): 79.

8. Alfred Vallette, "Le Théâtre du Peuple," *Mercure de France* 19 (août 1896): 383.

9. Alfred Jarry, "Of the Futility of the 'Theatrical' in the Theatre," in *Selected Works of Alfred Jarry*, ed. Roger Shattuck and Simon Watson Taylor (New York: Grove Press, 1965), pp. 74–75.

10. Maurice Pottecher, *Le Théâtre du Peuple de Bussang* (Paris: P. V. Stock, 1913), p. 13.

11. See Fisher, pp. 78–81.

12. See Robert Withington, *English Pageantry: An Historical Outline* (1918; reprint ed., New York: Benjamin Blom, 1963), vol. 2, pp. 197–296.

13. Louis N. Parker quoted in Withington, vol. 2, p. 291.

14. Dickinson, p. 177.

15. Cheney, p. 137; see also Chapter 1, n. 3.

16. Edward Gordon Craig, *The Theatre—Advancing* (Boston: Little, Brown, and Co., 1919), p. 45.

17. Ibid.

18. Raoul Auernheimer quoted in Dorothy Pam, *"Murderer, the Women's Hope,"* *The Drama Review* 19 (September 1975): 7.

19. Craig, p. 22.

20. Gordon Craig's theatre journal, *The Mask*, had been published from Florence since 1908 and his theories were widely known. Michael Kirby in his book, *Futurist Performance* (New York: E. P. Dutton & Co., Inc., 1971), pp. 75–76, details Craig's possible influence on the Futurists.

21. Filippo Tommaso Marinetti, Emilio Settemelli, and Bruno Corra, "The Futurist Synthetic Theatre," trans. Victoria Nes Kirby, in Kirby, p. 202.

22. Marinetti, "The Variety Theatre," trans. Victoria Nes Kirby, in Kirby, pp. 179–86.

23. See Kirby, pp. 28–32.

24. Kirby, p. 28.

25. Ibid., pp. 28–29.

26. Marinetti, "Dynamic and Synoptic Declamation," in *Marinetti: Selected Writings*, ed. R.

W. Flint, trans. R. W. Flint and Arthur A. Coppotelli (New York: Farrar, Straus and Giroux, 1972), p. 147.

27. Kirby, p. 149.

28. Ibid.

29. See Marinetti, "Tactilism," in *Selected Writings*, pp. 109–12.

30. Kirby, p. 48.

31. Fedele Azari, "Futurist Aerial Theatre," trans. Victoria Nes Kirby, in Kirby, pp. 218–21.

32. Ibid., p. 219.

33. See p. 21 and Chapter 2, n. 15

34. Robert Motherwell, eds., *The Dada Painters and Poets: An Anthology* (New York: Wittenborn, Schultz, Inc., 1951), pp. 159–61.

35. Aste d'Esparbes in *Comoedia* 7 (mai 1922), quoted in Michel Sanouillet, *Dada a Paris* (Jean-Jacques Pauvert, 1965), pp. 250–51. (Translated in part in "The Dada Spirit in Painting," Motherwell, pp. 179–80.)

36. Motherwell, pp. 115–16.

37. See Raoul Hausmann, "Dadatour," *The Drama Review* 18 (June 1974): 128–30.

38. Oliver M. Sayler, *Max Reinhardt and His Theatre* (New York: Brentano's, 1924), p. 64.

39. Ibid., p. 190.

40. Martin Esslin, "Max Reinhardt: High Priest of Theatricality," *The Drama Review* 21 (June 1977): 14.

41. Oscar Bie, "Germany's New Scenecraft," *International Studio* 75 (August 1922): 427.

42. See Silvio D'Amico, "Shakespeare and Goldoni," *Theatre Arts Monthly* 18 (November 1934): 849–59.

43. Huntly Carter, *The Theatre of Max Reinhardt* (New York: Mitchell Kennerley, 1914), p. 210.

44. Max Reinhardt, *Schriften*, quoted in Esslin, p. 10.

45. Ibid., pp. 9–10.

46. Carter, p. 123.

47. Ibid.

48. Firmin Gémier, quoted in Raymond Pentzell, "Firmin Gemier and Shakespeare For Everybody," *The Drama Review* 11 (Summer 1967): 118–19.

49. There are many documentations of *The Miracle* but the best description of the design is in Claude Bragdon, "A Theatre Transformed," *Architectural Record*, 55 (April 1924): 388–97. The scenario can be found in Sayler, pp. 249–322.

50. "*The Miracle*—A Collaboration," *Theatre Arts Monthly* 8 (March 1924): 172–73.

51. Bragdon, p. 395.

52. Georg Fuchs, *Revolution in the Theatre*, trans. and ed. Constance Connor Kuhn (Ithaca, N.Y.: Cornell University Press, 1959), p. 38.

53. Ibid., p. 46.

54. Ibid., p. 70.

55. See Adolphe Appia, *The Work of Living Art*, trans. H. D. Albright (1921; reprint ed. Coral Gables, Florida: University of Miami Press, 1960), pp. 49–50.

56. Claude Bragdon, "Towards A New Theatre," *Architectural Record* 52 (September 1922): 171–182.

57. MacGowan and Jones, p. 188.

58. Erwin Piscator, *Das Politische Theater*, quoted in C. D. Innes, *Erwin Piscator's Political Theatre: The Development of Modern German Drama* (Cambridge: University Press, 1972), p. 24.

59. The influence of Jessner, Meyerhold, and others on Piscator is discussed in Innes, passim.

60. Heinz Bernard, "The Theatre of Erwin Piscator," *Prompt* 3 (1963): 27.

61. See Innes, pp. 136–43.

62. Ibid.

63. See Cheney, "The Space Stage," *Theatre Arts Monthly* 11 (October 1927): pp. 762–74.

64. Frederick Kiesler, "Debacle of the Modern Theatre," *The Little Review* 11 (Winter 1926): 67.

65. Ibid., pp. 70–72.

Chapter 4

1. See Charles-Nicolas Cochin, *Projet d'Une Salle de Spectacle* (1765; reprint ed., Geneva: Minkoff Reprint, 1974).

2. Pierre Sonrel, "La Salle de Spectacle," *L'Architecture d'Aujourd'hui* 23 (mai 1949): 33.

3. Guillaume Apollinaire, "The Breasts of Tiresias," in *Modern French Theatre*, ed. and trans. Michael Benedikt and George E. Wellwarth (New York: E. P. Dutton & Co., Inc., 1966), p. 66.

4. Pierre Albert-Birot, "A Propos d'Un Théâtre Nunique," *Sic* 8, 9, 10 (aout–octobre 1916): n.p. *Sic*, which was founded in 1916, espoused many Futurist concepts including the ideas of speed, motion, and simultaneity. For more detail see Robert Motherwell, *The Dada Painters and Poets*, pp. xxxv and 103–4.

5. Henri Béhar, *Etude sur le Théâtre Dada et Surréaliste* (Editions Gallimard, 1967), p. 54.

6. Albert-Birot.

7. Ibid.

8. Ibid.

9. Margaret Dietrich, "Twentieth-Century Innovations in Stage Design, Stage Machinery and Theatre Architecture In Austria," in *Innovations in Stage and Theatre Design*, ed.

Francis Hodge (New York: American Society for Theatre Research/Theatre Library Association, 1972), p. 110.

10. Ibid.

11. *Oskar Strnad*, ed. Max Eisler (Vienna: Gerlach und Wielding, 1936), p. 69.

12. Ibid., p. 79.

13. Oskar Strnad, quoted in Dietrich, p. 111.

14. Walter Gropius, quoted in Oskar Schlemmer, *Oskar Schlemmer und die Abstrakt Bühne* (Munich: Die Neue Sammlung, 1961), p. 54.

15. Walter Gropius, quoted in Erwin Piscator, *Le Théâtre Politique*, texte français d'Arthur Adamov (Paris: L'Arche Editeur, 1962), pp. 131-33. A partial translation appears in S. Giedion, *Walter Gropius: Work and Teamwork* (New York: Reinhold Publishing Corp., 1954), pp. 63-64.

16. Gropius, quoted in Sybil Moholy-Nagy, *Moholy-Nagy: Experiment In Totality* (Cambridge, Massachusetts: M. I. T. Press, 1969), p. 53.

17. Oskar Schlemmer, Laszlo Moholy-Nagy, Farkas Molnar, *The Theatre of the Bauhaus*, ed. Walter Gropius, trans. Arthur S. Wensinger (Middletown, Connecticut: Wesleyan University Press, 1961), pp. 67-68.

18. Ibid., p. 68.

19. Ibid.

20. See Schlemmer et al., *Theatre of the Bauhaus*, pp. 72-77.

21. Ibid., p. 74.

22. See Michael Kirby, *Futurist Performance* (New York: E. P. Dutton & Co., Inc., 1971), pp. 89-90.

23. From a Federal Theatre Project press release, "The Theatre of the Future." (Courtesy of the Research Center for the Federal Theatre Project.)

24. Ibid.

25. Ibid.

26. Antonin Artaud, *The Theatre and its Double*, trans. Mary Caroline Richards (New York: Grove Press, Inc., 1958), pp. 96-97.

27. See Joseph T. Shipley, "Finns Spin in a Novel Theatre," *Christian Science Monitor*, September 24, 1960, p. 4.

28. Ibid.

29. See "Théâtre Mobile de Jacques Polieri," *Aujourd'hui* 30 (février 1961): 56-57.

30. Jacques Polieri, "Le Théâtre Kaleidoscopique," *La Revue Théâtrale* 30 (1955): 25. "Théâtre kaleidoscopique" was Polieri's term for his theatre and may be considered as a 1950s version of such phrases as "total theatre."

31. Ibid.

32. André Wogenscky, quoted in "Theatre Inflation," *Progressive Architecture*, December 1970, p. 59.

33. Several examples may be found in *The Drama Review* 12 (Spring 1968). See also *Interscena* 67 2 (Spring 1967), and G. M. Kallmann, "Theatres," *Interiors* 116 (September 1956): 109-19.

34. See Hannelore Schubert, *The Modern Theatre: Architecture, Stage Design, Lighting*, trans. J. C. Palmes (New York: Praeger Publishers, 1971), p. 19 ff.

35. A 1930 article (K. Lönberg-Holm, "New Theatre Architecture In Europe," *Architectural Record* 67 (May 1930): 490-96) claimed that the Endless Theatre would hold 100,000 persons.

36. Frederick Kiesler, quoted in Thomas H. Creighton, "Kiesler's Pursuit of an Idea," *Progressive Architecture*, July 1961, pp. 110-11.

37. See Creighton, passim.

38. Ibid., p. 123.

39. Ibid., p. 116.

40. Ibid., p. 122.

41. Ibid., p. 111.

42. Ibid., p. 110.

43. See Morton Eustis, "A Universal Theatre," *Theatre Arts Monthly*, June 1933, pp. 447-57; Kiesler, "A Festival Shelter: The Space Theatre For Woodstock, N.Y.," *Shelter Magazine*, May 1932; "Frederick Kieslers Theaterprojekte," *Bauen + Wohnen* 11 (1951): 2-4.

44. See *Frederick Kiesler: Architekt* (Vienna: Organisation Herausgeber und Verleger: Galerie Nächst St. Stephen, n.d.), pp. 10-12, 54-57.

45. Kiesler, *Inside The Endless House* (New York: Simon and Schuster, 1966), p. 428.

46. Ibid.

47. *De Stijl* was an art group founded in 1916-17 and was characterized by the use of rectangular forms and primary colors. Among members of the group were Kurt Schwitters, Moholy-Nagy, and El Lissitzky.

48. In *Inside The Endless House*, pp. 513-15, Kiesler tells of a 1961 conference on flexible theatre space to which he was invited as a guest but was not allowed to speak.

49. Oskar Schlemmer, et al., p. 89.

50. Bernard Reder, quoted in John I. H. Baur, *Bernard Reder* (New York: Frederick A. Praeger, Inc., 1961), p. 28.

51. Margaret Weiss, "'Labyrinth': Film in a Framework," *Saturday Review*, July 8, 1967, p. 61.

52. See Douglas Haskell, "To-Morrow and the World's Fair," *Architectural Record* 88 (August 1940): 67-68.

53. Kenneth Lindley, *Seaside Architecture* (London: Hugh Evelyn, 1973), p. 71.

54. Otto Piene, "The Theatre That Moves," in Henning Rischbeiter, ed., *Art and the Stage in the 20th Century* (Greenwich, Connecticut: New York Graphic Society, 1969), pp. 258-59.

55. Ibid., p. 259.

56. Ibid.

57. Polieri, "Le Théâtre Kaleidoscopique," p. 25.

58. See Polieri, *Scénographie Sémiographie* (Paris: Editions Denoël, 1971), pp. 69–76.

59. Polieri, "Dove va l'avanguardia in Francia?" *Sipario* 19 (1961): 13.

60. Polieri, *Scénographie Sémiographie*, facing p. 229.

61. See Billy Klüver et al., eds., *Pavilion* (New York: E. P. Dutton, Inc., 1972).

62. Ibid., p. x.

63. According to Calvin Tomkins, artist Robert Breer referred to it as a "buckled Fuller" dome. (*Pavilion*, p. 114.)

Chapter 5

1. The active experimentation, however, had virtually ceased by 1935. The forces of Socialist Realism that began with Stalin became increasingly dominant from the late twenties onward. During the thirties, many artists repudiated, under pressure, their earlier avant-garde work and discontinued their experimenting. Vsevelod Meyerhold boldly refused to do so and was only temporarily spared because of the renewed support of Stanislavsky. With the latter's death in 1938, Meyerhold quickly lost all support. In 1939 his wife was found beaten to death in their apartment, and he himself was never found and presumed murdered.

2. Vladimir Markov, *Russian Futurism: A History* (London: MacGibbon & Kee, Limited, 1969), p. 149.

3. Camilla Gray, *The Russian Experiment In Art 1863–1922* (New York: Harry N. Abrams, Inc., 1971), p. 115.

4. Ibid., pp. 213–18.

5. Ibid., p. 216.

6. *Der Blaue Reiter* was a Cubist group founded in Munich in 1916 by Vassily Kandinsky and others.

7. See, for example, Alexander Tairov, *Notes of a Director*, trans., William Kuhlke (Coral Gables, Florida; University of Miami Press, 1969); and Vsevelod Meyerhold, *Meyerhold on Theatre*, trans. and ed., Edward Braun (New York: Hill and Wang, 1969).

8. Meyerhold, p. 21.

9. See, for example, Alexander Bakshy, *The Path of the Modern Russian Stage and Other Essays* (London: Cecil Palmer and Hayward, 1916); or Yevgeny Znosko-Borovski, *Ruskii Teatr Nachala XX Vyeka* (Prague, 1925).

10. Znosko-Borovski, pp. 300–2.

11. Meyerhold, pp. 112, 143–44.

12. Meyerhold may also have been demonstrating here the influence of Reinhardt whom he had seen in 1907.

13. Meyerhold, pp. 113-14 and Znosko-Borovski, pp. 311-12.

14. Meyerhold, p. 114 and Znosko-Borovski, p. 303.

15. Meyerhold, pp. 103, 114-15.

16. Ibid., p. 117.

17. Ibid., p. 170.

18. Quoted in Kenneth Frampton, "Notes On A Lost Avant-Garde," in *Art In Revolution* (London: Hayward Gallery, 1971), p. 21.

19. Montage staging is the juxtaposition of simultaneous or sequential scenes or actions to create a unified impression not necessarily inherent in any one scene. This is the idea that Eisenstein was to develop as the basis for his film work.

20. 1913 is the date given by Malevich himself as the beginning of Suprematism. The art was similar to *de Stijl*, using rectangular and primary colors. The figures seemed to float in space.

21. See Gray, pp. 166-67.

22. Frampton, p. 21.

23. Quoted in Gray, p. 226.

24. See Sophie Lissitzky-Küppers, *El Lissitzky: Life-Letters-Texts* (Greenwich, Connecticut: New York Graphic Society, 1968). Lissitzky has defined space as "That which is not looked at through a keyhole, nor through an open door. Space does not exist for the eye only: it is not a picture, one wants to live in it."

25. Andrei B. Nakov, *Russian Constructivism: Laboratory Period* (London: Annely Juda Fine Arts Gallery, 1975), n.p. See also El Lissitzky, "Proun Space," in Lissitzky, *Russia: An Architecture for World Revolution* (Cambridge, Massachusetts: M.I.T. Press, 1970), pp. 138-39.

26. Herbert Read, "Introduction," in Lissitzky-Küppers. See also Lissitzky, "Proun Space."

27. Ibid.

28. El Lissitzky, "The Painter On The Stage Progresses Towards Architecture," in *Art and the Stage in the Twentieth Century*, ed., Henning Rischbeiter (Greenwich, Connecticut: New York Graphic Society, 1969), p. 138.

29. Frampton, p. 25.

30. Ibid.

31. See S. O. Khan-Mahomedov, "Soviet Architecture and Town Planning of the Twenties," in *Art in Revolution* (London: Hayward Gallery, 1971), p. 36, and A. Chinyakov, "The Vesnin Brothers," in *Building in the USSR 1917-1932*, ed, O. A. Shvidovsky (New York: Praeger Publishers, 1971), p. 47.

32. Wall placards were common in many productions; Meyerhold used them again in the 1930 production of Mayakovsky's *Bathhouse*.

33. Meyerhold, pp. 163, 170-74.

34. Meyerhold, p. 166.

35. Ibid.

36. Ibid., p. 174.

37. El Lissitzky, "The Plastic Organization of the Electro-Mechanical Show *Victory Over the Sun*," in *Russia: An Architecture for World Revolution*, p. 136.

38. Meyerhold, p. 189. See also Andrei B. Nakov, *Stenberg* (London: Annely Juda Fine Arts Gallery, 1975), pp. 47–48.

39. Meyerhold, pp. 188–89.

40. Descriptions of these performances can be found in Meyerhold.

41. Meyerhold, p. 233.

42. Ibid.

43. Meyerhold, pp. 241–42.

44. The theatre was inspired in part by Lissitzky. In a 1930 conversation with Meyerhold and Pavel Tsetnerovich (who later directed for Okhlopkov) Lissitzky stated: "If anyone were to ask me what the stage area should be, I would reply: a *floor*, just like the deck of a ship. . . . Secondly, we need extensive breadth on the sides. Thirdly . . . the profile of the auditorium should be like an amphitheatre. . . . We go one step more. The stage is arranged so that it is on the level as the street; in this way we would be able to let cars, trams, cannons, horses, regiments and demonstrations pass through." (*El Lissitzky* [Cologne: Galerie Gmurzynska, 1976], pp. 77–78.)

45. H. W. L. Dana, "Meyerhold's New Theatre," *New Theatre* 44 (January 1935): 10–11. See also Mikhail Barkhin and Sergei Vakhtangov, "A Theatre For Meyerhold," *Theatre Quarterly* 2 (July-September 1972): 69–74.

46. Meyerhold, p. 257.

47. Lee Strasberg and Sidney Kingsley, "An Interview With Okhlopkov," *The Drama Review* 17 (March 1973): 122.

48. Marie Seton, *Sergei M. Eisenstein* (New York: A. A. Wyn, Inc., 1952), pp. 65–66.

49. Sergei Eisenstein, "Through Theatre To Cinema," *Theatre Arts Monthly* 20 (September 1936): 738.

50. Ibid., p. 739

51. Ibid., p. 746.

52. Ronald Hunt, "The Demise of Constructivism," *Art and Artists* 6 (April 1971): 7.

53. Andre van Gyseghem, *Theatre In Soviet Russia* (London: Faber and Faber Ltd., 1943), p. 132.

54. The official title was "Poem of Happy Events of Life, of Great Discoveries, of Amazing Spectacles of the Moon, of New Stars and Innumerable Seas, of Sun Spots and New Sciences."

55. From a TASS new release. (Courtesy Slavic Collection, New York University.)

56. Most of the mass spectacles were presented in the years 1919 to 1921. After that, with the stabilization of the political situation and the reduced need for such propaganda, few spectacles were presented.

57. Spencer E. Roberts, *Soviet Historical Drama* (The Hague: Martinus Nijhoff, 1965), p. 30.

58. Quoted in Roberts, p. 30.

59. Adrian Piotrovsky referred to "the topographic understanding of theatrical space" in *Za Sovetskii Teatr*. Quoted in František Deàk, "Russian Mass Spectacles," *The Drama Review* 19 (June 1975): 14.

60. For a complete discussion of this theory see Nikolai Evreinov, *The Theatre in Life*, ed. and trans. Alexander I. Nazaroff (1927; reprint ed., New York: Benjamin Blom Inc., 1970).

61. I. Korolev. "Contemporary Stage Decoration in the U.S.S.R.," *The Drama* 20 (January 1930): 101–102. Korolev was president of the Association of Theatrical Artists of Moscow.

62. Most reports indicate 8,000 performers and 100,000 spectators. See Rene Fülop-Miller and Joseph Gregor, *The Russian Theatre: Its Character and History* (London: George G. Harrap & Co., Ltd., 1930), and Arthur Holitscher, *Das Theatre im Revolutionaren Russland* (No publication information).

63. Nikolai Evreinov, *Le Théâtre en Russe Sovietique*, texte français de Madeleine Eristov (Paris: Les Publications Techniques et Artistiques, 1946), p. 273.

64. *Istoria Sovetskogo Teatra* 1917–1924 (Leningrad: Gosudarstvenoi Akademiya Iskustvoznanya, 1933), vol. 1, p. 273.

Chapter 6

1. *Teatralnya Entsiklopedia* (Moscow: 1961), vol. 4, pp. 238–39. See also Gail Lenhoff, "The Theatre of Okhlopkov," *The Drama Review* 17 (March 1973): 91.

2. Ya. Varshavskii, "Nevereye v Teatr," *Teatr* 5 (1937): 111; and Lenhoff, pp. 92–93.

3. Nikolai Okhlopkov, "Ob Uslovnosti," *Teatr* 11 (1959): 60.

4. Lee Strasberg and Sidney Kingsley, "An Interview With Okhlopkov," *The Drama Review* 17 (March 1973): 122.

5. Ibid.

6. Quoted in Norris Houghton, *Moscow Rehearsals* (New York: Harcourt, Brace and Co., 1936), pp. 148–49.

7. Andre van Gyseghem, *The Theatre in Soviet Russia* (London: Faber and Faber Ltd., 1943), p. 191.

8. Houghton, p. 100.

9. Stephen Karnot, "Krasny Presny," *New Theatre*, July-August 1934, p. 7.

10. van Gyseghem, pp. 193–95.

11. Karnot, p. 8.

12. Strasberg and Kingsley, p. 122.

13. Boris Alpers, "Razbeg," *Sovetskii Teatr* 5 (1932): 12.

14. Strasberg, "Lee Strasberg's Russian Notebook," *The Drama Review* 17 (March 1973): 117.

15. Varshavskii, p. 112.

16. Okhlopkov, p. 52. Note, also, his fifth principle, above.

17. Some of the best examples of his stylized effects are to found in *Aristocrats*. In a scene in which a performer was supposed to be skiing down a mountainside, a stationary actor pantomimed the motions of skiing, as black-clad performers rushed past her with branches. In another scene, two men fighting in a stormy sea, the sea was indicated by a turbulently undulating tarp (controlled by other performers) and the men appeared through various slits.

18. Karnot, p. 7.

19. van Gyseghem, p. 198.

20. Varshavskii, p. 120.

21. Ibid.

22. A description of the performance can be found in Houghton, pp. 21–23, and van Gyseghem, pp. 189–193.

23. Varshavskii, p. 112.

24. This experience is described in amusing detail by van Gyseghem, pp. 190–91.

25. This enthusiasm is evident not only in written accounts but can be seen in a rare film of the performance owned by Professor Mel Gordon of New York University.

26. van Gyseghem, p. 192.

27. Varshavskii, p. 120.

28. TASS press release, May 22, 1937. (Courtesy Slavic Collection, New York University.)

29. Lenhoff, p. 102.

30. Houghton, *Return Engagement* (New York: Holt, Rinehart and Winston, 1962), p. 107.

31. See Vitaly Gankovsky, "New Directions in Soviet Theatre," *Theatre Design and Technology* 33 (May 1973): 18–24.

32. Varshavskii, passim.

33. It was printed in *La Revue internationale du théâtre et des Beaux Arts* and has been reprinted in *Myśl Teatralna Polskiej Awangardy 1919–1939* (Warsaw: Wydawnictwa Artystyczne i Filmowe, 1973), pp. 209–13. *Myśl Teatralna* also contains essays by and about Szymon Syrkus and Andrej Pronaszko.

34. *Myśl Teatralna*, p. 209. See also Michel Corvin, *Le Théâtre Récherche Entre les Deux Guerres: Le Laboratoire Art et Action* (Paris: La Cité—l'Age d'Homme, [1975]), p. 296.

35. See Corvin, Part 3, Chapter 1.

36. Syrkus, in his essay "On the Simultaneous Theatre" (*Myśl Teatralna*, p. 220), also cites Apollinaire's introduction to *The Breasts of Tiresias*.

37. Corvin, p. 36. Pronaszko also noted that the annular stage had been proposed by the poet Adam Mickiewicz in the 1840s. (See "Rebirth of the Theatre," *Myśl Teatralna*, p. 293.)

38. Syrkus, p. 223.

39. Tonecki, "Theatre of the Future," *Myśl Teatralna*, p. 211.

40. Syrkus, passim.

41. Pronaszko, passim.

42. See Akakia-Viala, "Théâtre, Temps, Espace," *Intermède* 2, 16e année (1947), 16–17.

43. Zygmunt Tonecki, quoted in Corvin, p. 296.

44. Michel Corvin, who reproduced the ground plan in his book, does not give a date for the production.

45. Denis Bablet, "Art et Action," *Interscena 67* 2 (Spring 1967): 34.

46. Corvin, p. 300.

47. Ibid. The technology of television was known by the thirties, even if it was not yet practical, and Marinetti and Tonecki, as well as Autant, optimistically included it in their theatre proposals. The closed-circuit television, however, was not installed at the Paris Exposition.

48. Ibid.

49. Syrkus, p. 221.

50. While Pronaszko's designs for Schiller were certainly of interest, they were all frontal.

Chapter 7

1. See Allan Pierce, "Black Mountain College: A Survey of Theatrical Performances" (unpublished paper, New York University, 1976), pp. 4–6.

2. George Randall, quoted in Pierce, p. 6.

3. Happenings are defined by Michael Kirby as "a form of theatre in which diverse elements, including nonmatrixed performing, are organized in a compartmented structure." For a thorough discussion of the history and esthetics of Happenings see the introduction to his book, *Happenings* (New York: E. P. Dutton & Co., Inc., 1965). See also Allan Kaprow, *Assemblage, Environments, and Happenings* (New York: Harry N. Abrams, Inc., 1966).

4. Kirby, pp. 24ff.

5. Jean-Jacques Lebel, "Theory and Practice," in *New Writers IV* (London: Calder and Boyars, Ltd., 1967), p. 42.

6. Ibid.

7. Other art historians attribute the first collage to Georges Braques.

8. Christian Norberg-Schulz, *Existence, Space and Architecture* (New York: Praeger Publishers, 1971), pp. 41–42.

9. Umberto Boccioni, quoted in Jennifer Licht, *Spaces* (New York: Museum of Modern Art, 1969), n.p.

10. Ibid.

11. Ibid.

12. Naum Gabo and Antoine Pevsner, "The Realistic Manifesto," in *Naum Gabo: The Constructive Process* (London: The Tate Gallery, 1976), pp. 21-26.

13. See Chapter 4.

14. Piet Mondrian, quoted in Licht.

15. From a description by Kate Steinitz, quoted in W. C. Seitz, *The Art of Assemblage* (New York: Museum of Modern Art, 1961), p. 50.

16. Kirby, p. 22.

17. There are several so-called folk artists who have created more or less similar environments, although generally not as total or elaborate as those of Schwitters or Schmidt. Also, none of these artists have had a visible impact on avant-garde art as Schwitters and Schmidt did. See Elinor Lander Horwitz, *Contemporary American Folk Artists* (Philadelphia and New York: J. B. Lippincott Company, 1975).

18. Calvin Tomkins, *The Bride and the Bachelors* (New York: The Viking Press, 1965), p. 62.

19. Ibid.

20. Ibid., p. 63.

21. See Thomas H. Creighton, "Kiesler's Pursuit of an Idea," *Progressive Architecture* (July, 1961), 104-24.

22. H. H. Arnason, *History of Modern Art* (Englewood Cliffs, New Jersey and New York: Prentice-Hall, Inc. and Harry N. Abrams, Inc., 1968), p. 569.

23. Ibid., p. 554.

24. Kaprow, p. 165.

25. Martin Duberman, *Black Mountain: An Exploration in Community* (New York: E. P. Dutton & Co., Inc., 1972), p. 350.

26. John Cage, quoted in Duberman, p. 350.

27. Michael Kirby and Richard Schechner, "An Interview With John Cage," *Tulane Drama Review* 10 (Winter 1965): 52.

28. Ibid.

29. Duberman, p. 352.

30. Kirby and Schechner, p. 50.

31. Tomkins, p. 118.

32. Kirby and Schechner, pp. 65-66.

33. Also in that class were Jackson MacLow, George Brecht, Dick Higgins, and Al Hansen.

34. Allan Kaprow, "The Legacy of Jackson Pollock," *Art News*, October 1958, pp. 56-57.

35. Kirby, *Happenings*, p. 54.

36. Ibid.

37. Ibid.

38. Allan Kaprow, quoted in Richard Kostelanetz, *The Theatre of Mixed Means* (New York: The Dial Press, Inc., 1968), pp. 107–8.

39. Ibid., p. 108.

40. Ibid.

41. Kaprow, *Assemblage, Environments and Happenings*, pp. 165–66.

42. Kirby, *Happenings*, p. 71.

43. Kaprow, *Assemblage, Environments and Happenings*, pp. 190–96.

44. Ibid., p. 164.

45. Described in Kaprow, *Assemblage, Environments and Happenings*, pp. 227–32.

46. Ibid., pp. 255–68.

47. For detailed accounts of these Happenings see *Tulane Drama Review* 10 (Winter 1965).

48. See Kirby, *Happenings*.

Chapter 8

1. Richard Schechner, "6 Axioms for Environmental Theatre," *The Drama Review* 12 (Spring 1968): 41.

2. Stuart Sherman, for instance, a so-called conceptual artist, performs on street corners and in parks, as well as on conventional stages without any visible change in style. (See Brooks McNamara, "Stuart Sherman's Third Spectacle," *The Drama Review* 20 [June 1976]: 47–55).

3. Richard Schechner, interview in New York City, January 9, 1976, and "Post Proscenium," in *Theatre 3: The American Theatre 1969-1970* (New York: Charles Scribner's Sons, 1970), p. 28.

4. Schechner, interview.

5. Ibid.

6. See Head, "Kill Viet Cong," *Tulane Drama Review* 10 (Summer 1966): 153. A scenario for *Guerilla Warfare* appears in the *Village Voice*, September 7, 1967.

7. See Schechner, "6 Axioms," pp. 55–56, and *New York Times*, October 29, 1967.

8. Henry Lesnick, *Guerilla Street Theatre* (New York: Avon Books, 1973), p. 11.

9. R. G. Davis, "Guerilla Theatre," *Tulane Drama Review* 10 (Summer 1966): 134.

10. For a complete scenario see Lesnick, pp. 160–62.

11. Schechner, "Guerilla Theatre: May 1970," *The Drama Review* 14 (Spring 1970): 166.

12. Schechner, personal files.

13. Peter Schumann, "Program Notes for the Newport Folk Festival," quoted in Arthur Sainer, *The Radical Theatre Notebook* (New York: Avon Books, 1975), p. 165.

14. Helen Brown and Jane Seitz, "With The Bread and Puppet Theatre," *The Drama Review*

12 (Winter 1968): 70. Despite this statement the Bread and Puppet Theatre has performed on conventional stages, although they do so only occasionally.

15. Stefan Brecht, "Peter Schumann's Bread and Puppet Theatre," *The Drama Review* 14 (Spring 1970): 46.

16. For a discussion of the application of multiple and random focus in theatre design see Hugh Hardy, "Designing Random Focus," *The Drama Review* 12 (Spring 1968): 121–26.

17. Peter Schumann, "Bread and Puppets," *The Drama Review* 14 (Spring 1970): 35.

18. Peter Schumann, quoted in Brown, pp. 66–67.

19. Ross Lumpkin, "Last Bread and Puppet Circus," review of *The Domestic Resurrection Fair and Circus* in *Soho Weekly News*, August 22, 1974, p. 16.

20. An earlier version—the "Anti-Bicentennial Circus"—was performed in California in 1975. See Theodore Shank, "The Bread and Puppet's Anti-Bicentennial: A Monument to Ishi," *Theatre Quarterly* 5 (September-November 1975): 73–88.

21. Ron Argelander, "The War Is Over," review of *The Domestic Resurrection Fair and Circus* in *Soho Weekly News*, August 19, 1976, pp. 14–15.

22. For discussions and descriptions of the Living Theatre's work see especially *The Drama Review* 13 (Spring 1969); *Yale Theatre* (Spring 1969); Pierre Biner, *The Living Theatre* (New York: Horizon Press, 1972); A. Rostagno and G. Mantegna, *We, The Living Theatre* (New York: Ballantine Books, Inc., 1970); Jean Jacquot, ed., *Les Voies de la Création Théâtrale*, (Paris: Editions du Centre National de la Recherche Scientifique, 1970).

23. Pierre Biner, *The Living Theatre*, Chapter 10, passim.

24. Ibid., p. 48.

25. Schechner, "An Interview with the Becks," *The Drama Review* 13 (Spring 1969): 37.

26. Biner, p. 85.

27. Ibid., p. 86.

28. Schechner, "Becks," p. 34.

29. Biner, p. 149.

30. Jean Jacquot, "The Living Theatre," in *Les Voies de la Création Théâtrale*, vol. 1, p. 229.

31. The description of *Antigone* is based on Biner, Chapter 28 and Jacquot, pp. 217–44.

32. Julian Beck and Judith Malina, *Paradise Now* (New York: Random House, 1971). For descriptions of the performance see also Biner and Jacquot.

33. Biner, p. 186.

34. Ibid., p. 192.

35. Jacquot notes that at the Sports Palace in Geneva (which the Becks claim was their favorite auditorium because of the "fluidity") in which there was seating on four sides of a central stage, one section of the audience was somewhat removed. While these spectators had a better view of the earlier stage activities it was essentially left out of the "free theatre" sections. The spectators in that section generally remained in their seats for most of the performance.

36. Beck and Malina, p. 140.

37. Paul Ryder Ryan, "The Living Theatre in Brazil," *The Drama Review* 15 (Summer 1971): 22.

38. Ibid., p. 23.

39. For a complete description see Claudio Vicentini, "The Living Theatre's *Six Public Acts*," *The Drama Review* 19 (September 1975): 80–93.

40. For a detailed account of the performance and its background see A. C. H. Smith, *Orghast at Persepolis* (New York: The Viking Press, 1972).

41. Smith, p. 61.

42. The idea for the enclosed space and movable scaffolds was first tried by Brook in his production of *The Tempest* in July 1968 at the Round House Theatre in London. (See Smith, p. 24, and Margaret Croyden, "Brook's Tempest Experiment," *The Drama Review* 13 [Spring 1969]: 125–28.)

43. Peter Brook, quoted in Smith, p. 109.

44. Quoted in Ossia Trilling, "Peter Brook In Persia," *Theatre Quarterly* 2 (January-March 1972): 37.

45. Ibid., p. 39.

46. Ibid., p. 40.

47. For a partial description of the piece see Ossia Trilling, "Robert Wilson's *Ka Mountain*," and Basil Langton, "Journey To Ka Mountain," *The Drama Review* 17 (June 1973): 33–47.

48. Trilling, "Ka Mountain," p. 43.

49. Ann Halprin, "Yvonne Rainer Interviews Ann Halprin," *Tulane Drama Review* 10 (Winter 1965): 147

50. Ibid., pp. 149–50.

51. Sainer, p. 54.

52. Robert Morris, "Notes On Dance," *Tulane Drama Review* 10 (Winter 1965): 184–85.

53. Ibid., p. 185.

54. Joan Jonas with Rosalind Krause, "Seven Years," *The Drama Review* 19 (March 1975): 13.

55. Ibid.

56. Ibid., p. 14.

57. Ibid., pp. 14–15.

58. See Jonas, p. 15.

59. For a complete description see Janelle Riering, "Joan Jonnas' *Delay Delay*," *The Drama Review* 16 (September 1972): 142–50.

60. Riering, p. 144.

61. Joan Jonas, quoted in Riering, p. 145.

62. For a complete description see Trisha Brown, "Three Pieces," *The Drama Review* 19 (March 1975): 26–27.

63. Brown, p. 26.

64. See Sally Sommer, "Equipment Dances: Trisha Brown," *The Drama Review* 16 (September 1972): 137.

65. Brooks McNamara, "Vessel: The Scenography of Meredith Monk" *The Drama Review* 16 (March 1972): 89.

66. Don McDonagh, *The Complete Guide To Modern Dance* (Garden City, N.Y.: Doubleday and Company, Inc., 1976), p. 416–17.

67. McNamara, p. 90

68. Ibid.

69. Ibid., p. 102.

70. Ibid., p. 100.

71. Ibid., p. 97.

Chapter 9

1. Grotowski refers to Meyerhold in "Towards the Poor Theatre," (*Tulane Drama Review* 11 [Spring 1967]: 60). Since Grotowski studied at the Academy of Stagecraft (GITIS) in Moscow when Okhlopkov was still active, it is hard to believe that Grotowski was not familiar with his work.

2. Jerzy Grotowski, "For a Total Interpretation," *World Theatre* 15 (1966): 20.

3. Grotowski, "Towards the Poor Theatre," p. 63.

4. Grotowski, "Interview," *The Drama Review* 13 (Fall 1968): 39.

5. Ibid.

6. Eugenio Barba, "Theatre Laboratory 13 Rzedow," *Tulane Drama Review* 9 (Spring 1965): 162.

7. Ibid.

8. Boleslaw Taborski, *Byron and the Theatre* (Salzburg, Austria: Institut für Englische Sprache und Literatur, 1972), p. 354.

9. Barba, p. 162.

10. Grotowski, quoted in Barba, p. 156.

11. Barba, p. 162.

12. Grotowski noted that those spectators whom the actors treated as sick "were furious; the others were very proud because they had been judged 'sane.'" ("Interview," p. 39.)

13. Ludwig Flaszen, "Wyspianski's *Akropolis*," *Tulane Drama Review* 9 (Spring 1965): 177.

14. Grotowski, "Towards the Poor Theatre," p. 63.

15. Grotowski, "Interview," p. 42.

16. Ibid., p. 41.

17. Grotowski, *"Doctor Faustus* in Poland," *Tulane Drama Review* 8 (Summer 1964): 120–21.

18. Grotowski, "Interview," p. 43.

19. Ibid.

20. This may be seen in a statement by the German director Peter Stein, who has said about his work: "It is not a question of integrating the spectator with the action as Grotowski attempts to do; no, not at all: it is a question of finding a rapport between what occurs on the stage or performance place and the spectator who watches." (Bernard Dort, "La Schaubühne am Halleschen Uffer: Entretien avec Peter Stein," *Travail Théâtrale* 9 [octobre-decembre 1972]: 32.)

21. See Marc Fumaroli, "Eugenio Barba's *Kaspariana,"* *The Drama Review* 13 (Fall 1968): 46–56; and Christiane Aubert and Jean-Luc Bourbonnaud, "Kaspariana" in *Les Voies de la Création Théâtrale* ed. Jean Jacquot (Paris: Editions du Centre National de la Recherche Scientifique, 1970), vol. 1, p. 131–70.

22. Aubert and Bourbonnaud, p. 166.

23. Ibid., p. 167.

24. Fumaroli, "Funeral Rites: Eugenio Barba's *Ferai,"* *The Drama Review* 14 (Fall 1969): 48.

25. Ibid.

26. See "A Letter from Eugenio Barba in Southern Italy," *The Drama Review* 19 (December 1975): 47–57.

27. See Richard Mennon, "Grotowski's Paratheatrical Projects," *The Drama Review* 19 (December 1975): 58–69.

28. Jacques Polieri, "Systematisation de l'Espace Scénographique," in *Scénographi Sémiographie* (Paris: Editions Denoël, 1971), pp. 99–108.

29. Polieri, "Dove va l'avanguardia in Francia?" *Sipario* 19 (1964): 4.

30. See Polieri, "Gamme de 7: Argument Pour Un Ballet Spectacle," in *Scénographie Sémiographie*, pp. 125–32. (A partial translation appears in *World Theatre* 15 [1966]: 17.)

31. Polieri, "Scale of 7," *World Theatre* 15 (1966): 17.

32. See Polieri, "Le Livre de Mallarmé," in *Scénographie Sémiographie*, pp. 133–40. (A partial, and somewhat rearranged, translation appears in *The Drama Review* 12 [Spring 1968]: 179–82.)

33. Polieri, "Le Livre de Mallarmé: A Mise en Scéne," *The Drama Review* 12 (Spring 1968): 181.

34. See Polieri, "Ballet-paragramme Miro," in *Scénograpahie Sémiographie*, pp. 149–81.

35. Milan Pásek, "On Experience with New Forms of Theatre Space," *Interscena* 67, 1 (Autumn 1967): 47–48.

36. Ibid., p. 48.

37. Ibid., p. 50.

38. Tadeusz Kantor, "Evolution of Stage Settings: 1945–1962," in Henning Rischbeiter, ed.,

Art and the Stage in the Twentieth Century (Greenwich, Connecticut: New York Graphic Society Ltd., 1969), p. 245.

39. Denis Bablet, "Entretien avec Tadeusz Kantor," *Travail Théâtrale* 6 (janvier-mars 1972): 55.

40. Wieslaw Borowski, "The Happenings of Tadeusz Kantor," *The Theatre in Poland* 15 (May 1973): 23.

41. Bablet, p. 56–57.

42. Ibid., p. 73.

43. See Denis Calandra, "Experimental Performance at Edinburgh," *The Drama Review* 17 (December 1973): 61–68.

44. René Haineaux, *Stage Design Throughout the World Since 1960* (London: George G. Harrap & Co., Ltd., 1973), p. 224.

45. Michael Smith, "Theatre Journal," review of *Automobile Graveyard* in *Village Voice*, April 21, 1966, p. 27.

46. See Odette Aslan, "Le Cimétière des Voitures," in *Les Voies de la Création Théâtrale*, pp. 309–40.

47. Aslan, p. 320.

48. Ibid.

49. See Ilka Marinko Zanotto, "An Audience Structure for *The Balcony*," *The Drama Review* 17 (June 1973): 58–65.

50. Ibid., p. 60.

51. See Zanotto, "The Voyage," *The Drama Review* 17 (June 1973): 66–72.

52. Ann Halprin, "Yvonne Rainer Interviews Ann Halprin," *Tulane Drama Review* 10 (Winter 1965): 151–52.

53. Ibid., p. 157.

54. Richard Schechner, Interview in New York City, January 9, 1976.

55. See Richard Schechner, "6 Axioms for Environmental Theatre," *The Drama Review* 12 (Spring 1968): 41–64.

56. Schechner, Interview.

57. The New Orleans Group was founded by Franklin Adams, Paul Epstein, and Richard Schechner in New Orleans in 1966.

58. Schechner, *Environmental Theatre* (New York: Hawthorne Books, Inc., 1973), pp. 67–68.

59. Ibid., p. 68.

60. See Brooks McNamara, Jerry Rojo, Richard Schechner, *Theatres, Spaces, Environments: Eighteen Projects* (New York: Drama Book Specialists, 1975), pp. 154–63. Interestingly, a *Village Voice* review noted that the production "might be described as a very good happening on the same themes as Ionesco's play . . . or as an environment in which "Victims of Duty" was the dominant element." (Michael Smith, "Theatre Journal," review in *Village Voice*, May 11, 1967, p. 24.)

61. Jerry Rojo, "Interview: Environmental Theatre," *Performing Arts Journal* 1 (Spring, 1976): 20.

62. McNamara, et al., pp. 154–55.

63. Schechner, "6 Axioms," p. 49.

64. Schechner, "On Environmental Design," *Educational Theatre Journal* 23 (December 1971): 379–80. This essay was later incorporated into *Environmental Theatre*.

65. Schechner, Interview. This is closely echoed by Jerry Rojo: "Environmental theatre in the broadest sense has come to mean for me an organic production process in which an ensemble of performers, writers, designers, directors, and technicians participate on a regular basis in the formation of the piece through workshops and rehearsals." (McNamara, et al., p. 14.)

66. Schechner, Interview.

67. Schechner, "On Environmental Design," p. 385.

68. Ibid.

69. Schechner, ed., *Dionysus In 69* (New York: Farrar, Straus & Giroux, Inc., 1970), n.p.

70. See McNamara, et al., pp. 130–37.

71. Interview with Spalding Gray and Elizabeth LeCompte in New York City, August 1975.

72. Rojo, p. 21.

73. Schechner, Interview.

74. McNamara, et al., p. 102.

75. Schechner, "On Environmental Design," pp. 396–97.

76. See McNamara, et al., pp. 164–81. This book contains descriptions of many projects worked on by the three authors.

77. Eugene Lee, quoted in "Unit Sets as Entire Theatres," *Theatre Crafts* 5 (September 1971): 13.

78. Ibid.

79. Franco Quadri, *"Orlando Furioso,"* *The Drama Review* 14 (Spring 1970): 118. This article contains a detailed description of the production.

80. John Lahr, "On Stage," review of *Orlando Furioso* in *Village Voice*, November 12, 1970, p. 51.

81. Quadri, p. 119.

82. Quadri, p. 121.

83. Ettore Capriolo, *"Le Roland Furieux* sur la place publique," program of the Théâtre des Nations (Paris: May 1970).

84. Quadri, p. 124.

85. Ibid., p. 122.

86. See Colette Godard, "Luca Ronconi's *XX*," *The Drama Review* 15 (Fall 1971): 9–28.

87. Thomas Quinn Curtiss, "Drama Festival Opens in Pandemonium," review of *XX* in *International Herald Tribune*, April 15, 1971.

88. Godard, p. 19.

89. Ibid., p. 21.

90. Quadri, "Luca Ronconi," *The Drama Review* 21 (June 1977): 105-6. This might be compared with Norman Bel Geddes' 1933 proposal for a Water Pageant Theatre for the Chicago Century of Progress Exposition. There was to be a 2000 seat auditorium as well as space for spectators in 500 canoes. The stage, to be built in Lake Michigan, would be a pyramid structure of platforms ranging from eight inches to thirty-six feet above water level. (See Norman Bel Geddes, "Six Theatre Projects," *Theatre Arts Monthly* 14 [September 1930]: 762-79.)

91. Quadri, "Luca Ronconi," p. 107.

92. Emile Copferman, "Entretien avec Ariane Mnouchkine," *Travail Théâtrale* 2 (janvier-mars 1971): 9.

93. *Gambit*, 5, 20 is devoted entirely to *1789* and includes the script. A full description of the performance can also be found in Victoria Nes Kirby, "1789," *The Drama Review* 15 (Fall 1971): 73-92.

94. Irving Wardle, "Interview with Ariane Mnouchkine," *Performance* 1 (April 1972): 135.

95. Ibid.

96. Ariane Mnouchkine, "From Production to Collective Creation," *Gambit*, p. 60.

97. Christophe Campos, "Experiments for the People of Paris," *Theatre Quarterly* 2 (October-December 1972): 60.

98. See Bablet, "Une Scénographie pour '1793'," *Travail Théâtrale* 23 (janvier-mars, 1976): 97-104.

99. Bablet, "Avec Guy-Claude François," *Travail Théâtrale* 18-19 (janvier-mars, 1975): 36-39.

100. Ibid.

101. Ibid., p. 38.

102. Copferman, "An Interview With Ariane Mnouchkine," *Gambit*, p. 73.

103. See, for example, Rino Mele, "Memé Perlini's *Yellow Whiteness*," *The Drama Review* 19 (December 1975): 9-18; Peter Lackner, "Stein's Path to Shakespeare," *The Drama Review* 21 (June 1977): 79-102; "Andrei Serban," *Yale/Theatre* 8 (Spring 1977): 66-77.

Appendix A

1. From *Sic*, 8, 9, 10 (août-octobre, 1916).

Appendix B

1. 1929. Reprinted in *Myśl Teatralna Polskiej Awangardy 1919-1939* (Warsaw: Wydawnictwa Artystyeznei i Filmowe, 1973), pp. 209-13.

2. Cf. no. 45 of *Wiadomości literackie* [*Literary News*]. (Author's note.)

3. Here one can draw an interesting analogy with trends in modern painting, which is passing from the easel into freer form, dispensing with the artificial boundary of the frame and tending toward the creation of oneness with its surroundings and unification with the external world. (Author's note.)

4. See Chapter 4.

Bibliography

Akakia-Viala. "Théâtre. Temps, Espace." *Intermède*, No 2, 16ᵉ année (1947), 5–20.

Albert-Birot, Pierre. "A Propos d'Un Théâtre Nunique." *Sic* 8, 9, 10 (août–octobre 1916).

Allix, André. "The Geography of Fairs." *Geographical Review* 12 (1922): 532–69.

Alloway, Lawrence. "Art in Escalation." *Arts Magazine*, December, 1966–January, 1967, pp. 40–43.

Alpers, Boris. "Razbeg." *Sovetskii Teatr*, 5 (1932), 12–24.

Altman, George; Freud, Ralph; Macgowan, Kenneth and Melnitz, William. *Theatre Pictorial.* Berkeley, California: University of California Press, 1953.

Apollinaire, Guillaume. "The Breasts of Tiresias." *Modern French Theatre*. Edited and translated by Michael Benedikt and George E. Wellworth. New York: E. P. Dutton & Co., Inc., 1966.

Appia, Adolphe. *Music and the Art of the Stage*. Translated by R. W. Corrigan and M. D. Dirks. Coral Gables, Florida: University of Miami Press, 1962.

_____. *The Work of Living Art*. Translated by H. D. Albright. Coral Gables, Florida: University of Miami Press, 1960.

Argelander, Ron. "The War Is Over." Review of *The Domestic Resurrection Fair and Circus*, by the Bread and Puppet Theatre. *Soho Weekly News*, August 19, 1976, pp. 14–15.

Arnason, H. H. *History of Modern Art*. Englewood Cliffs, New Jersey: Prentice-Hall, Inc., and New York: Harry N. Abrams Inc., 1968.

Artaud, Antonin. *The Theatre and its Double*. Translated by Mary Caroline Richards. New York: Grove Press, 1958.

Art et Action. "Le Théâtre Populaire." *Anthologie*, no 3, 16ᵉ année (février–mars 1936): 5–8.

Art in Revolution. London: Hayward Gallery, 1971.

Aslan, Odette. "Le Cimétière des Voitures." *Les Voies de la Création Théâtrale*. Edited by Jean Jacquot. Paris: Editions du Centre Nationale de la Recherche Scientifique, 1970.

Aubert, Christiane and Jean-Luc Bourbonnaud. "Kaspariana." *Les Voies de la Création Théâtrale*. Edited by Jean Jacquot. Paris: Editions du Centre Nationale de la Recherche Scientifique, 1970.

Aujourd'hui 17 (mai 1958). Special issue on theatre architecture and design.

Awasthi, Suresh. "The Scenography of the Traditional Theatre of India." *The Drama Review* 18 (December 1974): 36–46.

Bablet, Denis. "Art et Action." *Interscena 67*, 2 (Spring 1967): 27–35.

_____. "Avec Guy-Claude Francois." *Travail Théâtrale* 18-19 (janvier-juin, 1975): 36–39.

_____. "Entretien avec Tadeusz Kantor." *Travail Théâtrale* 6 (janvier-mars 1972): 50–61.

_____. *Esthétique Générale du Décor de Théâtre de 1870 a 1914*. Paris: Editions du Centre Nationale de la Recherche Scientifique, 1965.

_____. "Une Scénographie pour '1793'." *Travail Théâtrale* 23 (janvier-mars 1976): 97:104.

Bakshy, Alexander. *The Path of the Modern Russian Stage and Other Essays*. London: Cecil Palmer and Hayward, 1916.

_____. *The Theatre Unbound*. London: Cecil Palmer and Hayward, 1923.

Barba, Eugenio. "A Letter from Eugenio Barba in Southern Italy." *The Drama Review* 19 (December 1975): 47-57.

_____. "Theatre Laboratory 13 Rzedow." *Tulane Drama Review* 9 (Spring 1965): 153-71.

Barkhin, Mikhail and Vakhtangov, Sergei. "A Theatre for Meyerhold." *Theatre Quarterly* 2 (July-September 1972): 69-74.

Baur, John I. H. *Bernard Reder*. New York: Frederick A. Praeger, Inc., 1961.

Beck, Julian. *The Life of the Theatre*. San Francisco: City Lights Books, 1972.

_____ and Malina, Judith. *Paradise Now*. Collective Creation of the Living Theatre. New York: Random House, Inc., 1971.

Béhar, Henri. *Etude sur le Théâtre Dada et Surréaliste*. Editions Gallimard, 1967.

Bernard, Heinz. "The Theatre of Erwin Piscator." *Prompt*, 3 [n.d.], 26-28.

Bie, Oscar. "Germany's New Scenecraft." *International Studio* 75 (August 1922): 425-29.

Biner, Pierre. *The Living Theatre*. New York: Horizon Press, 1972.

Borowski, Wieslaw. "The Happenings of Tadeusz Kantor." *The Theatre in Poland* 15 (May 1973): 17-29.

Bragdon, Claude. "A Theatre Transformed." *Architectural Record* 55 (April 1924): 388-97.

_____. "Towards a New Theatre." *Architectural Record* 52 (September 1922): 171-82.

Braithwaite, David. *Fairground Architecture*. New York: Frederick A. Praeger, Inc., 1968.

Brecht, Stefan. "Peter Schumann's Bread and Puppet Theatre." *The Drama Review* 14 (Spring 1970): 44-90.

Brody, Alan. *The English Mummers and Their Plays*. Philadelphia: University of Pennsylvania Press, 1970.

Brook, Peter. *The Empty Space*. New York: Avon Books, 1968.

Brown, Helen and Seitz, Jane. "With the Bread and Puppet Theatre." *The Drama Review* 12 (Winter 1968): 62-73.

Brown, Trisha. "Three Pieces." *The Drama Review* 19 (March 1975): 26-32.

Bunt, Cyril G. E. "The Art of the Pageant." *Connoisieur* 115 (1945): 71-78.

Burdick, Elizabeth; Hansen, Peggy C.; and Zander, Brenda. eds. *Contemporary Stage Design USA*. New York: ITI/US, 1974.

Burian, Jarka. *The Scenography of Josef Svoboda*. Middletown, Connecticut: Wesleyan University Press, 1974.

Calandra, Denis. "Experimental Performance at Edinburgh." *The Drama Review* 17 (December 1973): 53-68.

Campos, Christophe. "Experiments for the People of Paris." *Theatre Quarterly* 2 (October-December 1972): 57-67.

Canadian Theatre Review 6 (Spring 1975). Special issue on theatre space.

Capriolo, Ettore. "*Le Roland Furieux* sur la place publique." *Program of the Théâtre des Nations*. Paris: May 1970.

Carlson, Marvin. *The Theatre of the French Revolution*. Ithaca, New York: Cornell University Press, 1966.

Carter, Huntley. *The New Spirit in the European Theatre 1914-1924*. New York: George H. Doran Company, 1925.

_____. *The Theatre of Max Reinhardt*. New York: Mitchell Kennerley, 1914.

Cawte, E. C.; Helm, Alex; Marriott, R. J. and Peacock, Norman. *English Ritual Drama*. London: 1967.

Chambers, E. K. *The English Folk Play*. Oxford: Oxford University Press, 1933.

_____. *The Medieval Stage*. Oxford: Oxford University Press, 1903.

Cheney, Sheldon. *The Art Theatre*. 2nd ed. New York: Alfred A. Knopf, 1925.

———. *The Open Air Theatre*. 1918: rpt. New York: Kraus Reprint Co., 1971.

———. "Renaissance Entries." *Theatre Arts Monthly* 13 (August 1929): 611–14.

———. "The Space Stage." *Theatre Arts Monthly* 11 (October 1927): 762–74.

———. *Stage Decoration*. 1928; rpt. New York: Benjamin Blom, 1966.

Cheronnet, Louis. "Le Spectacle dans la Rue." *L'Architecture d'Aujourd'hui* 23 (mai 1949): 4–7.

Chevalier, Denys. "Spectacle Jacques Polieri." *Aujourd'hui* 27 (juin 1960): 60–61.

Cochin, Charles-Nicolas. *Projet d'Une Salle de Spectacle*. 1765: Reprint. Geneva: Minkoff Reprint, 1974.

Cole, Toby and Chinoy, Helen Krich. *Directors on Directing*. Revised edition. Indianapolis: Bobbs-Merrill Company, Inc., 1963.

Copferman, Emile. "Entretien avec Ariane Mnouchkine." *Travail Théâtrale* 2 (janviers–mars 1971).

Corvin, Michel. *Le Théâtre Récherche Entre les Deux Guerres: Le Laboratoire Art et Action*. Paris: La Cité—l'Age d'Homme, [1975].

Craig, Edward Gordon. *On the Art of the Theatre*. New York: Theatre Arts Books, 1956.

———. *The Theatre—Advancing*. Boston: Little, Brown and Co., 1919.

Creighton, Thomas H. "Kiesler's Pursuit of an Idea." *Progessive Architecture*, July, 1961, pp. 104–24.

Croyden, Margaret. "Brook's Tempest Experiment." *The Drama Review* 13 (Spring 1969): 125–28.

Cummings, E. E. "Coney Island." *Vanity Fair*, June 1926.

Curtiss, Thomas Quinn. "Drama Festival Opens in Pandemonium." Review of Luca Ronconi's *XX. International Herald Tribune*, April 15, 1971.

D'Amico, Silvio. "Shakespeare and Goldoni." *Theatre Arts Monthly* 18 (November 1934): 849–59.

Dana, H. W. L. "Meyerhold's New Theatre." *New Theatre* 44 (January 1935): 10–12.

Davis, R. G. "Guerilla Theatre." *Tulane Drama Review* 10 (Summer 1966): 130–36.

Deàk, František. "Russian Mass Spectacles." *The Drama Review* 19 (June 1975): 7–22.

Dickinson, Thomas Herbert. *The Case of American Drama*. Boston: Houghton, Mifflin Co., 1915.

Dietrich, Margaret. "Twentieth-Century Innovations in Stage Design, Stage Machinery, and Theatre Architecture in Austria." *Innovations in Stage and Theatre Design*. Edited by Francis Hodge. New York: American Scoiety for Theatre Research/Theatre Library Association, 1972.

Dort, Bernard. "La Schaubühne am Halleschen Uffer: Entretien avec Peter Stein." *Travail Théâtrale* 9 (octobre–décembre 1972): 16–36.

Dowd, David Lloyd. *Pageant Master of the Republic: Jacques-Louis David and the French Revolution*. Lincoln, Nebraska: University of Nebraska Press, 1948.

Drama Review, The 12 (Spring 1968). Special issue on theatre architecture.

Duberman, Martin. *Black Mountain: An Exploration in Community*. New York: E. P. Dutton & Co., Inc., 1972.

Dupavillon, Christian. "Scénographie d'un Spectacle." *Travail Théâtrale* 1 (octobre–décembre 1970): 135–38.

Eisenstein, Sergei. "Through Theatre to Cinema." *Theatre Arts Monthly* 20 (September 1936): 735–47.

Eisler, Max, ed. *Oskar Strnad*. Vienna: Gerlach und Wielding, 1936.

El Lissitzky. Cologne: Galerie Gmurzynska, 1976.

Esslin, Martin. "Max Reinhardt: High Priest of Theatricality." *The Drama Review* 21 (June 1977): 3–24.

Eustis, Morton. "A Universal Theatre." *Theatre Arts Monthly*, June 1933, pp. 447–57.

Evreinov, Nikolai. *The Theatre in Life*. Edited and translated by Alexander I. Nazaroff. 1927; Reprint. New York: Benjamin Blom, Inc., 1970.

──────. *Le Théâtre en Russe Sovietique*. Texte français de Madeleine Eristov. Paris: Les Publications Techniques et Artistiques, 1946.

Farwell, Arthur. "The Pageant and Masque of St. Louis." *American Review of Reviews*, August, 1914, pp. 187-93.

Federal Theatre Project. "The Theatre of the Future." Press release, 1937. Courtesy Research Center for the Federal Theatre Project, Fairfax, Virginia.

50 Let Sovetskogo Iskusstova Khydozhuiki Teatra. Moscow: 1969.

Fisher, David James. "Romain Rolland and the French People's Theatre." *The Drama Review* 21 (March 1977): 75-90.

Flaszen, Ludwig. "Wyspianski's *Akropolis*." *Tulane Drama Review* 9 (Spring 1965): 175-82.

Forbes-Robertson, Johnston. *A Player Under Three Reigns*. Boston: Little, Brown, and Co., 1925.

Fox, Terry Curtis. "Does Mack the Knife Belong Outdoors?" Review of *Threepenny Opera*. *Village Voice*, July 18, 1977, p. 63.

Frederick Kiesler: Architekt. Vienna: Organisation Herausgeber und Verleger: Galerie Nächst St. Stephen, n.d.

Fuchs, Georg. *Revolution in the Theatre*. Translated and edited by Constance Connor Kuhn. Ithaca, New York: Cornell University Press, 1959.

Fuerst, Walter René and Hume, Samuel J. *Twentieth-Century Stage Decoration*. 1929. Reprint. New York: Dover Publications, Inc., 1967.

Fülop-Miller, René. *The Mind and Face of Bolshevism*. New York: Harper and Row, 1965.

────── and Gregor, Joseph. *The Russian Theatre: Its Character and History*. London: George G. Harrap and Co., Ltd., 1930.

Fumaroli, Marc. "Eugenio Barba's *Kaspariana*." *The Drama Review* 13 (Fall 1968): 46-56.

──────. "Funeral rites: Eugenio Barba's *Ferai*." *The Drama Review* 14 (Fall 1969): 46-56.

Gambit, 5, 20 (n.d.). Special issue on the Théâtre du Soleil.

Gankovsky, Vitaly. "New Directions in Soviet Theatre." *Theatre Design and Technology* 33 (May 1973): 18-24.

Gassner, John. *Form and Idea in Modern Theatre*. New York: The Dryden Press, 1956.

Geddes, Norman Bel. "Six Theatre Projects." *Theatre Arts Monthly* 14 (September 1930): 762-79.

Giedion, S. *Walter Gropius: Work and Teamwork*. New York: Reinhold Publishing Corporation, 1954.

Godard, Colette. "Luca Ronconi's *XX*." *The Drama Review* 15 (Fall 1971): 9-28.

Gorchakov, Nikolai. *The Theatre in Soviet Russia*. New York: Columbia University Press, 1957.

Gorelik, Mordecai. *New Theatres for Old*. New York: E. P. Dutton & Co., Inc., 1962.

Gray, Camilla. *The Russian Experiment in Art 1863-1922*. New York: Harry N. Abrams, Inc., 1971.

Gray, Spalding and Elizabeth LeCompte. Interview in New York City, August, 1975.

Grotowski, Jerzy. "*Doctor Faustus* in Poland." *Tulane Drama Review* 8 (Summer 1964): 120-33.

──────. "For a Total Interpretation." *World Theatre* 15 (1966): 18-23.

──────. "Interview." *The Drama Review* 13 (Fall 1968): 29-45.

──────. *Towards a Poor Theatre*. New York: Simon and Schuster, 1968.

──────. "Towards the Poor Theatre." *Tulane Drama Review*, 11 (Spring, 1967), 60-67.

Haineaux, René. *Stage Design Throughout the World Since 1960*. London: George G. Harrap & Co., Ltd., 1973.

Halpert, Herbert and Story, G. M., eds. *Christmas Mumming in Newfoundland.* Toronto: University of Toronto Press, 1969.

Halprin, Ann. "Yvonne Rainer Interviews Ann Halprin." *Tulane Drama Review* 10 (Winter 1965): 142–67.

Hardy, Hugh. "Designing Random Focus." *The Drama Review* 12 (Spring 1968): 121–26.

Haskell, Douglas. "To-morrow and the World's Fair." *Architectural Record* 88 (August 1940): 65–72.

Hausmann, Raoul. "Dadatour." *The Drama Review* 18 (June 1974): 128–30.

Head, Robert. "Kill Viet Cong." *Tulane Drama Review* 10 (Summer 1966): 153.

Hewitt, Barnard. "Erwin Piscator." *The High School Thespian*, May, 1974, pp. 6–7.

Hodge, Francis, ed. *Innovations in Stage and Theatre Design.* New York: American Society for Theatre Research/Theatre Library Association, 1972.

Holitscher, Arthur. *Das Theater im Revolutionaren Russland.* No publication information.

Horwitz, Elinor Lander. *Contemporary American Folk Artists.* Philadelphia and New York: J. B. Lippincott Company, 1975.

Houghton, Norris. *Moscow Rehearsals.* New York: Harcourt, Brace and Co., 1936.

––––––. *Return Engagement.* New York: Holt, Rinehart and Winston, 1962.

Hunt, Ronald. "The Demise of Constructivism." *Art and Artists* 6 (April 1971): 7–9.

Innes, C. D. *Erwin Piscator's Political Theatre: The Development of Modern German Drama.* Cambridge: University Press, 1972.

International Theatre Institute. *Stage Design Throughout the World Since 1950.* New York: Theatre Arts Books, 1964.

Isaac, Dan. "The Death of the Proscenium Stage." *The Antioch Review* 31 (1971): 235–53.

Isaacs, Mrs. Edith Juliet. *Architecture for the New Theatre.* New York: National Theatre Conference, 1935.

Jacquot, Jean, ed. *Les Voies de la Création Théâtrale.* Paris: Editions du Centre Nationale de la Recherche Scientifique, 1970.

Jarry, Alfred. *Selected Works of Alfred Jarry.* Edited by Roger Shattuck and Simon Watson Taylor. New York: Grove Press, 1965.

Jonas, Joan with Rosalind Krause. "Seven Years." *The Drama Review* 19 (March 1975): 13–17.

Joseph, Stephen. *New Theatre Forms.* New York: Theatre Arts Books, 1968.

Kallmann, G. M. "Theatres." *Interiors* 116 (September 1956): 109–19.

Kaplan, Donald M. "Theatre Architecture: A Derivation of the Primal Cavity." *The Drama Review* 12 (Spring 1968): 105–16.

Kaprow, Allan. *Assemblage, Environments and Happenings.* New York: Harry N. Abrams, Inc., 1966.

––––––. "The Legacy of Jackson Pollock." *Art News*, October, 1958, pp. 24–26ff.

Karnot, Stephan. "Krasny Presny." *New Theatre*, July–August 1934, pp. 6–8.

Kiesler, Frederick. "Debacle of the Modern Theatre." *The Little Review* 11 (Winter 1926): 61–72.

––––––. "A Festival Shelter: The Space Theatre for Woodstock, N.Y." *Shelter Magazine*, May, 1932.

––––––. *Environmental Sculpture.* Solomon R. Guggenheim Museum of Art.

––––––. *Inside the Endless House.* New York: Simon and Schuster, 1966.

––––––. "Notes on Improving Theatre Design." *Theatre Arts Monthly* 18 (September 1934): 726–28.

Kirby, E. T., ed. *Total Theatre.* New York: E. P. Dutton & Co., Inc., 1969.

Kirby, Michael. *The Art of Time: Essays on the Avant-Garde.* New York: E. P. Dutton & Co., Inc., 1969.

––––––. *Futurist Performance.* New York: E. P. Dutton & Co., Inc., 1971.

_____. *Happenings.* New York: E. P. Dutton & Co., Inc., 1965.

_____. "Marta Minujin's Simultaneity." *The Drama Review* 12 (Spring 1968): 149–52.

_____ and Schechner, Richard. "An Interview with John Cage." *Tulane Drama Review* 10 (Winter 1965): 50–72.

Kirby, Victoria Nes. "1789." *The Drama Review* 15 (Fall 1971): 73–92.

Kirkland, Christopher D. "The Golden Age, First Draft." *The Drama Review* 19 (June 1975): 53–60.

Klüver, Billy; Martin, Julie; and Rose, Barbara, eds. *Pavilion.* New York: E. P. Dutton & Co., Inc., 1972.

Korolev, I. "Contemporary Stage Decoration in the U.S.S.R." *The Drama* 20 (January 1930): 101–3.

Kostelanetz, Richard. *The Theatre of Mixed Means.* New York: The Dial Press, Inc., 1968.

Kourilsky, Françoise. *Le Bread and Puppet Theatre.* Lausanne: La Cité Editeur, 1967.

Lackner, Peter. "Stein's Path to Shakespeare." *The Drama Review* 21 (June 1977): 79–102.

Lahr, John. "On Stage." Review of *Orlando Furioso* by Luca Ronconi. *Village Voice,* November 12, 1970, p. 51.

Langton, Basil. "Journey to Ka Mountain." *The Drama Review* 17 (June 1973): 48–57.

Lebel, Jean-Jacques. "Theory and Practice." *New Writers IV: Plays and Happenings.* London: Calder and Boyars, Ltd., 1967.

Lehman, Arnold L. *1930's Expositions.* Dallas: Dallas Museum of Fine Arts, 1972.

Lenhoff, Gail. "The Theatre of Okhlopkov." *The Drama Review* 17 (March 1973): 90–105.

Lesnick, Henry. *Guerilla Street Theatre.* New York: Avon Books, 1973.

Lewy, Thomas. *The Audience in Modern Theatre.* Unpublished Ph.D. Dissertation. New York University, 1971.

Leyda, Jay. "News from Moscow." *Theatre Arts Monthly,* 18 (April 1934): 281–94.

Ley-Piscator, Maria. *The Piscator Experiment.* Carbondale, Illinois: Southern Illinois University Press, 1967.

Licht, Jennifer. *Spaces.* New York: Museum of Modern Art, 1969.

Lindley, Kenneth. *Seaside Architecture.* London: Hugh Evelyn, 1973.

Lissitzky, El. *Russia: An Architecture for World Revolution.* Cambridge, Massachusetts: M.I.T. Press, 1970.

Lissitzky-Küppers, Sophie. *El Lissitzky: Life-Letters-Texts.* Greenwich, Connecticut: New York Graphic Society, 1968.

Living Theatre, The. *The Living Book of the Living Theatre.* Greenwich, Connecticut: New York Graphic Society, 1971.

Lönberg-Holm, K. "New Theatre Architecture in Europe." *Architectural Record* 67 (May 1930): 490–96.

Loney, Glenn M. "Remembering Reinhardt." *Theatre Crafts* 7 (November/December 1973): 22ff.

Lumpkin, Ross. "Last Bread and Puppet Circus." Review of *The Domestic Resurrection Fair and Circus,* by the Bread and Puppet Theatre. *Soho Weekly News,* August 22, 1974, p. 16.

McDonagh, Don. *The Complete Guide to Modern Dance.* Garden City, New York: Doubleday and Company, Inc., 1976.

Macgowan, Kenneth. *The Theatre of Tomorrow.* New York: Boni and Liveright, 1921.

_____ and Jones, Robert Edmond. *Continental Stagecraft.* New York: Harcourt, Brace and Company, 1922.

MacGregor Robert M. *Stages of the World: A Pictorial Survey of the Theatre.* New York: Theatre Art Books, 1949.

McKechnie, Samuel. *Popular Entertainments Through the Ages.* Reprint. New York: Benjamin Blom, 1969.

McNamara, Brooks. "Popular Scenography." *The Drama Review* 18 (March 1974): 16–24.

———. "Stuart Sherman's Third Spectacle." *The Drama Review* 20 (June 1976): 47–55.

———. "Vessel: The Scenography of Meredith Monk." *The Drama Review* 16 (March 1972): 87–103.

———; Rojo, Jerry; and Schechner, Richard. *Theatres, Spaces, Environments: Eighteen Projects.* New York: Drama Book Specialists, 1975.

Marinetti, Filippo Tommaso. *Marinetti: Selected Writings.* Edited by R. W. Flint. Translated by R. W. Flint and Arthur A. Coppotelli. New York: Farrar, Straus, and Giroux, 1972.

Markov, Vladimir. *Russian Futurism: A History.* London: MacGibbon & Kee, Limited, 1969.

Melchinger, Siegfried, ed. *Max Reinhardt: Sein Theater in Bildern.* Hanover: Friedrich Verlag Velber, 1968.

Mele, Rino. "Memé Perlini's Yellow Whiteness." *The Drama Review* 19 (December 1975): 9–18.

Mennen, Richard. "Grotowski's Paratheatrical Projects." *The Drama Review* 19 (December 1975): 58–69.

Meyerhold, Vsevelod. *Meyerhold on Theatre.* Translated and edited by Edward Braun. New York: Hill and Wang, 1969.

Mielziner, Jo. *The Shapes of Our Theatre.* New York: Clarkson N. Potter, Inc., 1970.

"Miracle—A Collaboration, The." Theatre Arts Monthly 8 (March 1924): 171–83.

Mnouchkine, Ariane. "From Production to Collective Creation." *Gambit,* 5, 20 (n.d.).

Moholy-Nagy, Sybil. *Moholy-Nagy: Experiment in Totality.* Cambridge, Massachusetts: M.I.T. Press, 1969.

Morris, Robert. "Notes on Dance." *Tulane Drama Review* 10 (Winter 1965): 179–86.

Motherwell, Robert, ed. *The Dada Painters and Poets: An Anthology.* New York: Wittenborn, Schultz, Inc., 1951.

Mullin, Donald C. *The Development of the Playhouse.* Berkeley: University of California Press, 1970.

Munk, Erika. "The Price is the Mind and the Spirit." Review of *Fefu and Her Friends* by Maria Irene Fornes. *Village Voice,* May 19, 1977.

Myśl Teatralna Polskiej Awangardy 1919–1939. Warsaw: Wydawnictwa Artystyczne i Filmowe, 1973.

Nakov, Andrei B. *Russian Constructivism: Laboratory Period.* London: Annely Juda Fine Arts Gallery, 1975.

———. *Stenberg.* London: Annely Juda Fine Arts Gallery, 1975.

Neff, Renfreu. *The Living Theatre: USA.* Indianapolis: Bobbs-Merrill Co., 1970.

Newman, Teresa. *Naum Gabo: The Constructive Process.* London: The Tate Gallery, 1976.

New Writers IV: Plays and Happenings. London: Calder and Boyars Ltd., 1967.

Nicoll, Allardyce. *The Development of the Theatre.* 5th ed. New York: Harcourt, Brace, Jovanovich, Inc., 1968.

Niedermoser, Otto. *Oskar Strnad 1879–1935.* Vienna: Bergland Verlag, 1965.

Norberg-Schulz, Christian. *Existence, Space and Architecture.* New York: Praeger Publishers, 1971.

Okhlopkov, Nikolai. "Ob Uslovnosti." *Teatr,* 11 (1959), 52–73.

Pam, Dorothy. "Murderer, the Women's Hope." *The Drama Review* 19 (September 1975): 5–12.

Pásek, Milan. "On Experience with New Forms of Theatre Space." *Interscena 67* 1 (Autumn 1967): 47–51.

Pentzell, Raymond. "Firmin Gémier and Shakespeare for Everybody." *The Drama Review* 11 (Summer 1967): 113–24.

———. "A Hungarian Christmas Mummers' Play in Toledo, Ohio." *Educational Theatre Journal* 29 (May 1977): 178–98.

Pierce, Allan. "Black Mountain College: A Survey of Theatrical Performances." Unpublished paper, New York University, 1976.

Piscator, Erwin. *Le Théâtre Politique*. Texte français d'Arthur Adamov. Paris: L'Arche Editeur, 1962.

———."'Totaltheater' (theatre of totality) and 'totales theater' (total theatre)." *World Theatre* 15 (1966): 5–9.

Polieri, Jacques. "Dove va l'avanguardia in Francia?" *Sipario* 19 (1964): 2–13.

———. "Le Livre de Mallarmé: A Mise en Scène." *The Drama Review* 12 (Spring 1968): 179–82.

———. "New Production and Scenography." *World Theatre* 15 (1966): 10–15.

———. "Pour une Nouvelle Dimension Scénique." *La Revue Théâtrale* 34 (1956): 39–42.

———. *Scénographie Sémiographie*. Paris: Editions Denoël, 1971.

———. "Le Théâtre Kaleidoscopique." *La Revue Théâtrale* 30 (1955): 23–25.

Pottecher, Maurice. *Le Théâtre du Peuple de Bussang*. Paris: P. V. Stock, 1913.

Prampolini, Enrico. "The Magnetic Theatre and the Futurist Scenic Atmosphere." *The Little Review* (Winter 1926): 101–8.

Progressive Architecture (December, 1970). Special issue: "Theatres for the Seventies."

Pronaszko, Andrzej. "Rebirth of the Theatre." *Myśl Teatralna Polskiej Awangardy 1919–1939*. Warsaw: Wydawnictwa Artystyczyne i Filmowe, 1973.

Quadri, Franco. "Luca Ronconi." *The Drama Review* 21 (June 1977): 103–18.

———. "Orlando Furioso." *The Drama Review* 14 (Spring 1970): 116–24.

Riering, Janelle. "Joan Jonas' *Delay Delay*." *The Drama Review* 16 (September 1972): 142–50.

Rischbeiter, Henning, ed. *Art and the Stage in the Twentieth Century*. Greenwich, Connecticut: New York Graphic Society, 1969.

Roberts, Spencer E. *Soviet Historical Drama*. The Hague: Martinus Nijhoff, 1965.

Rojo, Jerry. "Environmental Design." *Contemporary Stage Design USA*. Edited by Elizabeth Burdick, Peggy C. Hansen and Brenda Zanger. New York: ITI/US, 1974.

———. "Interview: Environmental Theatre." *Performing Arts Journal* 1 (Spring 1976): 20–28.

———. "The Modern Theatre Environment as Architecture." Unpublished manuscript, January, 1970.

Roose-Evans, James. *Experimental Theatre from Stanislavski to Today*. New York: Avon Books, 1971.

Rosenberg, Harold. "Art World: Environmental Art." *New Yorker*, October 21, 1967.

Rostagno, Aldo and Mantegna, G. *We, the Living Theatre*. New York: Ballantine Books, Inc., 1970.

Ryan, Paul Ryder. "The Living Theatre in Brazil." *The Drama Review* 15 (Summer 1971).

Sainer, Arthur. *The Radical Theatre Notebook*. New York: Avon Books, 1975.

Sanouillet, Michel. *Dada à Paris*. Jean-Jacques Pauvert Editeur, 1965.

Sayler, Oliver M. *Max Reinhardt and His Theatre*. New York: Brentano's, 1924.

Schechner, Richard. "Actuals: Primitive Ritual and Performance Theory." *Theatre Quarterly* 1 (April–June 1971): 49–66.

———. "An Interview with the Becks." *The Drama Review* 13 (Spring 1969): 24–44.

———, ed. *Dionysus in 69*. New York: Farrar, Straus & Giroux, Inc., 1970.

———. *Environmental Theatre*. New York: Hawthorne Books, Inc., 1973.

———. "Guerilla Theatre: May 1970." *The Drama Review* 14 (Spring 1970): 163–68.

———. "Interview in New York City, January 9, 1976.

———. "On Environmental Design." *Educational Theatre Journal* 23 (December 1971): 379–97.

————. Personal files.

————. "Post Proscenium" *Theatre 3: The American Theatre 1969-1970.* New York: Charles Scribner's Sons, 1970.

————. *Public Domain.* New York: Avon Books, 1969.

————. "Public Events for the Radical Theatre." *Village Voice,* September 7, 1967, pp. 27-28.

————. "Selective Inattention." *Performing Arts Journal* 1 (Spring 1976): 8-20.

————. "6 Axioms for Environmental Theatre." *The Drama Review* 12 (Spring 1968): 41-64.

Schlemmer, Oskar. *Oskar Schlemmer und die Abstrakt Bühne.* Munich: Die Neue Sammlung, 1961.

————. Moholy-Nagy, Laszlo, and Molnar, Farkas. *The Theatre of the Bauhaus.* Edited by Walter Gropius. Translated by Arthur S. Wensinger. Middletown, Connecticut: Wesleyan University Press, 1961.

Schubert, Hannelore. *The Modern Theatre: Architecture, Stage Design, Lighting.* Translated by J. C. Palmes. New York: Praeger Publishers, 1971.

Schumann, Peter. "Bread and Puppets." *The Drama Review* 14 (Spring 1970): 35.

Seitz, W. C. *The Art of Assemblage.* New York: Museum of Modern Art, 1961.

Seton, Marie. *Sergei M. Eisenstein.* New York: A. A. Wyn, Inc., 1952.

Shank, Theodore. "The Bread and Puppet's Anti-Bicentennial: A Monument to Ishi." *Theatre Quarterly* 5 (September-November 1975): 73-88.

Shipley, Joseph T. "Finns Spin in a Novel Theatre." *Christian Science Monitor,* September 24, 1960.

Shvidovsky, O. A., ed. *Building in the USSR 1917-1932.* New York: Praeger Publishers, 1971.

Simmer, Bill. "The Theatrical Style of Tom O'Horgan." *The Drama Review* 21 (June 1977): 59-66.

Simonson, Lee. *The Stage Is Set.* New York: Theatre Arts Books, 1963.

Smith, A. C. H. *Orghast at Persepolis.* New York: The Viking Press, 1972.

Smith, Michael. "Theatre Journal." Review of *Automobile Graveyard. Village Voice,* April 21, 1966, p. 27.

————. "Theatre Journal." Review of *Victims of Duty. Village Voice,* May 11, 1967, p. 24.

————. "Theatre Journal." *Village Voice,* January 18, 1968.

Sokolova, N. "Soviet Stage Design." *Art and Artists,* 6 (April 1971).

Sommer, Sally. "Equipment Dances: Trisha Brown." *The Drama Review* 16 (September 1972): 135-41.

Sonrel, Pierre. "La Salle de Spectacle." *L'Architecture d'Auhourd'hui* 23 (mai 1949): 22-36.

Southern, Richard. *The Seven Ages of the Theatre.* New York: Hill and Wang, 1961.

Steward, Dwight. *Stage Left.* Dover, Delaware: The Tanager Press, 1970.

Strasberg, Lee. "Lee Strasberg's Russian Notebook." *The Drama Review* 17 (March 1973): 106-21.

———— and Kingsley, Sidney. "An Interview with Okhlopkov." *The Drama Review* 17 (March 1973): 121-23.

Syrkus, Szymon and Helena. "On the Simultaneous Theatre." *Myśl Teatralna Polskiej Awangardy 1919-1939.* Warsaw: Wydawnictwo Artystyczne i Filmowe, 1973.

Szydlowski, Roman. *The Theatre in Poland.* Warsaw: Interpress Publishers, 1972.

Taborski, Boleslaw. *Byron and the Theatre.* Salzburg: Institute für Englische Sprache und Literatur, 1972.

TASS. "Flyer Vodopyanov's Play *Dream* at the Moscow Realistic Theatre." Press release, May 22, 1937.

————. "Moscow Planetarium Presents a Play *Galilei.*" Press release, March 28, 1937.

Theatre Crafts 5 (September 1971). Special issue on environmental theatre.

———— 6 (March/April 1972). Special issue on street theatre.

———— 9 (September 1975). Special issue on the history of outdoor stages.

"Theatre Inflation." *Progressive Architecture*, December, 1970, pp. 48–64.

"Théâtre Mobile de Jacques Polieri." *Aujourd'hui* 30 (février 1961): 56–57.

"Theatre Out-of-Doors, The." *Theatre Arts Monthly* 13 (August 1929).

Theatre Quarterly 2 (October–December 1972). Special issue on street theatre.

Tomkins, Calvin. *The Bride and the Bachelors.* New York: The Viking Press, 1965.

Tonecki, Zygmunt. "The Theatre of the Future." *Myśl Teatralna Polskiej Awangardy 1919-1939.* Warsaw: Wydawnictwa Artystyczne i Filmowe, 1973.

Trilling, Ossia. "Peter Brook in Persia." *Theatre Quarterly* 2 (January–March 1972): 32–47.

———. "Robert Wilson's *Ka Mountain.*" *The Drama Review* 17 (June 1973): 33–47.

Tulane Drama Review 10 (Winter 1965). Special issue on Happenings.

"Unit Sets as Entire Theatres." *Theatre Crafts* 5 (September 1971): 10–15ff.

Vallette, Alfred. "Le Théâtre du Peuple." *Mercure de France* 19 (août 1896): 383.

van Gyseghem, Andre. *Theatre in Soviet Russia.* London: Faber and Faber Ltd., 1943.

Varshavskii, Ya. "Neveriye v Teatr." *Teatr* 5 (1937): 111–20.

Veinstein, André. "Dialogue avec Jacques Polieri." *Quadrum* 8 (1960): 116–68.

Velekhova, N. "Obraz Okhlopkovskogo Spektaklya." *Teatr* 6 (1954): 70–80.

Vicentini, Claudio. "The Living Theatre's *Six Public Acts.*" *The Drama Review* 19 (September 1975): 80–93.

Wardle, Irving. "Interview with Ariane Mnouchkine." *Performance* 1 (April 1972): 132–35.

———. "Rare Moments of Distinction." Review of Ronconi's *Utopia. London Times,* September 11, 1975, p. 12.

Waugh, Frank A. *Outdoor Theatres.* Boston: Richard G. Badger, 1917.

Waugh, Mark, ed. *Fairground Snaps.* Photos by Dick Scott-Stewart. London: Pleasant Pastures Ltd., 1974.

Weiss, Margaret. "'*Labyrinth*': Film in a Framework." *Saturday Review,* July 8, 1967, pp. 51–53ff.

Wickham, Glynne. *Early English Stages.* 2 vols. New York: Columbia University Press, 1959.

Withington, Robert. *English Pageantry: An Historical Outline.* 1918. Reprint. New York: Benjamin Blom, 1963.

World Theatre 14 (November/December 1965) and 15 (January 1966). Special issues on "Total Theatre."

Yale/Theatre 2 (Spring, 1969). Special issue on The Living Theatre.

Young, Marjorie. "Performance in Polish Villages." *The Drama Review* 18 (December 1974): 16–21.

Zanotto, Ilka Marinko. "An Audience Structure for *The Balcony.*" *The Drama Review* 17 (June 1973): 58–65.

———. "The Voyage." *The Drama Review* 17 (June 1973): 66–72.

Znosko-Borovski, Yevgeny. *Ruskii Teatr Nachala XX Vyeka.* Prague: 1925.

Zucker, Paul. *Theater und Lichtspielhäuser.* Berlin: Verlag Ernst Wasmuth A. G., 1926.

Index